Industrial Invasion of Nonmetropolitan America

Gene F. Summers
Sharon D. Evans
Frank Clemente
E. M. Beck
Jon Minkoff

The Praeger Special Studies program—utilizing the most modern and efficient book production techniques and a selective worldwide distribution network—makes available to the academic, government, and business communities significant, timely research in U.S. and international economic, social, and political development.

Industrial Invasion of Nonmetropolitan America

A Quarter Century of Experience

Praeger Publishers   New York   Washington   London

PRAEGER SPECIAL STUDIES IN U.S. ECONOMIC, SOCIAL, AND POLITICAL ISSUES

Library of Congress Cataloging in Publication Data
Main entry under title:

Industrial invasion of nonmetropolitan America.

(Praeger special studies in U.S. economic, social, and
political issues)
    Bibliography: p.
    1. Industries, Location of—United States. 2. United
States—Economic conditions—1945-   I. Summers,
Gene F., 1936-
HC110.D5I53   338'.0973   75-25026
ISBN 0-275-56080-5

PRAEGER PUBLISHERS
111 Fourth Avenue, New York, N.Y. 10003, U.S.A.

Published in the United States of America in 1976
by Praeger Publishers, Inc.

Printed in the United States of America

In recent years industries have been looking to rural areas and small towns for new plant locations. For a variety of reasons such as labor costs, land costs, and tax advantages, this trend is likely to continue. The existence of previous experience of industrial location in rural areas should provide a source of insights to the potential consequences of a national population redistribution policy which follows the strategy of encouraging the mobility of capital into nonmetropolitan areas in the form of industrial development.

Between 1960 and 1970 manufacturing employment in metropolitan areas grew 4 percent but 22 percent in nonmetropolitan areas. In less urbanized and sparsely populated nonmetropolitan areas the rate of increase was even higher. Such growth is consistent with the policy goals of federal legislation such as the Economic Opportunity Act of 1964, the Public Works and Economic Development Act of 1965, the Appalachian Regional Development Act of 1965, and the Rural Development Act of 1972. Clearly, the intent of Congress in recent years has been to encourage the mobility of capital into nonmetropolitan areas of the nation on the presumption that industrial development of such communities will generate a more equitable distribution of economic opportunities as well as other elements of high quality living conditions.

But regardless of the existence of federal programs devised to encourage this migratory process, it is almost certain to continue. There are strong market forces operative which also encourage industrial capital migration. It seems to us that the potential impact of this process on the nation can hardly be overstated for it is a process of societal realignment with a scope and magnitude rivaling the emergence of industry in the last century or the mechanization of agriculture in this century.

During and since World War II there has been a considerable number of impact studies of industrial location in rural areas and small towns. Most such research efforts have focused on only a few variables among the many which may be affected by plant location. Fortunately, population characteristics have been among the variables most frequently included. Almost always the research monitors a single community, county, or cluster of counties. Such studies generally are done at one point in time with an effort made to reconstruct the history of events up to that point. While these features of the research efforts are limitations, if one considers each study in isolation, in the aggregate they provide a valuable source of information.

Viewed thusly, they represent a considerable range of types of industry, size of plant, labor intensiveness, skill level, and other industry
characteristics. They also provide a sampling of communities with
regional representation. And, finally, they encompass a considerable array of dependent variables which one may examine for evidence
of change. In short the reserve of impact studies may be mined to
provide insights into the consequences of bringing new industry into
low density rural areas. These scattered documents on industrial
invasion into nonmetropolitan areas of the United States have been
assembled in this book and a review and synthesis of findings prepared with respect to the impact of rural industrial development.

A word about the use of "invasion" in the title of this book is
in order. "Invasion" was chosen as a key word in the conceptualiza-
tion of process of industry moving into nonmetropolitan areas of the
United States because it accurately denotes the introduction of a for-
eign or exogenous element into the local system. Moreover, it is an
"alarm" word. That is, we want to call attention to the fact that inmigration of industry holds potential problems as well as benefits
for the hosting local public. We hope that our use of the term "invasion" will arouse the reader's senses to be alert to potential dangers
as well as desirable outcomes.

The primary objective of this work is to draw empirical generalizations from the experience of 25 years as that is revealed in
case studies of specific plant locations in nonmetropolitan areas.
Having stated an empirical generalization such as "Having experienced industrial development the majority of the local citizenry wants
more," it is all too easy to forget those who dissent. And in forget-
ting, one no longer needs to consider the legitimacy of their dissent.
It is a possibility inherent in a system which incorporates the princi-
ple of majority rule. The latent danger in it, of course, grows as
the size of the numerical majority increases. A part of the hoped
for value of this work is in giving attention to the bases of dissent.
The exceptions to the empirical generalization can sometimes be as
insightful as the general rule.

The preparation of this summarizing work was supported by
Research Grant OER-465-G-7(99-7-13280) from the Office of Economic Research, Economic Development Administration, and the
College of Agricultural and Life Sciences at the University of Wisconsin at Madison. Clearly, our greatest debt of gratitude is to the
several hundred researchers who went before us and sifted the evidence of impact from nearly one hundred plant locations over the
past two and one half decades. Their identity is revealed in the 186
documents listed in Appendix B of this work. To them we wish to express our deepest sense of obligation for without them this work
would not exist.

Close behind in our list of persons to whom we are in debt are the several hundred persons who responded to our call for assistance in locating the documents just mentioned. We cannot name them individually but they include federal, state, and local governmental officials; editors of professional journals; private industrial managers; and colleagues in academia across the nation.

When one is dealing with disciplines and issues which extend beyond one's own expertise it is well to have colleagues who are willing to lend their time and skill in order to minimize the risks of ignorance. We are most fortunate in having two such colleagues, Lloyd Bender and Ronald Shaffer, whose criticisms and comments on earlier drafts of this work have saved us much embarrassment. Yet in spite of their excellent counsel we are still vulnerable to the limitations of our knowledge. Therefore, we wish to express our great debt to Lloyd and Ron and also beg the reader to hold them blameless for the remaining errors.

The expert counsel and guidance of Drs. Isidore Bogdanoff, Roger Prior, and Eli March, in the Office of Economic Research, have been extremely valuable in shaping the product of our joint effort. Their patience with inevitable delays in meeting deadlines within the exigencies of academia is virtuous.

And last, only because they are the last to add the expert touch to the manuscript before it reaches the reader, we wish to acknowledge our dependence upon the expertise, patience, and congeniality of our staff: Virginia Dymond, Sue Ward, Susie Cline, Mary Miron, Teri Summers, Debbie Schuckit, and Sandy Hicks.

CONTENTS

LIST OF TABLES AND FIGURE

The Constitution of the United States charges federal officials with the responsibility of promoting the general welfare. And public representatives often refer to that fact. But the constitutional goal stands so undefined as to be of little value in directing the day-to-day efforts of running programs which owe their being to its existence. It is, after all, a very long conceptual journey from the goal, "promote the general welfare," to the detailed issues of social engineering. Paralleling this road of conceptual abstractness is another which joins the opposing communities of faith and reason. The higher an issue is on the order of conceptual abstraction, the more its proponents rely upon articles of faith for their defense. Application of rational processes is more often to be observed when the issue is one readily expressed in concrete terms.

Consequently, it is not surprising that when social scientists are called upon to assist in the resolution of social problems they are thrown into the fray where the issue is most concrete and where they are least likely to disturb the articles of faith held by public administrators, policy makers, or the public-at-large. Social scientists are much more likely to be asked, "How may we get industry to locate in our community?" than "Should we attempt to attract industry to our community?" In the former instance the wisdom of the objective is assumed; in the latter it is not. Unfortunately, most of the social science research demand is for a product which is not designed to speak to social policy at higher levels of generality where articles of faith are intensely involved. Rather it is for detailed data on the "how to" front. There are some indications that, on a long-term projection, the market for policy-relevant social science research may open up, but it is slow to do so and subject to short-term reversals as political personages come and go. Thus, one of our objectives in preparing this work has been to juxtapose social science research findings and our understanding of governmental policy and operations so as to permit an assessment of the wisdom of the procedures being followed or being advocated with regard to nonmetropolitan industrial development as a tool for promoting the general welfare.

Our concern, therefore, is with the consequences of industrial invasion of small towns and rural areas in a nation which has already achieved a high level of industrial development. Because this is a focus that has not received extensive attention previously, research which bears directly on our interest is relatively limited. Most analyses of industrial development have taken the nation-state as the unit of analysis and have viewed industrialization as a relatively long-term historical process. Because our focus is more narrowly circumscribed it is not clear just how relevant will be the findings of these macrohistorical analyses. Therefore, it is especially important to note the consequences of industrial invasion of rural communities, small nonmetropolitan towns, and substate regions as reported in case study documents. In short, we have attempted to inventory and refine the stockpile of raw materials mined by our colleagues over the years since World War II.

One of the many national needs is to achieve greater equality of life among all segments of our population. A more balanced geographic distribution of population is regarded by many persons as a necessary condition for achieving greater equality, especially between rural and urban people. Without eigher accepting or rejecting that premise, clearly the heavy concentration of population in existing metropolitan centers has precipitated an urban crisis. At the same time, many of the people left behind in rural areas find themselves in pockets of poverty.

Rural poverty and the urban crisis are waste products of a geographic mismatch of labor supply and demand. As such they are not separable problems, but rather two manifestations of a single supply and demand imbalance which has been an integral element in the national social system for the past century. There are, of course, several factors which have contributed to this mismatch: mechanization of agriculture, technological developments in farming, efficiency of agglomeration, externalizability of social overhead costs by industry in urban areas, the labor intensive character of industry in its infant years followed by a trend toward capital intensiveness, and expansion of world commodity markets, to mention a few obvious ones. To these technological and economic considerations one also should add public policy.

At the outset the architects of U.S. public policy were inclined to view society from the vantage point of the free market economy model and treat the situation as reflective of the natural functioning of society. That model--intellectually akin to social Darwinism--rests on the proposition that in the long run the competitive mechanisms will lead to an optimal spatial patterning of economic activity. Experience, however, demonstrated that several major assumptions of the free market model were not completely substantiated in the real world. Uneven geographic distribution of industrial activity generated severe social, economic, and environmental problems and led to increasing governmental intervention.

The first interventionist solution to the spatial mismatch of labor demand and supply was to encourage the movement of surplus labor to places of higher demand. Programs of education, job training, relocation assistance, and financial inducements were initiated to increase the mobility of labor. Such efforts paralleled powerful economic forces encouraging concentration of economic activity and population in metropolitan areas. Thus, market forces, acting jointly with interventionist policies, which were designed to lubricate the mechanisms of labor mobility, resulted in massive concentrations of labor in urban areas to such an extent that overurbanization has come to be viewed as being causally linked to many facets of the urban crisis.

An obvious second solution to the limitations of the free market model, and the ineffective efforts to solve the resultant problems of spatial disequilibrium through encouragement of labor mobility, is to encourage the mobility of capital. Interventionists of this persuasion argue that both problems--overurbanization and economic stagnation of rural areas--can be relieved by encouraging capital migration into nonmetropolitan areas of the nation. It is precisely this mobility of capital into nonindustrial regions which constitutes the primary force in nonmetropolitan industrial development, regardless of whether it is achieved through market forces or by interventionist efforts.

There is no doubt that capital is migrating to nonmetropolitan areas. And it is arriving in several forms; it is invested in infrastructure development, land speculation, and more importantly for our immediate concern in the increased demand for industrial labor. There is considerable evidence that where capital investment increases the labor demand, there follows an upgrading of aggregate income, levels of living, and volume of business activity and a stabilization of population, in some instances population growth. Consequently, interventionist policies have a broad support base among both rural and urban sectors of the population. Much less is understood of the impacts nonmetropolitan industrial development has on social, political, and psychological characteristics of the host communities. Moreover we do not understand the distributional character of its effects, including economic effects.

What is needed, therefore, is a clarification of the mechanisms by which this capital inflow affects the lives and living conditions of people in the areas experiencing industrial development. The migration of capital which brings manufacturing activity into small cities, towns, and rural areas is a process of societal realignment with a strong potential for reshaping American society and deserves extensive monitoring and careful analysis.

In casting about for a meaningful framework to structure one's understanding of the dynamics of industrial invasion into the nonmetropolitan areas, there is a great temptation to adopt existing models of industrialization and modernization. But it would be a mistake to follow that inclination. The industrial development of a rural area within a technologically and industrially advanced nation is a process unlike the historical emergence of industrialized Western societies. Industrialization is an evolutionary process of social change which had its origin in scientific discovery and the corollary growth of technological innovation. Nonmetropolitan industrial development, on the other hand, is essentially a spatial redistribution of economic activity within a nation.

The classic industrialization literature has its origin in the writings of scholars such as Karl Marx, Max Weber, and Herbert Spencer, and takes as its central concern the social (including economic) and psychological consequences of the industrial revolution. The modernization literature is primarily a post-World War II development guided by sociologists and economists such as Wilbert Moore, Seymour Martin Lipset, Neil J. Smelser, Bert F. Hoselitz, and Simon Kuznets. Here, too, the concern is with societal transformations in which technological and industrial growth are seen as primary causal factors. However, there is a crucial difference in the contexts of social change treated by these two sets of scholars.

The earlier writers were examining the consequences of an emerging technology and industrial economy. Nowhere in history prior to the industrial revolution had these forms of knowledge existed. Consequently, they required the creation of new forms of human activity, new social values, and new normative orders. Analysis and interpretation of these nascent social and cultural forms constitutes a theory (or theories) of evolutionary social change. Modernization scholars are confronted with the problem of mapping social change in societies which borrow and adopt technology and economic patterns from other societies and enter into a world market already dominated by established industrial societies. Theirs is primarily a theory of social and cultural change through the twin processes of diffusion and adoption.

Neither of these bodies of literature deals precisely with the issues of nonmetropolitan industrial development--the spatial redistribution of economic activity within an already industrialized society and the consequences it has for social and cultural patterns in the subnational region experiencing industrial invasion. The necessity for treating nonmetropolitan industrial development as a third type of social change alongside industrialization and modernization lies in the fact that we are dealing with communities rather than nations and in the fact that such communities are, on the whole, much more extensively integrated into the nation of which they are a part than are nations integrated into an international system.

While communities vary considerably in the extensiveness of their integration into and dependence upon the national system, no community can escape the reality of being linked to other communities through institutions of government, commerce, education, religion, and social welfare. Even the most isolated Appalachia town, or Indian village in northern Arizona, is an integral part of the United States. Yet the interface between local and national systems is little understood and often overlooked.

Social policy intended to deal with local problems seems frequently to treat communities as though they existed independently of the nation. From this orientation we have programs which presume that local problems can be handled effectively by local officials if only they are provided with financial and technical resources. Thus, for example, the rising crime rate in communities was first approached by providing federal funds to strengthen law enforcement agencies. No doubt many communities needed the added services but the logic behind their provision begs the question of why the increases in crime rates.

It is quite evident that many community problems are problems in the community but not of the community. Unemployment, poverty, outmigration, inflation, and rising real estate taxes are a few of the instances where clearly the local manifestation is an outgrowth of decisions and events beyond the community. Therefore, any successful solution must deal with the interface between local systems and the national system. And in some instances even international linkages must be considered, especially in border communities.

Faced with the reality that many community problems are localized symptoms of regional or national system problems, there is a temptation to declare the local community irrelevant. But the truth is far from that. People live their lives in towns, villages, rural communities, cities, and neighborhoods. National or regional level policies and programs ultimately must be judged according to their effectiveness and efficiency in the communities where people seek employment, job training, medical services, and all the other items included in the general welfare catalog. Rather than discard the community as a policy- and program-relevant social organization, there is a pressing need to understand better the community as a social system with an integrity of its own but which also is interfaced with nonlocal systems.

It should be fairly evident that the community is, for us, an important entity in the arena of political economics. Communities are complex systems with many goals which must be arranged in some scale of relative urgency. Which goals--or more precisely, whose goals--prevail in a system with finite resources is a fundamental issue because its resolution determines many other facets of life in a community. Within any community there are many interested parties struggling to lift their goals to the highest possible position on the priority list. But it is useful to divide these parties into two sectors--the private and public.

The distinction is an important one because the proponents of industrial development frequently equate community welfare with the health of the private sector. This is a small town version of Charles Wilson's belief that what was good for General Motors was good for the United States. We are honestly skeptical of the universal truth of such a dictum at either the national or local level. Rather we regard the investigation of who benefits from industrial development to be incomplete at present. For that matter, we do not presume that all communities benefit from industrial development.

In the political economics of nonmetropolitan industrial development we discern four principal parties: the local private and public sectors and the nonlocal private and public sectors. The nonlocal sectors may be further divided into state, regional, or national, but the four party model is a sufficient analytical framework for beginning the business of understanding the dynamics involved. Presumably each of these parties will assess nonmetropolitan industrial development according to its own criteria of potential costs and benefits and will carry on activity in the arena of political economics to maximize benefits and minimize costs. However, it appears to us there are inequalities among the parties with respect to their ability to make informed assessments and act in their interests.

Both the private and public sectors of local communities generally are ill-prepared to determine the potential benefits and costs of industrial development. In many instances they lack well defined criteria for assessment as well as the expertise needed to collect and weigh the evidence. Within the local community the public sector is even more handicapped than the private sector. Thus, both local parties are relatively ineffective participants in the arena of political economics.

One of our objectives in preparing this work has been that of examining past experiences with nonmetropolitan industrial development from the point of view of local communities. Much of what has been written previously implicitly, if not explicitly, examines the process from the perspective of the nonlocal private sector. Governmental agencies, federal and state, represent the nonlocal public sector as is reasonable. However, we fail to find in these literatures data or discussion of some aspects of industrial development which are the unique concern of the local community sectors. We hope the review and discussion which follow will begin the process of expanding our understanding of the implications of industrial development for both the public and private sectors of nonmetropolitan communities.

In the postwar period manufacturing industries have been expanding into the nonmetropolitan areas of the United States and the rate of this industrial migration has been increasing. Between 1960 and 1970 manufacturing employment in metropolitan areas grew by 4 percent while nonmetropolitan areas had a 22 percent growth.

Some architects of public policy view the location of industry in small cities, towns, and rural areas as an important tool for solving the twin problems of rural poverty and urban crisis. It is regarded as a primary instrument for achieving the policy goals set forth in federal legislation. For example, its use is explicit in the Economic Opportunity Act of 1964, the Public Works and Economic Development Act of 1965, the Appalachian Regional Development Act of 1965, and the Rural Development Act of 1972.

This work attempts to assess the validity of this view of rural industrial development. To do so we draw upon case study documents for research results about the impact of industrial development upon (1) the population dynamics, (2) the private sector, (3) the public sector, and (4) the quality of individual well-being in the host communities. From these findings we induce generalizations which are then considered in light of publicly stated policy goals.

It is essential to describe the data base from which our generalizations are drawn. There have been many investigations of the impacts of locating an industrial plant in a nonmetropolitan community. Most often the investigation was started <u>after</u> the plant was constructed and in operation. In a few instances, investigation coincided with plant development. These case study research efforts are the raw material for this work. For nearly a year we sought documents reporting results of impact case studies and by June 1974 had retrieved the 186 documents which are digested in the following pages.

1

The studies summarized here offer a regional flavor and also involve many types and sizes of industrial plants. Moreover, the towns and counties which hosted new plants provide a sampling of the types and sizes of communities for which industrial development is purported to offer hope. Where findings are repeated across regions, types of communities, and types of industrial firms we feel reasonably confident that we have uncovered a valid generalization.

Yet, we feel compelled to caution that the plant sites selected by the original researchers and identified by us do not constitute a representative sample of all such new plant locations in the United States between 1945 and the present.

The studies come predominantly from the Midwest and the South. They often were done by economists or sociologists associated with a state's agricultural experiment station and land grant college. What biases may have influenced the researchers' site selections and problem specifications, we cannot know.

EMPIRICAL GENERALIZATIONS

With that caveat we turn to the empirical generalizations:

1. In a clear majority of plant locations, the host community experiences population growth.

2. The population growth effect of a new plant is concentrated in villages and towns nearest the plant site.

3. The rate of population growth clearly is a function of the size of the industrial firm.

4. The initial source of population growth is likely to be increased inmigration coupled with unchanged or decreased outmigration.

5. The majority (2/3 to 3/4) of inmigrants move no farther than 50 miles. Those who move farther are probably managers and technical personnel.

6. The proportion of the host county's population living in places of 2,500 or more is increased by industrial development, with some growth also in hamlets and the open country.

7. Nonmetropolitan industrial workers, as a group, are residentially more mobile that rural dwellers generally.

8. Nonmetropolitan workers often commute long distances for a period of time after employment, but in the long run they move closer to their place of work, or change jobs.

9. The labor sheds of nonmetropolitan industrial plants often are larger than those in metropolitan areas, their size depending on many factors including size of towns near the plant, local highway

system, wage differentials between the plant and other local employers, and personal attributes of the workers.

10. Employers prefer younger workers although in some instances, skill gained through experience may be competitive with youth.

11. Preferences for male versus female employees are related to the type of industry, with males predominating in the heavy manufacturing industries and females being favored in the light industries such as apparel, textile, and appliance assembly plants. The latter are low-skilled, low-wage industries.

12. There is considerable evidence that nonwhites are underrepresented in the work forces of nonmetropolitan industrial plants. Where they are hired they are concentrated in unskilled and semiskilled jobs. This situation may indicate outright discriminatory hiring practices, or insufficient skill level among local nonwhites, or both.

13. Nonmetropolitan industrial workers have larger households than the local area residents generally. This appears to be a function of their age relative to the local population; more are in the child bearing and child rearing stages of the family cycle.

14. There is virtually no evidence that industrial development increases the level of educational attainment in the host community. Where it does occur the evidence suggests it is due to changes in the age structure, younger adults generally having completed more years of schooling.

15. New jobs often do not go to the local unemployed, underemployed, minorities, and marginally employable persons likely to be near or below the poverty level.

16. High-skill, high-wage industries, which are most likely to increase the aggregate income and raise the percentage of families above the poverty level, are least likely to hire local disadvantaged. The apparent gains in aggregate income and unemployment rate often hide the failure to aid the local disadvantaged.

17. Low-skill, low-wage industries are more likely to employ the disadvantaged.

18. Most female workers expect to draw unemployment if laid off and retire from the labor market if no work can be found locally. Moving the household to secure the wife's employment is not regarded by most female workers as a viable alternative.

19. Most male workers expect to seek other industrial work if laid off. Few would consider returning to farm work. Moving to another community to secure employment is an undesirable, but viable alternative.

20. Worker dissatisfactions with wage work in industry are offset by higher standards of living, job security, shorter hours, easier work, and greater chances of advancement.

21. Industrial firms often are offered inducements by the local community to encourage their choice of the community as a plant site.

22. Increase in the fiscal resource base of the local community often is outweighed by increased costs of providing services to the new industry and the community.

23. Net fiscal gains to the local government do occur. This usually is when no local subsidy was offered the industry, or the plant work force is hired locally, or large proportions of the plant work force live outside the community and commute to work.

24. Where new industry is accompanied by population growth it often strains existing basic service delivery systems.

25. Anticipated benefits to the local community generally exceed perceived benefits after development. Even so, the percentage of local citizens perceiving benefits outweighs those expressing negative opinions.

26. Those not perceiving personal benefits are heavily concentrated among the old, the ethnic and racial minorities, the unemployed, and farmers.

27. Having experienced industrial development, a majority of the local citizens want more.

28. Many local residents express positive feelings about one or another aspect of industrial invasion; for example, population growth, inmigrants, economic diversification, improved local shopping, and opportunity for off-farm work. While there are contrary feelings expressed, the scale weighs heavier in favor of optimism and satisfaction.

29. Inmigrants express more dissatisfaction with the local community services than long-term residents, particularly when the inmigrants are of higher skill and income levels that the host community residents.

30. Participation rates of industrial workers in voluntary organizations (churches, civic clubs, recreational) are similar to other community residents.

31. There is some evidence that choices of types of organizations in which to be involved differ between newcomers and long-term residents. The inmigrants show a propensity to favor business, professional, and labor organizations which appears to reflect their educational and occupational characteristics.

POLICY IMPLICATIONS

The above generalizations were weighed against the following public policy goals of federal legislation: to achieve a more balanced population distribution; to decrease the percentage of families below

the poverty level; to achieve greater equality of income; to reduce unemployment; to upgrade the quality and availability of basic services.
The results of that exercise in logic are distilled in the comments
which follow. They are not intended to be policy statements, but
rather statements which convey ideas relevant to existing policy or
the need for future policy.

1. Use of public money to induce industrial migration is not
necessary because of the existence of market conditions which stimulate migration decisions among managers of industrial capital. But
public money may be quite valuably spent as a steering mechanism to
guide industry's site selections to where their presence would bring
maximum benefit to the local public.

2. Low-skill, low-wage industries should be encouraged to
locate in communities (areas) with a surplus of low-skill labor. This
is viewed as a first stage of development to be followed by high-skill,
high-wage industry. Where surplus labor is highly skilled as well,
the two stages might well be executed simultaneously.

3. Recognizing that managers of private capital must make decisions which maximize capital gains for the firm it is very likely
some communities which do not attract private capital could nevertheless support low-profit enterprises. In those instances it would
be equitable to use public money to subsidize the formation of local
cooperatives and/or public profit-making corporations.

4. In order to ensure that disadvantaged residents are not by-
passed by the employment benefits generated through rural industrial
development, training programs to upgrade the skills of the local
population should be established and antidiscrimination laws should
be enforced. For publicly assisted plants, stipulations should be
made as to the proportion of poor or unemployed persons that must
be hired.

5. The small towns which will receive assistance in building
infrastructure and attracting industry should be carefully selected so
that funds are not dissipated on areas with little self-generating
growth potential. For this purpose, greater use should be made of
comprehensive research techniques, whether by government, private, or academic analysts.

6. Broad-based, long-range development strategies, involving
a number of industries and not only manufacturing, should be created
in order to begin solving the areawide problems of unemployment and
economic stagnation. This would require expanded funding and functioning of regional planning bodies.

7. There is a need to create awareness among rural populations of the type and extent of changes that industrialization may
bring. Results commonly expected are new jobs and population

stabilization, while changes in the social structure and leadership are less often anticipated.

8. Strain on a community's public services may be minimized by attracting a plant of suitable size; that is, either one that makes few demands on existing facilities such as medical, police, and fire services, or one which is large enough to provide these for itself.

9. A comprehensive labor survey in the early planning stages of location may help match supply and demand. The size and skill levels of potential male and female employees should be documented.

10. Firms locating in rural areas could be made aware of, and encouraged to participate in, government minority training assistance programs, especially where a labor survey has shown a large potential supply of unskilled, racial minorities, and women.

11. Since many rural industrial workers are young people with families, provision of schools and other child-oriented services such as day care centers is important. Assistance may be required to establish and expand these facilities in order to attract skilled workers and utilize local female labor.

12. The pattern of population growth and residential location associated with industrial development in nonmetropolitan areas is certain to exacerbate the taxation of agricultural land and further weaken the economic viability of farm enterprises. Therefore, it would seem prudent to establish a national land use policy which safeguards the future of agricultural land.

13. A national level program of training and assistance to local government officials and public administrators should be established. The fiscal resource base of many communities appears to be inefficiently utilized because of ineptness and lack of knowledge about such matters on the part of local officials.

2

INDUSTRIAL LOCATION
IN THE UNITED STATES

Industrial location in the United States has received extensive attention in a wide variety of disciplines including geography, economics, and regional planning. Some of the most useful examinations of locational phenomena have been presented by Perloff et al. (1960), Chinitz and Vernon (1960), Fuchs (1962), and Creamer (1963). Since these major discussions have dealt with many facets of industrial location which are only tangential to this work, the bulk of their content will not be reviewed here. Our concern is primarily with the description of trends in industrial location rather than the development of an analytical framework of location. Those readers wishing to pursue the conceptual background of many assumptions in our discussion are referred to Smith's (1972) more theoretical treatment, Industrial Location.

The present chapter focuses on three trends in industrial location which are the harbingers of industrial decentralization in the United States: the shift of industrial development from the Northeast to the South and West; the suburbanization of industries within metropolitan areas; the industrial development of nonmetropolitan communities and of rural areas. To varying degrees, these trends have characterized industrial location since the end of World War II. They are critical processes in the ongoing decentralization of industry. While our primary concern is nonmetropolitan development, we believe a prior discussion of regional and intrametropolitan shifts in industrial location will provide a useful backdrop to subsequent chapters.

REGIONAL SHIFTS

Industrial development in the nineteenth century and the early 1900s resulted in a clear concentration of manufacturing in the Northeast and, to a lesser extent, the north central region. The nature and degree of this concentration has been documented by Thompson (1933) and McLaughlin (1938).

Since the 1920s, however, there has been a surge in industrial development in the western and southern regions. This growth has involved both the development of new industries and the relocation of industries from the northeastern section of the country. Perhaps Fuchs (1962) has most succinctly described this phenomenon: "since 1919 the direction of redistribution of manufacturing has been away from the Northeast and toward the South and West."

In 1929, for example, the South and West together accounted for less than one out of every four manufacturing jobs (Fuchs, 1962). By 1958, however, this proportion had increased to one in three. This trend accelerated after World War II. Table 2.1 shows the growth in manufacturing employment for each of the four regions during the period 1947-63. As the data in Table 2.1 indicate, postwar industrial growth occurred largely outside the northern regions. While the percentage growth in manufacturing employment in the West was a startling 100.9 percent and 50.7 percent for the South it was only 21.1 percent for the north central region. And in the Northeast, percentage growth was actually negative (-0.2 percent). These data demonstrate the marked industrial growth that characterized the South and West from 1947 to 1963.

TABLE 2.1

Manufacturing Employment Growth by Region, 1947-63

Region	Number of States	Percentage Growth
United States	48	45.2
Northeast	9	-0.2
North central	12	21.1
South	16	50.7
West	11	100.9

Source: Leonard F. Wheat, Regional Growth and Industrial Location (Lexington, Mass.: D. C. Heath and Co., 1973), p. 3.

Further, this regional shift has continued. In the 1960s, the Northeast had a growth of 11.8 percent in manufacturing employment. This compared to a national average growth of 19.4 percent. During the same period, the increase in the South was almost 30 percent and in the West it was about 26 percent (see Patrick, 1973).

While a variety of reasons for these regional shifts in industrial location have been advanced in the literature, some of the most important are as follows.

1. <u>Shifts in the location of markets</u> have been characterized as a major determinant of industrial location by McLaughlin and Robock (1949), Thompson and Mattila (1959), and Perloff et al. (1960). The general reasoning behind this argument is that shifts in the population generate concomitant shifts in industrial location. See Smith (1972, pp. 61-62) for a discussion of how the market influences plant location.

2. <u>Labor-oriented variables</u> have also been viewed as important determinants of industrial location. The lower degree of unionization in the South, for example, has often been advanced as a reason for rapid industrial growth in that region (see for example McLaughlin and Robock's early statement <u>Why Industry Moves South</u>).

Another labor-oriented determinant of location relates to the surplus labor force generated by the mechanization of agriculture in the South. Fuchs (1962) argued that four labor-oriented industries-- textiles, apparel, footwear, and furniture--substantially contributed to southern gains in manufacturing since World War II. At the same time, the Northeast showed marked losses in these labor intensive industries.

3. <u>Climate</u> is widely accepted as a major determinant of industrial location. The best example, of course, is the aircraft industry. Fuchs (1962) argued that since climate affects migration in general it spurs the growth of market-oriented industries in areas of heavy in-migration.

While these three factors, of course, are only a few of the determinants of regional shifts in industrial location, they do comprise a core of reasons for the shift West and South. A complete theory of these locational shifts, however, is yet to be forthcoming.

SUBURBANIZATION OF INDUSTRY

Just as early industrial location in the United States was concentrated in the Northeast so was much growth concentrated in the central city (Thompson, 1933). At least since the 1920s, however, the trend in location has been toward a diffusion of industry within large metropolitan areas. In the 48 largest metropolitan areas, for example, the proportion of manufacturing workers in the central city as opposed to the suburbs declined from 66.5 percent in 1929 to 57.5 percent in 1954 (Vernon, 1959).

Further, while the intrametropolitan diffusion of industry began
in the early part of the century it has dramatically increased since
1947. Dean (1973) presented data which indicate that the post-World
War II rate of diffusion was approximately three times as great as
that during the prewar decades. Kain's (1969) data for the 40 largest
standard metropolitan statistical areas (SMSAs) indicate this trend is
especially significant in these areas. From 1947 to 1963 the percent
of manufacturing employment in the central cities declined from 66.9
percent to 48.2 percent--a trend that continued into the 1970s (Dean,
1973).

Like regional shifts in industrial location, the suburbanization
of industry has been generated and spurred by a number of variables.
Some of the most important determining factors can be briefly described here.

1. Transportation variables have been depicted by Moses and
Williamson (1967) as associated with the intrametropolitan distribution of industry. They argue that before the rise of the truck and
automobile it was cheaper to move people to jobs than jobs to people
(Dean, 1973). With the availability of automotive transportation,
however, manufacturing firms tend to locate near the large pools of
labor in the suburbs.

2. Space has long been recognized as a determinant of industrial location. Fuchs (1962) pointed out the search for abundant, in-
expensive space is associated with the movement of industry to the
suburbs. Dean (1973) has noted that suburban sites are generally
less expensive than their central city counterparts. Hoover and
Vernon (1959), for example, demonstrated that the cost of locating a
modern metalworking plant in Manhattan was about $2.3 million more
than that of a comparable site in the suburbs.

3. Taxes have traditionally been lower in the suburbs than in
the central city. This differential undoubtedly resulted in a considerable amount of industrial growth in the suburbs during the 1950s and
1960s. As Dean (1973) has pointed out, however, dramatic increases
in state taxes have generally placed local taxes in a secondary role.
In short, local taxes now comprise only a small percentage of an industry's tax bill.

4. Population increases in the suburbs have stimulated industrial growth along at least two dimensions. First, many industries
have been attracted by the market created by a burgeoning suburban
population. Second, the tremendous post-World War II increase in
the suburban population has resulted in the emergence of a huge reservoir of professional, technical, and clerical labor in the suburbs
(Dean, 1973). As a result, many industries requiring such labor
have located in the suburbs.

These are just some of the factors influencing the suburbanization of industry after World War II. As Dean (1973) has pointed out,
intrametropolitan industrial location remains a fertile area of study,
particularly in regard to the impact of such location and the nature
of the phenomenon in younger metropolitan areas.

NONMETROPOLITAN INDUSTRIAL DEVELOPMENT

Even a cursory review of the literature indicates that the two
processes described above--regional shifts in industry and suburbanization of industry--have received a great deal of investigation and discussion. On the other hand, the third process of decentralization discussed here--nonmetropolitan industrial development--has been
largely ignored in the literature. Heretofore, there have been few
systematic attempts to evaluate industrial location in nonmetropolitan areas.

At least two reasons account for the paucity of research on industrial development outside metropolitan areas. First, the phenomenon itself is comparatively recent. While the movement of industry to the South and West began in the 1920s and intrametropolitan
diffusion of industry emerged even earlier, industrial development in
nonmetropolitan areas did not reach even modest proportions until
the 1960s. Thus, in terms of time alone, there has not been an opportunity for thorough research.

Second, the almost awesome growth of metropolitan areas in
the postwar period led to a concentration of research on the problems
and issues associated with metropolitan development. This metropolitan emphasis has led to less research on small population group-
ings and continues to dominate study in most relevant disciplines.
Indeed, some analysts foreseeing a metropolitanization of the country
have preferred to focus on this phenomenon (cf. Pickard, 1972).
Further, some regional geographers and economists have argued that
nonmetropolitan growth is insignificant compared with SMSA growth
(Till, 1973).

Fortunately, it appears that research on nonmetropolitan development is slowly increasing. On the one hand, there has been increased empirical investigation in the area (cf. Stuart, 1971; Summers,
1973; Till, 1973; Jordan, 1967). These studies provide the foundation
for more comprehensive efforts such as this work. In addition, the
argument that industrial growth in nonmetropolitan areas is unimpor-
tant has been successfully rebutted by a variety of writers including
Bird (1973), Haren (1970), and Beale (1969).

Further, the data indicate that the construction of industries in
small towns and rural areas is one of the major trends in industrial

development in the United States. As Haren (1970) has noted, in the 1960s about 20 percent of the national increase in manufacturing employment stemmed from new plant locations in nonmetropolitan areas. And in the South, the region some have called the economic pacesetter of the 1970s, rural industrial locations are even more pronounced. Between 1962 and 1972 over 600,000 manufacturing jobs were added in rural and nonmetropolitan areas of the Southeast (Haren, 1973). This increase was about twice the increase in the metropolitan areas and equaled one-third of the entire U.S. expansion over the ten-year period. Finally, as Lonsdale and Browning (1971) have pointed out, there is currently a strong tendency among southern manufacturers to locate in rural areas or small communities.

In short, then, there can be little doubt that nonmetropolitan industrial location has reached at least modest proportions. Even more important, there is reason to believe this trend will continue and even accelerate. With this argument in mind, we believe it is useful here to delineate several of the major reasons why nonmetropolitan industrial growth has become important and why it will increasingly comprise a significant segment of industrial location in the United States.

1. Federal dispersion policies. As Smith (1972) has pointed out, the extent to which government should intervene in industrial location and related business decisions is an important question facing the United States as well as several other Western countries. Advocates of a laissez faire policy have argued that in the long run the price system will produce an optimal spatial pattern of industrial activity at both the national and regional levels. Experience, however, has demonstrated that several major assumptions of the free market model are not substantiated in the real world (Hansen, 1970; Smith, 1972). Consequently, uneven distribution of industrial activity--a saturation in some areas and a negligible amount in others--has generated severe social, economic, and environmental problems and has led to increasing governmental intervention.

One facet of this intervention which is most apparent is the program to promote the flow of capital into areas of lagging economic growth (see for example the Appalachian Regional Development Act of 1965 and the Public Works and Economic Development Act of 1965). As was pointed out in the Rural Development Act of 1972: "Rural development means the planning . . . development and expansion of business and industry in non-metropolitan areas to provide increased employment and income. . . ." The act earmarks large sums of money to stimulate such development. The reasoning behind such efforts is that this mode of decentralizing industry will not only benefit economically depressed areas but at the same time will help relieve the environmental and demographic problems of areas of overindustrialization.

2. Local community support. From the local point of view industrial development represents additional revenue, increased employment, and general economic expansion. Most importantly, there
is the assumption that bringing industry to nonmetropolitan areas will
stifle outmigration and thereby stabilize the population. Indeed, as
Marshall (1965) has pointed out, these assumptions are so widespread
that there is ever increasing competition among small communities to
attract industry. There are over 14,000 agencies now engaged in actively promoting industrial development for the various geographic
and political subdivisions they represent (Hansen and Munsinger, 1972).
And, the U.S. Department of Agriculture's Yearbook of Agriculture,
1971 had a chapter entitled "How a Town Can Attract Industry." These
factors, coupled with the popularity of the pamphlet What Will Industry
Mean to My Town?, provide strong support for the argument that local
community leaders seek industrial development. In fact, a poll of
small town bankers in the United States has indicated that the majority
felt lack of industry was the major economic problem of their community (see Urban Life, October 1972, p. 2).

3. Willingness of industry. As was previously pointed out,
Lonsdale and Browning (1971) found strong preferences among southern manufacturers to locate new industry in small towns and rural
areas. This phenomenon appears to be increasing throughout the
country for a variety of reasons including (1) lower land and water
costs, (2) tax exemptions often offered by local communities, (3) in-
ability to attract skilled personnel to plants in the central city of an
SMSA, and (4) the belief of some industrial leaders that there is more
of a work ethic in small towns and rural residents.

4. Surplus labor pool in nonmetropolitan areas. As Till (1973)
has noted, drastic declines in farm jobs, not fully offset by outmigration, have created a surplus labor force that is attractive to labor-
intensive industries. Till argues that this abundance of low-wage
labor operates as a prime locational inducement.

5. Transportation advances have made it possible to locate
plants outside metropolitan areas. The national interstate system,
for example, has given firms increased flexibility in locating new
plants (Dean, 1973).

It seems reasonable to argue that this broad set of factors has
not only operated to stimulate nonmetropolitan industrial development
in the past, but will have a significant impact in the future. The dis-
persal policy of the federal government, for example, seems likely
to be greatly expanded. It has widespread public support. A majority of the population believe something must be done to inhibit metropolitan growth in the United States (see the Report of the President's
Commission on Population Growth, 1972).

CONCLUSION

Given our assumption of continued and increased industrial location in nonmetropolitan areas the question arises as to the social, economic, and demographic consequences of such development. More specifically, what will industrial development really mean to these small towns and rural communities? To date, there is only scattered information regarding the impact of the construction of industries in these areas. To our knowledge, while there are several dozen case studies of such construction the results have never been compared or synthesized. The underlying purpose of this work is to take the first step toward a grounded explanation of the consequences of nonmetropolitan industrial development by placing the results of the various case studies in a coherent framework.

3

THE CASE STUDIES:
1945-73

The 186 study documents on which the analyses in this work are based were collected from many sources in 1973 and 1974. They are the result of an extensive search, but do not include every relevant study due to the constraints of time and the law of diminishing returns. They are a large sample of all studies carried out on manufacturing plants locating outside the standard metropolitan statistical areas of the United States between 1945 and 1973.

Manufacturing plants in more than 245 locations were studied. The exact figure, in common with other figures in the following pages, is not known because some authors did not provide these data. These factories were located in 34 states, with some marked concentrations in the Midwest and the South. Every state in the North Central Census Region (North Dakota, South Dakota, Nebraska, Kansas, Minnesota, Iowa, Missouri, Wisconsin, Illinois, Michigan, Indiana, Ohio) contained at least one study location. In the South there were groups of locations in the Ozarks, Kentucky, Arkansas, Mississippi, and the Carolinas. West Virginia, Virginia, Tennessee, Alabama, Georgia, Louisiana, Oklahoma, and Texas also contained studied plants. In the Northeast only Pennsylvania and New York were represented. In the Western Census Region there were a group of plant sites in Utah, and small numbers in New Mexico, Arizona, California, Oregon, and Montana. This distribution of manufacturing locations did not represent that of all factories established in rural areas between 1945 and 1973, simply those that were chosen for examination by investigators with many different purposes. More than 728 plants were studied, some singly, but many in groups of up to 110. Usually the greater the number of plants in a study, the less detailed the description of each, and the more aggregated the data. A number of factories were studied by more than one author and their impacts described in more than one publication. By far the most comprehensive study was carried out on a large steel plant at Hennepin, Illinois. Between 1968 and 1974 33 researchers produced 72 documents discussing the impacts of the plant.

While the time frame of this review and synthesis was 1945 to 1973, a majority of the plants were established between 1950 and 1960. There was also a large group that began operating between 1960 and 1970, with very few beginning before 1950 or after 1970. In the latter case, it is likely that research on long-run impacts is still being done, rather than that a sharp decline in rural industrial development has occurred. In the 1950-70 period, more than half the new industries located in the South.

The authors of the documents used several units of analysis to describe industrialization impacts. The majority focused on the town and/or county where the factory was located. Some extended the impact area to encompass parts or all of several counties. In comprehensive studies describing many plants, the unit of analysis was frequently a state, several states, or even a whole region such as the Southern Census Region.

The data base for these analyses was collected by several methods, and many investigators used more than one to obtain the necessary information. A common technique was the survey, either by personal interview or mail, which was used to gather data from plant employers and employees, company executives, inmigrants, farmers, local leaders, ministers, residents, and others. Many authors used information from secondary sources such as census publications, company records, state and federal documents, and local administrative records. Researchers also undertook some participant observation in the communities they were studying. Based on the information thus collected, the authors produced documents ranging from descriptive pieces to publications involving complex statistical analysis. Some articles use the data as background material in the illustration of current sociological-methodological approaches.

A total of 143 people wrote the 186 documents; 73 were sole authors and the rest were coauthors in groups of up to four. They were affiliated with a variety of institutions, including universities, and federal and state departments. They worked in universities in Tennessee, Louisiana, Wisconsin, Oklahoma, Arkansas, Missouri, Virginia, Illinois, Utah, Kansas, New York, Iowa, Kentucky, Texas, North Dakota, Montana, Minnesota, Pennsylvania, Mississippi, Ohio, Massachusetts, South Carolina, Oregon, Indiana, California, West Virginia, and South Dakota. Their areas of competence were mainly in the social sciences and commerce-economics; sociology, rural sociology, anthropology, commerce, industrial development, geography, land economics, industrial management, and marketing.

Federal and state institutions were represented by those in the U.S. Department of Agriculture (both the economic Research Service and the Agricultural Marketing Service), the U.S. Department of Commerce (Economic Development Administration), and state departments of highways, and audit and control. Some authors were employed by county or state development commissions or by private corporations. Several were associated with the American Industrial Development Council, and one was employed by a museum.

The case study documents appeared in the form of theses, journal articles, papers, bulletins, and reports. Several were in the form of bulletins from agricultural experiment stations at universities including Ohio, Louisiana, Utah, Kansas, Mississippi, Missouri, North Dakota, Arkansas, Iowa, Oklahoma, West Virginia, Clemson, Purdue, and Illinois. The theses were prepared for degrees at the master's and doctoral levels from many universities and the American Industrial Development Council. Many papers and reports were published by research units within universities in the areas of applied sociology, rural development, business, labor and industrial relations, and industrial development. Other sponsors included industrial and economic development committees and commissions, government agencies (Office of Economic Opportunity, Atomic Energy Commission), and professional societies. Many of the findings of researchers were published in journals of various kinds. These included national professional journals (in sociology, economics, rural sociology, industrial development, business, labor, medicine, anthropology), and regional publications (farm science, geography).

The industries under study were of many types and sizes. The predominant types were metal production and fabrication, chemicals, and apparel. Some of the many manufacturing products studied were as follows.

farm equipment	woolen yarn
steel	shirts
auto parts	shoes
custom tools	synthetic fibers
magnets	carpets
copper tubing	cameras
watch bearings	electronic equipment
business machines	pharmaceuticals
aircraft parts	plastics
storm windows	luggage
boilers	bedding
mobile homes	monuments
boxes	medical supplies
furniture	athletic equipment
tissue paper	stadium bleachers
whisky barrels	

The factories ranged in size from fewer than ten workers to over four thousand. Plants with fewer than one hundred employees produced such items as tissue paper, electric meters, bedding, and particle board. Those with between one hundred and one thousand workers typically made furniture, metal products, chemicals, apparel, and rubber products. Plants employing more than one thousand workers (there were eight such plants) produced aluminum, steel, engines, synthetic fibers, chemicals, business machines, and rocket fuel.

The analyses of the impacts of rural industrialization--economic, demographic, and social--are based on this collection of case study documents.

4

**POPULATION
GROWTH AND CHANGE**

Historically, rural/urban population distribution in the United States has been greatly influenced by technology. Before 1920 the majority of people lived in rural areas, but during the Civil War era an important trend of population redistribution began. Technological developments in the middle of the nineteenth century set off the process of industrialization and accompanying urbanization. Increasing employment opportunities in the cities induced a stream of migrants from rural regions. At the same time, the advancing mechanization of agriculture made many farm workers redundant, and these people swelled the flow to the cities. Heavy rural-to-urban migration continued throughout the nineteenth and twentieth centuries, and since 1870 urban population growth has accounted for more than half of the nation's population growth. Major consequences of this long-term trend have been the concentration of people in urbanized areas, that is, uneven national distribution, due to disproportionate growth in the cities, and abnormal population composition in rural areas. In 1960, 82 percent of overall population growth in the previous ten years had occurred in urban places. The small amount of growth in rural areas, combined with high outmigration of certain age groups has left these populations unbalanced, especially as regards age structure. Outmigrants are likely to be young people, who doubly deplete the population. Their departure deprives rural communities of both current and future members, for they are potential contributors to growth by natural increase.

Both rural residents and national policymakers, hoping to halt rural outmigration, stabilize population, and bring about growth, see industrial development as a solution to these imbalances. Chapter 4 describes what happened to the population of some rural communities where industry was introduced. Population size, distribution, and structure are examined and the impacts of rural industrial development on them are discussed.

SIZE

Almost all of the studies describing nonmetropolitan industrial development provide information on demographic variables. However, in many cases population data are given as background information, while the main focus is on economic or other aspects; hence many gaps become evident when the data are summarized. Table 4.1 shows the distribution of demographic data in the studies. In addition, some studies do not provide information about the location of an industry, number of employees, or the type of manufacturing involved. The net result of these missing data is to make it difficult to describe relationships and unwise to draw detailed conclusions.

TABLE 4.1

Distribution of Demographic Data Provided in 79 Studies

| | Unit of Analysis | | | | |
Variable	Town	County	Other Area	Industrial Employees	Rural Residents
Population size	4	--	2	--	--
Population size and change	25	29	16	--	--
Migration	3	10	8	15	--
Commuting	--	1	9	14	--
Population distribution	3	10	7	13	1
Population composition					
age	1	7	6	15	2
sex	1	3	3	15	2
family and marital	--	2	2	8	2
Residential mobility	1	5	3	5	--
Education levels	3	10	7	12	1
Religion	--	1	--	--	--
Household size	--	2	1	1	--

Note: A variable may be discussed in the context of several units of analysis in the same study; dashes indicate data not provided by studies.

Source: Compiled by the authors.

Population Size and Change

One of the common predictions about the introduction of industry into small towns is that it will remedy the decline in population that most rural areas have suffered. This is seen to be a beneficial, immediate impact, and there is little conjecture as to the long-term effects. Less obvious questions, but ones which require answering are (1) What type of industry is associated, if at all, with population increase? and (2) What size of industrial plant is associated, if at all, with population increase?

In six case histories, population size is given only as part of the preplant description of the study area, and change over the period of industrialization is not stated.

Fifty-eight studies document changes in population size in towns, counties, and larger areas after industry became established. Table 4.2 shows the proportion of communities experiencing population gains.

TABLE 4.2

Proportion of Towns and Counties Showing Population
Increase Following Plant Establishment,
by Census Region

Unit of Analysis	Regions							
	West		North Central		South		All Regions	
	No.	%	No.	%	No.	%	No.	%
Town	2	100	16	93	9	78	27	86
County	2	100	17	35	12	67	31	52
All units	4	100	33	64	21	73	58	68

Source: Compiled by the authors.

A three-county area in the Southern region also showed population gains. Table 4.2 shows that nearly all the towns had gained population, while fewer than half the counties had done so. The Western Census Region is represented by two towns and two counties, all of which had gained. In the North Central Region approximately one-third of the counties had increased in size, while almost all the towns had population gains. In the South, two-thirds of the counties

and nearly four-fifths of the towns had experienced population growth.
In both the North Central and Southern regions, the percentage of
areas showing increased population was close to the national average
of 68 percent.

These figures suggest that towns are more likely to grow as a
result of industrial growth than counties; that the demographic effect
of the new plant is concentrated around its location. In many instances,
the towns containing, or nearest to, the factory grew, while the surrounding county declined, suggesting that outmigration was continuing
from rural areas. However, some workers who may otherwise have
moved out of the county in search of a job, may have moved to the locality of the plant, thus adding to migration into the towns, but having
no effect on county population levels.

As well as the towns which grew steadily with industrial development, there were two which grew, then declined. The net results
were increased population and no change respectively. In a study of
six Wisconsin cities Andrews et al. (1959) find that the three less
industrialized cities grew at a slower rate than the three that were
more industrialized.

Few towns lost population during the industrial immigation
period, but over half the counties did so. Three counties recorded
both losses and gains in a year by year breakdown of the study period.
These three showed one net gain, one net loss, and one unspecified
net effect. One study (Dietz, 1971) describes 13 towns, the total
population of which increased by 95 percent in 30 years, while the
total population of their respective counties decreased 10 percent,
pointing to heavy outmigration. Another study (Till, 1972) document-
ing changes in counties in 13 Southern states finds that in those up to
50 miles from a standard metropolitan statistical area (SMSA), there
was growth regardless of the size of the main city in the county.
Those 50 to 200 miles from an SMSA also grew, except for those
where the initial population of the main city was less than 2,500. In
this category there were slight losses.

While these results show that population increase associated
with new industry is more likely to occur in the town nearest the plant
site than in the surrounding county, the causal link between industrial
invasion and population growth is not explicitly discussed in many of
the studies, and some point out likely causes of growth other than new
industry.

Many rural areas had been losing population prior to industrial
inmigration and the increase associated with the coming of new industry affected the rate of decline in several ways. Table 4.3 shows the
effect of the population increase associated with industrial invasion
on the previous rate of decline.

TABLE 4.3

Effect of Population Increase on Previous Rates
of Population Decline
(18 studies)

Effect on Previous Rate of Decline	Proportion of Relevant Studies
Slowed	1/6
Halted	1/6
Reversed	2/3

Source: Compiled by the authors.

In studies where this effect was discussed or implied, a majority show that population had increased sufficiently to achieve stability or turn the rate of change from a negative to a positive one.
The length of the study period differs in each case so that some of
these effects are short-term in nature, and may not be indicative of
long-run impacts.

Size of Plant and Population Increase

One measure of the size of an industrial plant is the number of
employees it has. Table 4.4 uses this indicator to show population
growth in towns and counties according to the size of the combined
work force of new plants.

In towns and counties where the industrial work force is greater
than 100, there is a steady increase in the population growth rate as
size of industry increases. The exception to this trend is in the
50-100 employee category, of which there are probably too few examples for the result to be meaningful.

There is a weak correlation between the size of the work force
of new industry and the likelihood of population growth, indicating
that there are many other influences on growth.

On the basis of these limited data, it may be tentatively concluded that towns and counties where the new industry has either
50-100 or 1,000+ employees are slightly more likely to grow than
those where the plant has 500-1,000 workers, and much more likely
to grow than those where the plant employs 100-500.

TABLE 4.4

Proportions of Towns and Counties with Increased
Population by Size of Work Force

Number of Plant	Percentage Showing Population Increase			
Employees	Towns	Counties	All	Number Studied
50–100	100	50	80	5
100–500	82	27	50	21
500–1,000	83	50	70	10
1,000+	100	67	79	19
Total	88	48	69	55

Source: Compiled by the authors.

Type of Industry and Population Increase

When the studies are classified by industry for analysis of the
effect of type of industry on the likelihood of population gains for towns
and counties, there are too few in most categories to allow meaningful comparisons. However, in the cases of metal production and
fabricating plants, and electrical and electronic equipment manufacturers, there are indications that the towns receiving these industries
are more likely to experience population growth than the surrounding
counties. This is in keeping with the findings detailed above in Table
4.2. Many towns had several types of new industry; thus it is difficult to single out the effects of each.

From the data available, it may be concluded that where new
industry is established in a rural area, it is the town rather than the
surrounding county that is likely to experience population growth. It
is not possible to make definitive statements about the effects of the
size of the industrial work force and the type of manufacturing on
change in population size due to the inadequacies of the data. Other
likely influences on population growth are nearness to an SMSA, regional factors, and recent growth.

MIGRATION

As noted above, many newly industrialized areas experienced
stabilization or reversal of their population decline. In view of the
general long-term decline in the rates of natural increase, that is,

excess of births over deaths in rural areas, this trend is not likely to be caused by a dramatic upsurge in the rate of natural increase, but points to changes in the ratio of inward and outward movement of population. Most of the new factories would have been responsible for some inmigration, and possibly outmigration, but only about one-third of the studies that provide demographic data discuss these important components of population change, and very few of these do so in terms of changes in the direction of net migration. That migration has occurred is implied by the population changes in many communities, but cannot be substantiated because details of numbers of births and deaths and population size at different points in time are not included.

It is thought or hoped by many rural or small town residents that the existence of industry in their community will help prevent the outmigration of young people, who have been leaving in droves. Very few studies mention this belief, and most can only surmise that outmigration has decreased due to the retention of unspecified age groups. The only study to look at this question in detail (Andrews and Bauder, 1968) finds that of the young adults leaving home, more left the county during the time the factory was established, and afterwards, than left previously. Thus, the expected reduction of movement of young single persons out of the county did not occur.

Fourteen of the case histories discuss inmigration only in terms of individuals or families, not as a rate. In many of these, the numbers involved were small and would have little effect on net migration. Two studies (Gray, 1969; Ryan, Clark, and Schkade, 1963) also mention outmigration in these terms. Where the plant construction phase of the industrial invasion process is singled out, it is stated that all the workers who moved in for this period moved out again, producing zero net migration. One town experienced continuing net outmigration for some time after the new plant went in, then a turnaround to net inmigration in the latter part of the study period. In another the migration flows were linked with fluctuations in the economy. More people came in than went out during the plant's peak employment period and in two years when there were recessions, but the reverse took place in each year following an economic downturn. In one case the net inflow became an outflow when the factory closed down, and the overall result for the community was net outmigration. One large plant (Gray, 1969) created net inmigration for several years. However, once its employment requirements stabilized and applicants began to realize that they did not have the necessary skills for the few jobs available, outmigration resumed. In only one study (Martin, 1960) is there reported long-term net inmigration, although this may have occurred, unreported, in many areas.

After looking at migration patterns of industrial workers in five towns, Wilcock (1954) concludes that when industry locates in a rural area, there is likely to be a slowing of the rate of outmigration, accompanied by the return of previous outmigrants, but with little or no inmigration from other areas. He attributed this to the availability of "surplus" labor in the vicinity of the new plant, that is, persons previously underemployed, or not in the labor force, such as part-time workers, housewives, and school-leavers.

In two cases, inmigrants are described as returning former residents, which implies that at least some of the rural residents who move to more urban areas in search of jobs want to move back and will do so if economic opportunities are available in their home towns. Among workers in 26 plants in Olsen and Kuehn's 1974 study of counties in Southern and Western states, 22 percent were inmigrants, and in some cases up to half of these were returnees. Bender, Green, and Campbell (1971) find that in the populations of counties in the Ozarks, 65 percent of inmigrants in the previous five years were returnees. As a group these people are likely to face fewer adjustment problems than fellow inmigrants, and identify with and become a part of the community more quickly. From the information available in 30 studies, it appears that the short-run impact of industrial invasion is likely to be increased inmigration and unchanged or decreased outmigration. There are too few studies, and information is not precise enough to enable characterization of migration in and out of towns, counties, and larger areas that felt the impact of industrial invasion.

In 11 studies, an average of 30 percent of the work force (range was 11 percent to 69 percent) had moved into the vicinity of the plant to take the new jobs. Table 4.5 shows the percentage who moved into counties in each census region. The number of studies providing this information is too small to justify further breakdown by type of industry. Likewise, the data are too sketchy to permit a definitive statement concerning the correlation, if any, between the number of plant employees and the proportion of them who migrated to take jobs. Calculations based on available data show the correlation to be negligible.

TABLE 4.5

Proportion of Plant Workers Migrating to Take New Employment

Census Region	Number of Studies	Average Percent
North Central	6	32
South	4	32
West	1	18
All regions	11	30

Source: Compiled by the authors.

The origin of workers who migrated is not mentioned in five of the studies detailing their proportion of the plant's labor force. Seven studies discuss origin, in terms of the same county, the same state, contiguous states, other states, or other countries. Often the figures given encompass more than one category, for example, all areas outside the county containing the plant. However, all seven distinguished between migrants who made intracounty moves, and those who came from further afield. Among the seven, an average of 31 percent of all workers (range was 8 percent to 69 percent) had come from places outside the county where the plant was located. The plants to which they came were dissimilar, leaving no scope for comparison among types of manufacturing. One study (Sizer and Clifford, 1966) does not indicate what proportion of the workers moved into the county, only the origin of those who did so; 20 percent came from contiguous states, 17 percent from other parts of the country, and 63 percent from the same state as the plant site. The 63 percent, combined with similar data computed from five of the seven studies just discussed, shows that a majority of migrants (an average of 66 percent for the six plants) had not moved out-of-state to take new jobs. The relatively short distances involved are evident in the three studies where this aspect of migration is documented. An average of 68 percent (range was 67 percent to 69 percent) of migrants had moved 50 miles or fewer.

Several studies look at migration in more depth, with two making comparisons between control and experimental counties. One study (Andrews and Bauder, 1968) gives the proportion of young people expected to leave the county when they finished school. In the county where the plant was established, the percentage dropped substantially after the plant went in, while in the control county there was a slight increase. As mentioned above, the study finds that of the young adults leaving home, more left the county after the factory was established than left previously. In the control county the proportion decreased, which was not anticipated. Equally unexpected were the changes in migration intentions among young people. In the experimental county fewer intended to stay after the plant went in than before, and in the control county the proportion was identical. It is surmised that industrialization brought increased awareness of the need for and value of education among young single members of the population, and they moved away to obtain this education.

Summers (1973) discusses net migration in four counties of an experimental area and one control county, and concludes that in the decade the plant was established, only the county containing the plant recorded net inmigration, while another experimental county experienced population stabilization. Thus only these two were able to attract replacements for outmigrants. Although the control county showed increased inmigration and decreased outmigration there was a continuing overall negative effect. In the same experimental area, Ramana (1968) suggests a rough indicator of plant workers' future migration intentions. He notes from data obtained during the first year of plant operations that 70 percent could be seen as potential "long term" residents because they lived in permanent homes, whereas the remainder might be intending to move because they lived in hotels, motels, trailers, and apartments.

Sizer and Smith (n.d.) argue that an industrial plant can be viewed as a migration of an aggregation of job opportunities, and as such represents "intervening job opportunities" to an individual looking for employment. They contend that since fewer skilled positions are available than unskilled, workers with such skills see fewer intervening opportunities and would have to migrate further to find employment at their skill level. The hypothesis tested is that the greater an individual's income, that is, the higher his level of skill and knowledge, the greater the distance migrated, and vice versa. The distribution of income among plant workers supports the hypothesis. Those who migrated from noncontiguous counties had higher incomes than those who came from contiguous counties, who had higher incomes than those who were natives of the study county. The top income brackets contained a greater proportion of inmigrants than natives, as well as more long-distance than short-distance migrants. Similarly, Summers (1973) reports that a greater percentage of salaried workers had migrated than workers as a whole, and Olsen and Kuehn (1974) conclude that migrants received higher salaries than natives because they were likely to be managerial personnel. Sizer and Smith (n.d.) also find that the long-distance migrants moved to maintain an already high standard of living, that is, conservative migration, whereas the short-distance migrants moved in an effort to improve their standard of living (seen as innovative migration). Contiguous-county migrants reinforce the theory that people tend to migrate the shortest distance necessary to achieve their goals. Sizer and Smith (n.d.) conclude that the implication is that industry should establish itself where the required type of worker is located. Olsen and Kuehn (1974) report both economic and nonmonetary motivations for moving. Monetary or work-related reasons include promotion or transfer, having been fired or laid off, and dissatisfaction with the previous job. Nonmonetary considerations may encompass a desire for improved quality of life, family reasons, and life transition situations such as finishing military service.

In another study Sizer and Clifford (1966) hypothesized that the inmigrants brought with them a set of educational values and norms which differed from those of the natives. The conclusion reached is that migration is a factor in the differences in attitudes only at the lower socioeconomic levels.

In studying poverty households in the Ozarks, Bender, Green, and Campbell (1971) report that 12 percent of these consisted of in-migrants. Among this group 29 percent were retired, disabled, or unemployed, and a further 35 percent accepted a lower income after moving. This constitutes selective inmigration of poverty-prone people to an already poverty-prone region.

Although few authors discuss migration in detail, there is general recognition that inmigration is important to industry to supply needed labor and important to the community to stabilize or increase population.

POPULATION DISTRIBUTION

One likely impact of the geographical movement of people is to alter the spatial distribution and concentration of populations. It might be surmised that in rural areas industrial invasion rearranges the population by inducing households to become concentrated around the new plant, thus imitating the earlier rural-to-urban move initiated by the availability of industrial jobs in cities.

Twenty-seven studies describe population distribution of the study areas and/or the plant employees. Many of the studies discussing migration and residential mobility also contain implicit information on this subject. Four case histories document changes in distribution in the study area, providing insights into the process of urbanization, or concentration of population in the towns. Unfortunately, this number is too small to permit definite conclusions. Three studies-- a University of Virginia report (Bureau of Population and Economic Research, 1956), Klein (1959), and Andrews and Bauder (1968)--show changes in population distribution before and during their respective study periods. Each shows an increase in the proportion living in towns, gains made at the expense of surrounding rural areas. In Charlotte County, Virginia, there is a very slight increase. In Choctaw County, Oklahoma (Klein, 1959), the proportion of the population living in the towns grew by more than one-third during the study period, mainly by depletion of the rural farm group. At the end of the study about 40 percent of the county population lived in the towns, making the county as a whole moderately urbanized. In Monroe County, Ohio (Andrews and Bauder, 1968), both the experimental and control counties had experienced a slight increase in degree of urbanization, so that approximately one-third of the population in each lived in the town. Thus industrialization seemed to have little effect on urbanization levels. While all three studies show an increasing proportion of the population in the towns, such figures can be misleading. Summers points out that although the percentage in his experimental county classified as urban rose

during the decade the plant was established, this was not due to a
large rural-to-urban population movement (Summers and Beck, 1972,
and Summers, 1973). Rather, the inmigration of 332 persons to one
town qualified it to be classified as urban and thus added the whole
population of the town (2,610) to the urban sector. He cites these
figures to support his hypothesis that, in spite of their historical
association, urbanization and industrialization do not necessarily occur together in rural areas. He suggests that limited urbanization
followed the establishment of the steel plant because the district had
well-developed transportation, educational, and power conversion-
transmission systems, as well as a surplus of labor, and plant employees who commuted instead of moving to the towns.

Three case histories mention population distribution at one
time only, as background material. McElveen (1970) describes the
preindustrial distribution in a South Carolina county as 1/6 urban,
1/6 rural farm, and 2/3 rural nonfarm. After the establishment of
the plant, Sizer and Clifford (1966) find an urban/rural ratio of 36
percent/64 percent in their experimental county in West Virginia,
while Klimasewski's (1974) eight counties in eastern Tennessee were
at least 70 percent rural, and four of these had no urban population
at all.

Dietz (1971) documents the declining proportion of rural farm
dwellers in the population in 38 experimental and control counties.
During the 30-year period of industrial growth these counties lost
rural farm population at similar rates, so that in 1960 the experimental group was 36 percent farm people and the control group, 40
percent.

Two studies contrast residence patterns of plant employees and
open-country residents, with similar findings. Maitland and Wilber
(1958), and Bertrand and Osborne (1959) both find approximately 40
percent of the employees living in the towns, about 30 percent on
farms, and about 30 percent in rural nonfarm dwellings. They also
find roughly 70 percent of open-country residents in their samples
living on farms, and 30 percent elsewhere. This suggests that the
workers had not flocked to the towns where the plants were located,
but were distributed fairly evenly throughout the study counties. In
central Utah, Christiansen, Maitland, and Payne (1959) find two-
thirds of the workers living in the plant towns, with 81 percent in the
same county as the factory.

Among the 15 studies detailing the residential distribution of
the plant workers, most state the proportion of them living in the
same town as the plant site. The average is 62 percent. There is
not enough evidence in the case histories to reconcile these rates of
urban residences (40 percent and 62 percent), but possible causes of
variation are those mentioned by Summers (1973): transportation,

educational, and power conversion-transmission systems, commuting patterns, and surplus of labor, particularly female labor. Hiring policies of factory management are mentioned in several studies, usually to point out that local residents were given preference initially, and where carried out, this would influence the residential distribution of employees.

Some case histories describe the spatial distribution of the factory employees in more general terms. Five show that at least 70 percent of the workers lived in the county where their plant was located (average was 89 percent; range, 75 percent to 100 percent). In all three cases where fewer than 70 percent resided in the same county, the plant site was within ten miles of the county border, indicating that a better basis for comparison of employee distribution is actual distance in miles between place of residence and plant. This relationship is more fully explored in the discussion of commuting patterns which follows.

Among county populations, industrial invasion was associated with altered spatial distribution of people. Evidence from a small number of studies suggests that increased urbanization may be associated with the introduction of industry, but may also be caused by other factors in rural areas in the short run. Although substantial but varying proportions of plant employees lived in the same town as the factory, the magnitude of their influence on the process of urbanization is not made clear. Few, if any of the studies, provide information on rates of natural increase, net migration, residential origin of inmigrants, percentage of the town population who are plant employees, local labor supply, as well as county population distribution. These data are necessary for a discussion of the association between distribution of plant workers and changes in levels of urbanization, which may also be caused by factors unrelated to the industrial invasion.

Residential Mobility

Previously it was noted that an average of 30 percent of industrial workers, as detailed in 11 studies, moved into the plant area to take their new jobs. This describes one aspect of the geographical mobility induced by rural industrial invasion. Another is residential mobility, which is defined in Maitland and Friend's summary of five studies (1961), as "a move from one dwelling to another regardless of the distance or localities involved."

Fourteen of the studies discuss residential movers and stayers among the plant employees and other groups. One study by Ryan, Clark, and Schkade (1963) finds that half the population of Paris,

Texas, had moved in the five years prior to the establishment of the factory. Maitland and Friend (1961) conclude that there is residential mobility among all three groups of rural inhabitants--plant employees, and nonfarm and farm dwellers--but that the employees move far more often than the other two groups. This is spelled out in the individual case histories. Black, Fredrickson, and Maitland (1960) show that the inmigrant employees of a rocket fuel plant had lived in an average of 4.4 residences in the previous ten years, the native plant employees in 2.8 residences, and the native nonplant workers in 1.9 houses in that decade. In two central Utah counties (Christiansen, Maitland, and Payne, 1959), the respective average number of residences in the previous 11 years for plant employees was 1.5; for rural nonfarm dwellers, 1.3; and rural farm dwellers, 1.2. Both Bertrand and Osborne (1959), and Maitland and Wilber (1958) show that plant employees had moved more often than other rural residents. In their study of Monroe County, Ohio, Andrews and Bauder (1968) find that in both the control and experimental counties there was an increase in the number of moves per household when comparing the five-year period before and after industrialization, but that there was a greater increase in the experimental county. Their assumption is that this is associated with the new jobs created by the plant. Kaldor, Bauder, and Trautwein (1964) state that farm households containing one or more plant employees had made twice as many moves in the previous 7-1/2 years as those with no plant workers. This assertion reiterates the conclusion reached in all relevant studies: that the plant employees as a group were more residentially mobile than rural dwellers in general.

Few studies describe moving in terms of changes in residential classification, for example, farm to town. Bertrand and Osborne (1959), and the Arkansas Department of Labor (1958) both find that starting work in the plant did not cause large numbers of rural inhabitants to move into the town where the factory was located. In the former study this was because most of those who moved went to the same kind of residence, for example, farm to farm, town to town. In the Arkansas report most of the employees did not move at all when they began work in the factory. Apart from this reference, there is little direct evidence in the studies to indicate how often residential and job mobility coincide or are associated with each other. Obviously, the 31 percent of the work force who migrated across county lines to take new industrial jobs also changed residence, but it is difficult to determine whether job or residential mobility occurred first, or the two coincided. One study (Maitland and Wilber, 1958) indicates that among the workers at a wirebound box factory in Louisiana, 20 percent moved when they took the factory job, 40 percent moved before taking it, and 16 percent after. Thus, it is not clear that taking a new job was the sole motive for, or closely connected with, moving house among plant employees. Sizer and Smith (n.d.) hypothesize that residential mobility is influenced by such factors as being in the expansion stage of the family life cycle, ambition, lack of binding family ties, and availability of opportunity. Reasons given by a sample of residents in the central Utah study (Christiansen, Maitland, and Payne, 1959) partially support the hypothesis; 60 percent of the plant employees who moved said they did so to obtain their own homes, as did 44 percent of the farmers and 48 percent of open-country nonfarm respondents. Secondary reasons were the need to have more room for an expanding family, to obtain a garden, and to be close to work. Schneiderman (1971) sought to test his hypothesis that laborers will move closer to their workplace. He found that in the three years after the steel plant opened, the proportion of the work force living within the county rose from 10.6 percent to 20 percent. There was also a slight increase in the proportion living in the three adjacent counties (65 percent to 67.7 percent).

Several authors discuss possible causes of residential mobility. Black, Fredrickson, and Maitland (1960) suggest that the inmigrant plant employees' history of greater mobility may be due to moves associated with a college education. Kaldor, Bauder, and Trautwein (1964) surmise that workers at an Iowa factory are more mobile because they are adaptable and ready to try new situations. The Arkansas Department of Labor report (1958) concludes that the small amount of residential mobility associated with the establishment of a clothing factory resulted from the company's policy of hiring local people where possible. That 90 percent of this factory's workers were women is also likely to contribute to the lack of mobility.

There are too few studies providing details of residential mobility to enable the drawing of more than tentative conclusions. However, whether the establishment of an industry is the cause or not, the plant employees in these studies appear more likely to change residence than other rural dwellers. The movement that does take place often does not involve a change in residential classification.

COMMUTING

Industries moving into rural areas are often unable to recruit their whole labor force in the immediate vicinity of the plant site because of a mismatch between their requirements and the characteristics of local job-seekers. When they look further afield, some of those they hire become inmigrants and some commuters. Some who initially commute long distances later move closer to the factory, thus causing a shrinkage of the laborshed of that plant. Lonsdale (1966) finds that one-quarter of the employees in a fiber plant had moved closer to it since beginning work there. This had reduced the average one-way commuting distance from 28.8 to 8.4 miles. Summers (1973) notes that most of the workers who had moved after applying for their jobs had moved toward the plant, and the proportion driving 30 miles or more to work decreased between 1969 and 1972. In their study of six Wisconsin cities, Andrews et al. (1959) conclude that in the short run farmers who go to work in industry commute, and in the long run they move to town. These observations suggest that workers may be prepared to commute longer distances for a time after they begin work at the plant, but at a certain point, perhaps once they come to feel secure and settled in their jobs, they move toward the plant.

In discussing the extensive laborsheds of their four study areas, Olsen and Kuehn (1974) find that in three of these regions inmigrant plant workers were more likely to live close to the factory than either residents or returnees.

The journey to work can be measured in terms of distance or time. Of the 24 studies discussing commuting, 2 describe it both ways, 20 use distance as the measure, and 2 use time only. Presumably most studies use distance because it is directly measurable by the researchers. Lonsdale defends the use of time because it may be a better measure of the "effort" the worker puts into commuting. He finds, however, in his study (1966) that there is a close relationship between minutes and miles, suggesting that "one is about as satisfactory a measure as the other."

The distance between the plant and the worker's residence is described in road miles in some studies, in air miles (that is, within a certain radius of the plant) in some, while others are not explicit about which is used. Distance in highway miles seems more useful for comparisons. Clemente and Summers find that 42 air miles are equivalent to 57 highway miles in a study area in north central Illinois (Clemente and Summers, 1973b, 1973e, 1974, and 1975; and Summers, 1973). Most studies show the cumulative percentage of the work force traveling given distances to the factory. The cut-off points differ; so it is not easy to make comparisons. In the case histories where distance is measured in road miles, the proportion of plant workers journeying four miles or less (in four studies) ranges from 11 percent to 67.6 percent, with an average of 37.9 percent. At ten miles or less, the percentages in four studies range from 18.3 to 75. Lonsdale (1966) makes comparisons with a 1963 Bureau of the Census study of urban commuting patterns which states that "forty-five percent of American workers commute up to four miles, and seventy-six percent up to ten miles." The percentages for Lonsdale's workers are 11 percent and 40 percent respectively, and in almost all other case studies giving this information the percentages are low, suggesting that rural workers come from further afield than their urban counterparts. Four studies among the ten measuring commuting distance in highway miles describe the laborshed in terms of the longest one-way distance driven by a worker. This distance varies from 20 to 57 miles. Five studies give the average one-way commuting distance which ranges from 3.2 to 19 miles. Lonsdale (1966) sets up several models to explain the spatial pattern of commuter origin for one of the plants he studied. The best, but not complete, fit is obtained for the model which states that commuting diminishes directly with distance up to 20 miles, then at a pace proportional to three times the mileage. Influencing factors apart from distance are thought to be per capita income, population density, and intensity of agricultural employment.

Six studies encompassing ten towns discuss commuting distance in terms of air miles. In five cases the location of the most distant plant worker ranges from 14 to 35 miles, and the proportion of workers up to ten miles from the plant averages 75 percent (range is 70 percent to 78 percent). Although this is close to the figure for urban workers, it is likely that the conversion of air miles to road miles would produce a different pattern, one which might tend to support further the conclusion that rural industrial employees commute further than urban workers.

The two studies discussing the journey to work only in terms of time both observe that the vast majority of workers traveled for 20 minutes or less.

The variation in commuting distances among the studies indicates that many factors are influential, and that different combinations of these factors underlie patterns of movement around industrialized rural towns. Lonsdale (1966) cites some causal differences: degree of urbanization, city size, terrain, availability of paved roads, mode of transportation, job opportunities, and wage level differentials between the plant and other employers. In his study, and in one of a Ravenswood, West Virginia, plant which he quotes, job opportunities and wage differentials appear to be important in producing a wide spatial distribution of plant workers. Both these plants were established in "low income" environments where agricultural wages were low and job opportunities limited, and they had a wide spread of workers. He compares this with another South Carolina plant (Plaxico, 1947) which was located in a similar environment but had a narrower distribution, and concludes that the difference is in the wage differentials. The latter plant paid a wage comparable to that of nearby employers, while at Ravenswood and Kinston (Lonsdale's study area) the workers received higher wages than the local average.

These workers were prepared to pay the time and money costs of commuting to hold more highly paid jobs. Factory managers interviewed by Abt Associates (1968) saw their plant laborsheds as having two sets of boundaries. One was the area the managers thought their plants capable of drawing from, and a second, smaller area was that encompassing the residences of the current labor force. Employers in the two cities in this study perceived their laborsheds to be larger than those in the two towns, and reported more frequent and longer distance commuting. The suggestion is that a large town can serve as an employment center for a wider geographical area than can a small one for similar reasons to those cited above by Lonsdale. The presence of intervening job opportunities is discussed by two authors. McElveen (1970) suggests that the large city near his study area had usurped the town's labor supply so that workers for the new factory had to be recruited from further afield. Schneiderman (1971) finds that the percentage of workers at a given distance from the plant increases up to 30 miles, then decreases, and he surmises that this represents the limit of the plant's attractive power, after which it faces strong competition for labor from other employers. Andrews et al. (1959), looking at six cities, conclude that additional plants in lightly industrialized cities cause commuting numbers and distances to rise, while in more heavily industrialized cities there is a much less pronounced effect on commuting patterns. The former conclusion is supported by a small number of studies giving information about city size and the journey to work. This limited evidence suggests that the smaller the town where a new place is located, the larger that plant's laborshed will be and vice versa.

Several studies discuss the type of worker who commutes, particularly trying to characterize those who travel long distances. Summers (1973) finds a slight tendency for older, better-educated, higher-status employees to commute short distances. Somers (1958) had a similar finding for plant employees at Ravenswood. Hourly rated workers were more willing to commute long distances than salaried employees, perhaps because the latter were often inmigrants who could easily choose to live close to the factory. Clemente and Summers (1973b, 1974) find that neither age alone, nor family status predict work-residence separation. Similarly, Lonsdale (1966) reports that younger, newly hired workers were slightly more likely to commute further. Summers (1973) also documents a very weak tendency for workers on higher incomes and with a longer work history to travel further. McElveen (1970) notes that in his South Carolina study area near a large city, black workers commuted further than whites, the limit being 60 miles, compared with five miles for white workers. Howard (1973) reports that male workers were willing to commute further than female. Stepp and Plaxico (1948) find that among plant workers, farm residence and work cause variation. Those living on farms commuted further than nonfarm residents, but farm-dwelling workers who also did part-time farm work traveled shorter distances.

These studies do not provide a complete picture of the characteristics of rural industrial employees that are related to their commuting activities. Rather, they delineate areas for further investigation.

Approximately one-third of the studies discuss the commuting patterns around new industrial plants. From the information they provide it may be concluded that the laborsheds of such plants tend to be larger than those in urban areas, their size depending on many factors including city size, wage differentials between the plant and other local employers, and personal characteristics and preferences of the plant employees.

POPULATION COMPOSITION

Many of the case histories provide demographic information about the population groups in the study areas. The characteristics of plant workers are frequently given as background material for the analysis of economic and other variables. Other groups described include total population of the town, county, or larger area surrounding the plant site, as well as such subpopulations as farm operators, rural nonfarm dwellers, and employed heads of households.

Age

Twenty-six studies give details of the breakdown of groups by age. Most provide these data in written form, while a few graphically portray them in population pyramids. The age composition of the study area as a whole is dealt with by a small number of authors, who are concerned with the proportions of the population in three general age groups--the young, the work force, and old people. In Paris, Texas (Ryan, Clark, and Schkade, 1963), there were changes in the representation of these groups during the industrial development period. The proportion in the older group rose, while the youth group decreased. Andrews and Bauder (1968) find the population pyramids in both their experimental county and the state to be hourglass-shaped due to heavy outmigration of the 20-34 age segment. However, in their experimental county this proportion remained stable, but its decline in the control county points to continued outmigration. In their study in Wisconsin, Andrews et al. (1959) observe that the more industrialized cities have a larger 25-54 age group, that is, active labor force, and a slightly smaller proportion of people over 65 than less industrialized towns.

The age dependency ratio is a summary measure of the age composition of a population. It is a number representing the number of dependents (those aged under 15 years and those over 65 years), per 100 in the 15-64, or "productive" age group. This ratio is discussed or implied in eight studies, most of which show change over the study period. In almost all cases the ratio increased, indicating that industrial invasion was associated with altered balance of the three age groups in these populations, due to a decreased proportion in the productive group and/or an increased percentage of children and old people. However, it is unclear precisely what effect industrial invasion had because increasing age dependency ratios are also a product of the recent rural population trends of outmigration among young people, and high birth rates. Table 4.6 shows age characteristics of plant workers in 12 studies. It is clear that a large proportion of these work forces are in the younger age groups. The reason given or implied for the lack of older workers is the employers' desire for workers able to handle the physically hard work, that is, younger workers. However, Merrill and Ryther (1961), in looking at several types of factories, observe that the age composition of the work force may vary with the degree of skill required; so that older, more skilled workers may be in demand, although the overall age grouping of the plants they studied shows that the work force was predominantly young people. In the clothing factory in Star City, Arkansas (Arkansas Department of Labor, 1968), no age limit was set by the employer, who thought that older women were good workers. However, the report suggests that the work force was in fact made up of younger people because of the skill level required and the physical demands of doing piece-rate sewing by machine. Many of the employees in these plants were under 30 years of age. Schneiderman (1971) finds that it was plant policy to hire younger workers, while Uhrich's (1974) study area contains a college which accounts for the characteristically larger younger age groups containing many potential job seekers. Howard's (1973) data on job applicants shows that 50 percent of these were under 25 years of age.

Several authors characterize the workers by sex as well as age. Maitland and Wilber (1968) and the Arkansas Department of Labor report (1958) find the modal and median ages of the females to be greater than for the males, and suggest this may be due to the women's unavailability for employment while their children are young. Brady (1974) says that the same pattern in Wynne, Arkansas, indicates that few jobs are available for female high school graduates.

TABLE 4.6

Age Characteristics of Plant Workers

Study	Under 30	30-50	Over 50	Modal Age Group	Median Age
	(cumulative percent)				
Merrill and Ryther (1961)	43.1	94.1	100	20-29	28 males, 27.3
Maitland and Wilber (1961)	54	99	100	males, 25 and under	females, 33.5
				females, 30-34	35.7
Bertrand and Osborne (1959)	30	86	99	--	
Arkansas Department of Labor (1958)					
total	44	85	100		33
males	69	92	100	under 20	24
females	41	96	100		34
Helgeson and Zink (1973)	63.3	92.8	100	--	--
Schneiderman (1971)	50	94.4	100	--	--
Uhrich (1974)				males, 25-29	30
				females, 20-24	
Somers (1958)	--	--	--	25-34	--
Brady (1971)	--	--	--	--	males, 33.2
					females, 27.6
Kuehn et al. (1972)	--	--	--	--	32.5
Debes (1971)	--	--	--	--	30.4
Lonsdale (1966)	--	--	--	--	males, 32.3
					females, 31.4

Note: Dashes indicate data not provided by study.

Source: Compiled by the authors from studies indicated.

39

Evidence from this small number of studies appears to indicate that older age groups do not have the representation in the work force that their numbers warrant due to company policies and requirements for physically active and younger workers. Women in these plants are, on the whole, older than their male counterparts because many return to work after rearing young children, and because there may be a lack of jobs for young women.

Seven studies discuss age composition in terms of intergroup comparison relevant to their analysis. They find that the plant workers are younger than other groups in the area populations--younger than local nonplant workers (Black, Fredrickson, and Maitland, 1960; Summers, 1973; Bertrand and Osborne, 1958; Maitland and Wilber, 1958); farmers (Christiansen, Maitland, and Payne, 1959; Kaldor, Bauder, and Trautwein, 1964); and native residents (Sizer and Clifford, 1966). They suggest this is due to the plants' recruiting younger people, and the provision of jobs which prevented outmigration of younger workers.

Two studies examine changes in the median ages of the populations of experimental and control counties with differing results. Dietz (1971), whose study period spanned 30 years, finds that the median age rose in that time, but that there was a smaller increase in the experimental counties because the plants attracted young people with families. The median age in Andrews and Bauder's (1968) experimental county also increased slightly, probably due to the continued slight outmigration of young people. In their control county, however, the decrease in the median age of the population is attributed to net outmigration among those aged 55 and older.

Thus rural industrial invasion is associated with changes in the age composition of host towns and counties because it affects some of the basic demographic processes (mainly migration) which determine population size and structure.

Sex

Twenty-one studies describe the sex distribution of the population around the plant site, or of the workers of the plant.

Only three studies provide information about changes in the sex ratio (usually defined as the number of males per 100 females) of the host populations.

Table 4.7 shows that in two cases industrial invasion was not associated with any great change in the sex ratio at the county level. In Lamar County, Texas (Ryan, Clark, and Schkade, 1963), the drop parallels the general U.S. trend for the decade 1950-60. In the town of Paris, Texas, the ratio was stable, but low, as are all the postindustrial figures. The U.S. rural sex ratio for 1960 was 104.3, indicating an excess of males, whereas these study areas showed an excess of females, a characteristic more in line with the overall national figure for 1960, which was 97.1. Historically, rural/urban differences in the sex ratio have been caused in part by greater migration of females to the cities. It is possible that males and females now have been leaving these areas in equal numbers, and this, combined with the aging of the whole rural population, has contributed to the low sex ratios.

TABLE 4.7

Changes in Sex Ratios of Host Populations
(number of males per 100 females)

| | | Sex Ratios | |
Study	Unit of Analysis	Before Industrialization	After Industrialization
Wilson (1965)	county	97	97
Walraven (1962)	3 counties	slightly over 100	almost exactly 100
Ryan, Clark, and Schkade (1963)	county	98.7	92.4
	town	87.2	87.4

Note: Figures given for after industrialization are for 1960.

Source: Compiled by the authors from studies indicated.

Table 4.8 shows the proportion of female employees in different types of factories, and some of the studies relevant to the table explain these percentages. There were very few women involved in the production of steel, or bricks, or in some of the metalworking plants. At the other end of the spectrum, female labor was predominant in the manufacturing of apparel, electronic systems components, and in one metalworking plant. An examination of the nine metalworking labor forces shows that in all but three cases, women made up less than 16 percent of the workers, and it is likely that the majority were employed in office jobs. In Bucher's 1971 study, in plant "D" many women were employed in production because the

TABLE 4.8

Distribution of Plant Employees by Sex and Plant Product

Study	Percent Male	Percent Female	Plant Product
Maitland and Wilber (1958)	84	16	furniture
Bertrand and Osborne (1959)	73	27	wirebound boxes
Summers (1973)	96.4	3.6	steel
Stepp and Plaxico (1948)	57	43	textile spinning
Graham (1973)	hourly workers		
	17.9	82.1	electronic systems component
	hourly workers		
	37	63	electronic systems component
Bucher (1971)	51	49	metal products
	95+	5	aluminum products
	24	76	metal products
	89	11	metal products
	76	24	"cut and sew"
	85	15	metal products
Howard (1973)	45	55	textiles
Helgeson and Zink (1973)	77.6	22.4	aerospace equipment, farm machinery, mobile homes
Arkansas Department of Labor (1968)	11	89	apparel
Uhrich (1974)	46.8	53.2	medical supplies
Black, Fredrickson, and Maitland (1960)	67	33	missile fuel
Brady (1971)	5	95+	apparel
	40	60	shoes
	100	0	copper tubing
Lonsdale (1966)	83	17	synthetic fiber
McElveen (1970)	65	35	plastic products, metal products
	96	4	instruments, transportation equipment, bricks
Abt Associates (1968)	70	30	sheet metal working
	95	5	steel products
	5	95	"cut and sew"
Ritzenthaler (1953)	25	75	electric meters

Note: Some of the studies examined more than one plant.
Source: Compiled by the authors from the studies indicated.

manager felt that they performed better than men at most jobs. This firm intended to continue hiring females. In plant "A" (studied by Bucher), men had initially been sought and hired, but this produced a high labor turnover, possibly due to the low wage rate. At the same time, there was a shortage of employable males in the area. The company began hiring women and found their work highly satis- factory. Both the plants in Graham's 1973 study were located on Indian reservations. One initially hired females in the belief that they would be more capable of the type of work involved in assembling electronic circuits, as white women had proved to be. In an effort to lower male unemployment, the company hired men, who proved equally adept at the work. Observing these events, the second com- pany initially decided on a 50/50 sex balance, but allowed a natural equilibrium to develop, and this produced a work force that was 63 percent female.

These studies show that some preconceived ideas about the suitability of either sex for a particular type of work proved false. It is possible that the representation of women in the work forces of other plants in Table 4.8 was also influenced by managers' beliefs and policies, more than by the availability and suitability of potential female job-seekers.

Household Size and Family Status

Andrews and Bauder (1968), and Summers and associates (Beck, 1972a; Beck, Dotson, and Summers, 1973; and Summers, 1973) both looked for an association between industrialization and change in household size, but found none. Andrews and Bauder ex- pected an increase due to the halted outmigration of young people. That this did not occur may be due, among other things, to a simul- taneous change in the birth rate. Summers notes that household size declined in both the experimental and control areas. In the five studies making the comparison, all find that the plant workers had larger households than the study populations in general. In his Louisiana study area Osborne (1959) attributes this in part to a larger proportion of rural residents among plant workers than among the area population. He also notes that blacks had a larger average family size than whites and were more likely to have extremely large households. Kaldor, Bauder, and Trautwein (1964), and Andrews and Bauder also draw the same general conclusion. Sizer and Clifford's (1966) inmigrant workers had bigger households than did the natives of Jackson County, West Virginia. Similarly, in two central Utah counties (Christiansen, Maitland, and Payne, 1959) plant employees' families were larger than those of the farmers and nonfarm workers. Both this study and the Sizer and Clifford study also compare these groups in terms of their division among the different stages of the family life cycle.

Sizer and Clifford find that the modal stage for the two groups was the same--that of being married with children in school. Christiansen, Maitland, and Payne find plant workers and farmers both had a modal stage of couples with preschool and school children, while the nonfarmers were typically in the old adult phase, that is, where the family consists of adults of advanced age, with a smaller proportion having preschool and school children. This distribution is influenced by the age structure (45 percent of the nonfarmers were 60 years of age or older), as is the proportion of workers who were married. This ranges from 66 to 82 percent in six studies, and the older the work force, the larger the percentage married. Family size is also tied to the age distribution by Helgeson and Zink (1973) who observe that their workers had an average of less than one child per family and that this was understandable in light of the fact that 44 percent of them were aged 19 to 24. There are several explanations given for the proportion of married women in factory work forces. The Arkansas Department of Labor report (1958) ascribes the high percentage in an apparel factory to the type of work; Uhrich (1974) hypothesizes that in Brookings, South Dakota, many married women were working to put their husbands through university, and Kaldor, Bauder, and Trautwein (1964) see it as a function of the willingness of farmers' wives to work while they still had a preschool child at home.

This small number of relevant studies seems to suggest that the plant workers had larger households than the study populations, and also that the proportion married and family size were associated with their age distribution rather than the onset of industrial invasion.

Education

Thirty case histories discuss the educational attainment levels of various segments of the study populations. Very few describe changes occurring during the industrial invasion period; however, three that do so find differential increases in education levels in experimental and control areas. Summers and associates (Beck, 1972a; Beck, Dotson, and Summers, 1973; and Summers, 1973), and Dietz (1971) each note increases in both areas, but a greater change in their experimental counties. They ascribe this to substantial inmigration of males with more education, and retention of the younger, better-educated portion of the population respectively. Andrews and Bauder (1968) also describe an increase in both experimental and

control areas, with a greater rise in the latter. They conclude that
the difference is due to the counties' different age structure and
levels of schooling. These authors, along with Maitland and Wilber
(1958), Helgeson and Zink (1973), and Stepp and Plaxico (1948) see
age as an important determinant of levels of education. They suggest
that young people are likely to have more education than older age
groups. Seven studies report that the plant employees were more
educated than various groups in the study population, including heads
of households, nonfarmers, native residents, open-country dwellers,
and outmigrants. Six of these seven also report that the workers
were younger than the comparison groups in the population, thus
accounting for some of the differences. Three studies note that the
plant employees had less education than farmers, open-country heads
of households, and the national average. The industrial employers'
location and hiring policies appear to be associated with the educational level of plant workers. Christiansen, Maitland, and Payne
(1959) report that plant policy was to hire well-educated people. The
decision to locate the factory in Juab County, Utah, was heavily influenced by the high level of educational attainment among the potential work force. Davis (1963) reports that plant managers in White
County, Arkansas, followed an unwritten law of normally not hiring
persons who had not finished high school, while Maitland and Wilber
(1958) state that the employer considered the schooling of job applicants. Abt Associates (1968) find that where a minimum level of education was required by employers in four South Carolina and Mississippi towns it was usually completion of the ninth or tenth grade.
One exception was the employer who set the standard at sixth grade
for Negroes and ninth grade for whites. Less than a third of the
firms surveyed set a minimum level, but these plants, which tended
to be large establishments, had better-educated work forces. More
than half of the employers administered their own tests of educational
achievement, and others had access to the results of similar tests
given by state labor agencies. Level of education requirements appeared to fluctuate according to labor supply and demand, that is,
the standard was lowered when the labor market tightened, and this
disparity suggests that the requirements may have often been artifi-
cial and arbitrary.

In addition to age, other determinants of education levels cited
in several studies are sex and race. In the population of study areas
in four southern states and Utah, women had more years of formal
education than men, while in two cases the reverse was true. The
differences in levels between the sexes ranged from .1 to 1 year,
but in two studies where the information is given, the gap between
blacks and whites was large--5.8 and 3.7 years. In one of these
studies, Walker (1973), both blacks and whites showed higher levels

after industrial invasion than before, but the gap between them was only slightly lessened.

In describing the education levels of the general study populations, some authors make comparisons. Four areas in the South had levels below those of their respective states, while one in the same region was above the state average. Similarly, one area in Utah was above the national average. These studies were done at different times between 1945 and 1973; hence it is not possible to make direct comparisons. However, where the data are given, it appears that the South was at the bottom of the education ladder, in terms of average level of education of the population, proportion functionally illiterate, and percentage completing high school. However, Abt Associates do report that although there was much illiteracy among the nonwhites, and that Negro children were at a disadvantage at school, some improvement was occurring in the form of low and falling school dropout rates. School principals in these southern towns thought industrial invasion was positively associated with lower dropout rates.

The information in these studies suggests that the plant workers on the whole were more educated than the general study populations, largely due to their youth. Industrial invasion may be associated with changes in levels of education through its stimulation of migration which alters the age composition of the population. Young people moving in are likely to have completed more years of formal learning, thereby raising the overall level.

CONCLUSIONS

The information in these studies points to migration as the key to the analysis of demographic impacts of industrial invasion of rural areas in the United States. The important questions about how industrial invasion affects population size and composition can be explained largely by knowledge of the changes in migration patterns associated with, or brought about by the coming of industry. While the characteristics of inmigrants in these studies are similar to those of migrants in other times and places, their numbers, which determine changes in population size, depend on the compatibility of the employers' quantitative and qualitative labor needs with both the current and potential supply of workers.

5

IMPACTS ON
EMPLOYMENT AND
INCOME

EMPLOYMENT

The creation of employment opportunities lies at the heart of most discussions of rural industrial development. New manufacturing jobs form the basis of hopes for reversing the trends of population decline, unemployment, poverty, and general economic stagnation which have been plaguing rural areas for several decades. The establishment of rural industries is expected to have substantial positive effects on employment in two ways: by the direct hiring of workers from the indigenous labor force, and by the indirect, or multiplier, effects which they have on employment in other sectors of the local economy.

Direct Employment Effects

Many of the studies point to the finding that rural industrial development created new jobs as if it were surprising or significant. Yet this truism forms merely the very first step on the way to any analysis of the impacts of that development. The important question about the new manufacturing employment is not how many jobs were created, but who gets them. The assumption underlying a great deal of the current promotion efforts and policy-making has been that the workers will be recruited largely from the ranks of the local disadvantaged residents--the unemployed, the poor, racial minorities, etc., thereby helping to alleviate some of the economic distress in rural areas. But the studies show that often this is not the case.

Unemployed and Poor

Table 5.1 summarizes the findings reported on the hiring of previously unemployed workers. (The term "unemployed" is used here in its most general sense; that is, the person is not gainfully employed. This differs from the more restrictive technical usage in labor statistics wherein a person is unemployed only when he or she has been out of work for a period of time [usually six weeks] and is actively seeking employment.) In the majority of cases only a small proportion of the jobs were filled by previously unemployed persons; in only three instances was the proportion above 14 percent and over half the studies report hiring rates below 10 percent. In two studies the proportion of new jobs filled by previously unemployed is reported as being .25 or higher. Wadsworth and Conrad (1966) found that 25 of the 100 new jobs at the aluminum chair plant in Linton, Indiana, were filled by previously unemployed persons. Even more striking is the 43 percent rate found in Miernyk's (1971) survey of 33 plants in Area Redevelopment Administration areas.

We found only one study which examined the number of below poverty level persons employed by new plants. Kuehn and Associates (1972) studied 26 newly located or recently expanded plants in developing areas of Arizona, southern Appalachia, the Mississippi Delta, and the Ozarks. The relevant results from their study are summarized in Table 5.2.

In the Appalachia and Ozark areas nearly 20 percent of the jobs were filled by persons whose previous income was below poverty level. (Previous income was determined as the annual earnings in the last job held or 1965 family income if the person had no previous job.) In sharp contrast is the findings from the Mississippi Delta and Arizona areas where nearly 50 percent of the new hires were previously below poverty level.

As one would expect, the higher-skill, higher-wage firms attract few unemployed or poor individuals who typically lack the qualifications necessary to compete for such jobs. Thus, even in areas with significant rates of unemployment and poverty new plants may not alleviate these twin problems if the skill level of the surplus labor pool and new labor demand are not closely matched. This can be seen in the Paden, Krist, and Seaton study of five communities in Iowa (1972). Where the plants required more technical skills and where the net increases in average wage level were the highest (Grinnell and Jefferson), the percentage of jobs filled by previously unemployed persons was lowest (1 percent and 3 percent respectively; see Table 5.1). The point is also illustrated with respect to poverty relief by reference to the Kuehn et al. study (see Table 5.2). The Appalachia and Ozark areas were predominantly white while the Arizona area was

TABLE 5.1

Percentage of New Plant Workers Previously Unemployed

Study Area	Industry	Number of Jobs	Percent of Jobs Filled by Previously Unemployed
Linton, Ind. [a]	aluminum chairs	100	25.0
Wynne, Ark. [b]	apparel; copper tubing	1,900	11.2
Rochester, Minn. [c]	business machines	1,862	14.0
Ravenswood, W. Va. [d]	aluminum	894	11.0
Eastern Oklahoma community [e]	12 plants (mixed)	554	7.7
Area Redevelopment Administration area survey [f]	33 plants (mixed)	1,262	43.0
Mt. Airy, N.C. [f]	appliances	435	8.0
Jefferson, Iowa [g]	stamping, athletic equipment	369	3.0
Orange City, Iowa [g]	10 plants (mixed)	364	19.0
Creston, Iowa [g]	appliances, chemicals, oil filters	424	1.0
Grinnell, Iowa [g]	farm machinery, stadium bleachers, plastics	200	7.0
Decorah, Iowa [g]	screws	212	8.0
Star City, Ark. [h]	apparel (shirts)	336	9.5

Sources: Wadsworth and Conrad (1966)[a]; Brady (1974)[b]; Morris (1960)[c]; Somers (1958)[d]; Shaffer (1972)[e]; Miernyk (1971)[f]; Paden et al. (1972)[g]; Arkansas Department of Labor (1958)[h].

49

TABLE 5.2

Impact of New Jobs on Poverty in Four Developing Areas

Area and Poverty Status	Jobs	Percent of Total Jobs	Percent of Determined Jobs
Arizona: Apache and Navajo counties			
Total number of jobs	1,270	100.0	--
Number of determined jobs	373	29.4	100.0
New hires previously poor	183	14.4	49.1
New hires escaping poverty	93	7.3	24.9
Appalachia: Alcorn and Tippah counties, Miss.			
Total number of jobs	2,600	100.0	--
Number of determined jobs	2,368	91.1	100.0
New hires previously poor	441	16.9	18.6
New hires escaping poverty	315	12.1	13.3
Ozarks: Benton and Washington counties, Ark.			
Total number of jobs	1,980	100.0	--
Total of determined jobs	1,572	79.4	100.0
New hires previously poor	310	15.7	19.8
New hires escaping poverty	219	11.0	13.9
Mississippi Delta: Cross, Lee, and St. Francis counties, Ark.			
Total number of jobs	879	100.0	--
Number of determined jobs	809	92.0	100.0
New hires previously poor	389	44.3	48.1
New hires escaping poverty	220	25.0	27.2

Note: A 25 percent random sample was drawn within skill strata of each cooperating plant (26 of 56 through the four areas). Overall approximately 19 percent of the total estimated workers returned usable questionnaires. Number of jobs were estimated by expanding the sample by plants and rounding to whole numbers. A "determined job" is one for which Kuehn and associates could determine the poverty status of the employee in 1970 and at his or her previous employment. "Usage of these percentages assumed that sampled responses were typical of unsampled employees and sampled refusals by plant. Percentages based on unrounded data" (Kuehn et al., 1972, fn. 3, p. 7).

Source: Adapted from Kuehn et al. (1972).

largely American Indian and the Delta area was nearly 50 percent black. Skill level in the latter two areas would appear to be somewhat lower than in the former two. Moreover, the skill level requirements of the new jobs in the Appalachia and Ozark areas were somewhat higher. Thus, it would appear that a better match of skill demand and its supply among poverty families was achieved in the Arizona and Delta regions.

Areas in which poor and unemployed workers are most likely to be hired are those with substantial labor surpluses and high rates of poverty. This should be true when there is a reasonable match between job requirements and the ability of poor and/or unemployed persons to fill them and when there is not deliberate discrimination in hiring practices. This appears to have been the case with the 33 new plants that were induced through Area Redevelopment Administration loans to locate in areas of high unemployment and poverty. At these plants 43 percent of the jobs were filled by previously unemployed persons. While Miernyk (1971) suggests that this was due to the nature of the location decision--federal grants which stipulated that many unemployed be hired, as opposed to solely market considerations--it probably results also from the especially large pool of unemployed workers in the areas and the fact that over two-thirds of the jobs required only unskilled labor. The same set of factors appear to lie behind the 32 percent figure which was found for Economic Development Administration (EDA) growth center projects (Milkman et al., 1972, p. 146).

Racial Minorities

Only six of the case studies have investigated the impact of rural industrial development on the employment of blacks but among the six reports 14 sets of data are presented with one involving 244 southern counties (Walker, 1973). The study areas, percentage of jobs filled by blacks, and other pertinent data are presented in Table 5.3. In several cases rather large proportions--59 percent or more-- of those hired were black: a wirebound box factory in Louisiana (Bertrand and Osborne, 1959); an auto circuitry parts plant in Mississippi (Graham, 1973); and a brick factory in South Carolina (McElveen, 1970) employed mostly blacks; and primarily native Americans worked in two companies producing camera and missile components in Arizona (Graham, 1973) and in a meter manufacturing plant in Wisconsin (Ritzenthaler, 1953). On the other hand, no blacks were among the 130 workers hired at a furniture factory in Chickasaw County, Mississippi, even though 43 percent of the county was black (Wilber and Maitland, 1963) and it was found that blacks "overshared" in employment declines and "undershared" in manufacturing growth in two areas of Mississippi (Till, 1972).

TABLE 5.3

Percentage of Employees at New Plants Who Were Black

Study Area	Industry	Percent in Area Population	Number of Jobs	Percent of Jobs Filled by Blacks
Southeastern Louisiana parishes[a]	wirebound boxes	30	204	59
Summerville, S.C.[b]	brick factory	--	25	60
Chickasaw County, Miss.[c]	furniture	43	130	0
Adams County, Miss.[d]	all manufacturing	--	2,954	35
Jefferson City, Miss.[d]	all manufacturing	--	494	59
Alcorn County, Miss.[d]	all manufacturing	--	4,142	6
Tippah County, Miss.[d]	all manufacturing	--	2,121	9
244 southern counties[e]	nonagriculture	40	429,000	16
Miss. town[f]	sheet metalworking	--	--	45
Miss. city[f]	sheet metalworking	--	--	16
S.C. city[f]	sheet metalworking	--	--	50
Miss. town[f]	steel products	--	--	75
Miss. city[f]	steel products	--	--	55
S.C. town[f]	cut and sew	--	--	30

Note: Dashes indicate data not provided.

Sources: Bertrand and Osborne (1959)[a]; McElveen (1970)[b]; Wilber and Maitland (1963)[c]; Till (1972)[d]; Walker (1973)[e]; Abt Associates (1968)[f].

52

The key issue, however, is not how many blacks or other minorities are employed at particular plants, but rather, what are the overall tendencies for the employment of nonwhites in rural industries. For this purpose, the case study approach is inadequate as a basis for generalization unless the study sites were chosen as a probability sample of all possible sites in the United States or some selected region, which they are not (cf. Summers, Seiler, and Clark, 1970). Fortunately Walker has completed the needed type of analysis for 244 southern nonmetropolitan counties (1973) and his findings corroborate the case studies. His major finding was that

> blacks did not share equitably in the economic growth and development in the Deep South. Even though they represented almost 40 percent of the population in 1960, blacks captured only 16 percent of the non-agricultural employment growth between 1960 and 1970, or only 68,000 out of 429,000 new jobs. With the continuing large declines in black agricultural employment, the result was a net loss of over 97,000 jobs, while whites simultaneously gained 287,000 jobs [Walker, 1973, p. 170].

Furthermore, he found that black employment has been confined largely to low-wage, blue-collar occupations (Walker, 1973, p. 167), a result that is supported by every one of the above case studies (for native Americans as well as blacks) and by an analysis of several plants in four southern communities (Abt Associates, 1968). In each instance, only whites held managerial positions. While to some extent these trends are undoubtedly related to the prior question of work qualifications, the common view presented by the researchers is succinctly stated by Merrill and his associates: "There is ample evidence, despite the education and skill issue, that racial discrimination is . . . a major factor in the hiring practice of firms" (Abt Associates, 1968, p. 70).

Reasons Disadvantaged Are Not Hired

The reasons behind the low number of jobs filled by the unemployed, the poor, and racial minorities are not difficult to discover, for they are mentioned repeatedly in the case studies and background literature.

First, the new employment opportunities created by the establishment of a plant are often taken by workers from outside the immediate area, both commuters and inmigrants. Possessing more

education, better skills, or the "right" racial heritage, these newcomers intervene between the jobs and the local residents, especially the disadvantaged; they would be the targets for an industrialization program. The frequency and extent of inmigration and commuting which occurs is considerable, as was discussed in Chapter 4.

The extent in inmigration and return migration is especially
significant when considering the plight of the rural disadvantaged. It
is possible to reduce the rate of unemployment, underemployment,
or poverty in a community or region without providing a single new
job to the disadvantaged who live there. If every new job is filled
by a nondisadvantaged person who moves into the community, the
rate of unemployment (or underemployment or poverty) must decrease
since the labor force size is increasing faster than the number of persons unemployed. Yet the absolute number of persons in economic
distress may be unchanged or even increasing slightly. Thus, one
must consider more than gross rates of unemployment, underemployment, or poverty in order to assess adequately the effect of public
policy designed to deal with the economic distress of selected groups.

Second, jobs are also taken by new entrants to the labor force
from within the community, primarily women. We have seen that
many rural industries, particularly textiles and electronics assembly,
utilize female labor. While the income from these jobs may go toward
replacing that of an unemployed or underemployed male in the family,
they do not reduce the number of unemployed persons in the area. In
point of fact, increased labor force participation often is accompanied
by increased unemployment (Jordan, 1967; Scott and Summers, 1974).
In general, the studies show that local labor markets operate in ways
which often work against the needs of the people for whom rural industrial development has been promoted (cf. Abt Associates, 1968;
Bryant, 1969; Bender, Green, and Campbell, 1971, 1973; Miernyk,
1971). These factors must be taken into account if future policies
are to correct the problems of the past.

Multiplier Effect

The employment benefits generated by rural industrial development are not restricted to the workers hired by the new plants. Additional, secondary jobs are also created in other sectors of the local
economy, such as retail and wholesale trade and service industries,
as a result of the expenditures of the firms and their employees.
This process is often analyzed and compared in terms of an employment "multiplier," which measures the total direct and indirect effects as some multiple of the initial increase in jobs (see Andrews,
1953-56; Alexander, 1954; Tiebout, 1956a; 1956b; 1962; Palmer

et al., 1958; Isard, 1960; Pfouts, 1960; Brinkman, 1973). Table
5.4 lists all of the multipliers reported in the case studies.

A multiplier of 1.0 would mean that there was no net effect beyond the direct employment increase caused by the new industry;
higher multipliers indicate the extent of the indirect effects. There
are some differences in how the multipliers were computed but they
are not serious enough to prevent useful comparisons.

The most significant aspect of these findings is the number of
very low multipliers--half of them are below 1.2. This would not be
surprising if it were not for the fact that the most widely known figures are those given by the U.S. Chamber of Commerce studies
(1.65 and 1.68). As Till (1972, p. 27) cautions, "With such wide
variation it is useless to automatically apply a multiplier derived
from one area to the study of another. Yet this is frequently done."
The importance of such variation in multipliers can be grasped by
recognizing that with a multiplier of 1.02, it would take 50 jobs in
manufacturing to create one in nonmanufacturing, but with a multiplier of 1.65, it would take only about 1 2/3 jobs in manufacturing to
do so. Based on the data provided in the case studies, we can begin
to locate and analyze some of the reasons behind these differences.

Existing Economic Diversity
and Multipliers

A number of interrelated structural attributes condition the
multiplier effect of new industrial jobs in a number of respects.
First, the size of the existing manufacturing, commercial, and service sectors has a strong effect on whether local residents, retail-
ers, and manufacturers make their purchases within the town or in
another. Communities with only a few or no commercial and industrial establishments are more dependent on outside trade, and therefore do not gain many indirect or induced jobs through increased
business activity generated by new plants; just the opposite is the
case for economically more diversified communities. This is illustrated in Table 5.4 by the high multipliers from the Chamber of Commerce studies (1968, 1973), Pittman's study of Leflore County,
Mississippi (1965), and Davis's analysis of White County, Arkansas
(1963).

The criteria by which counties were chosen for the Chamber
analyses insured that all of them had relatively large manufacturing
sectors and were undergoing substantial economic growth. To be
included a county had to meet the following criteria: (1) manufacturing employment had to have more than doubled over the decade; (2) a
numerical increase of over 1,000 manufacturing employees; (3) manufacturing employment had to be more than 15 percent of total employment in the study of the 1950s and more than 20 percent in the study

TABLE 5.4

Employment Multipliers

Study Site	Unit of Analysis	Research Time Period	Industrial Product	Direct Employment	Employment Multiplier
Linton, Ind.[a]	city	1964	aluminum chairs	119	1.02
Gassville, Ark[b]	8-county area	1960-63	shirts	750	1.11
Summerville, S.C.[c]	4-county area	1963	bricks	25	1.36
Pickens, Miss.[d]	4-county area	1964-65	tissue paper	57	1.14
Braxton Co., W. Va.[e]	county	1963	particle board	77	1.50
Hart Co., Ky.[f]	county	1963	bedding	111	1.06
Fleming Co., Ky.[g]	county	1958-63	auto and appliance trim, shoes	328	1.11
Laurel Co., Ky.[g]	county	1958-63	yarn	107	1.18
Lincoln Co., Ky.[g]	county	1958-63	apparel	380	1.00
Marion Co., Ky.[g]	county	1958-63	barrels, communications equipment, apparel	496	1.11
Russell Co., Ky.[g]	county	1958-63	apparel	206	1.03
Howard Co., Ind.[h]	county	1949-60	all manufacturing	4,006	1.44
Box Elder Co., Utah[i]	county	1955-61	chemicals	5,688	1.34
Lawrence Co., Tenn.[j]	county	1954-63	bicycles	2,270	1.36
Select U.S. counties[k]	11 counties	1950-60	all manufacturing	17,116	1.65
Select U.S. counties[l]	10 counties	1960-70	all manufacturing	25,677	1.68
Leflore Co., Miss.[m]	county	1959-64	all manufacturing	1,430	1.59
White Co., Ark.[n]	county	1951-59	all manufacturing	590	1.71

Sources: Wadsworth and Conrad (1965)[a]; Jordan (1967)[b]; McElveen (1970)[c]; Crecink (1970)[d]; Hoover (n.d.a)[e]; Hoover (n.d.b)[f]; Garrison (1967)[g]; Stevens and Wallace (1964)[h]; McArthur and Coppedge (1969)[i]; Wilson (1965)[j]; Chamber of Commerce (1968)[k]; Chamber of Commerce (1973)[l]; Pittman (1965)[m]; Davis (1963)[n].

of the 1960s; and (4) the increase in manufacturing had to be the major employment change in the decade, excluding agriculture in the first study but not in the second. Leflore and White counties were explicitly selected for study on the basis of these requirements, and they both met all criteria but one. White County had an increase of 590, not 1,000 manufacturing jobs, and Leflore County's manufacturing employment accounted for 12 percent, not 15 percent of total employment. Considering the high multipliers found in these cases, it is unfortunate that very few rural counties can meet the above criteria. Only 20 counties in the entire United States in 1960 and 30 in 1970 met the full set of criteria. Therefore, considering them to be representative of what new industrial jobs mean to any community is clearly misleading.

Further evidence of the importance of existing industrial and commercial sectors for secondary employment impacts can be found in other case studies in which multipliers were not computed. The analysis of six small Wisconsin towns found that the more industrialized cities gained more nonmanufacturing jobs than the less industrialized, suggesting to the authors that "in a more industrialized city when employment expands in manufacturing there is a sympathetic growth in non-manufacturing segments of the economy" (Andrews et al., 1959, p. 27). Also, in Rochester, Minnesota, which already possessed a well-developed commercial sector (due mainly to its sizable medical establishments), the large IBM plant which located there had a significant positive effect on employment in local retail and service businesses (Morris, 1960).

Another of the reasons that economically less diversified communities tend to have lower employment multipliers is the greater likelihood of incommuters, who often spend most of their salaries in their place of residence rather than their place of employment. In such instances, the purchasing power added through industrial employment "leaks" out and does not contribute to the creation of new local jobs (cf. Daoust, 1954; Wadsworth and Conrad, 1965; Stevens and Wallace, 1964; Shaffer, 1972; Summers, 1973; Uhrich, 1974). This is a factor of considerable importance when one remembers that studies report a great deal of commuting in connection with rural plants (see Chapter 4).

One might expect multipliers to increase when they are measured over large geographic areas, reasoning that more of the effects occurring outside the immediate community would then be included. However, the figures for Gassville, Arkansas, and Pickens, Mississippi (1.11 and 1.14), which involved eight county and four county areas respectively, show that the impacts may still be minor (see Table 5.4). The failure of this expectation results from the fact that geographic size of an area is basically irrelevant. Rather, the

important factor is the range of services available within the area being considered. It is reasonable, of course, that often in extending
the geographic boundaries of a system one increases the range of
services and therefore also increases the degree to which the indirect
and induced effects of new industry can be internalized. But this does
not always occur.

Another important factor in the reduction of employment multipliers is the existence of considerable excess business capacity and
underemployment in many small towns. As a result, the firms can
handle increases in sales without hiring additional workers or enlarg-
ing their capital stock at a commensurate rate. Garrison (1972) considers this to be a key reason for the low multipliers (1.00-1.18) he
found in his study communities, as do Wadsworth and Conrad (1965)
for theirs (see Table 5.4). It was also singled out by Helgeson and
Zink (1973, p. 34) in their analysis of Jamestown, North Dakota, as
being largely responsible for the fact that "the nearly 400 jobs provided in manufacturing had little employment multiplier effect within
the region."

In certain towns, however, even with a relatively undeveloped
economy, particular quantities or types of industry may interact with
local conditions in such a way as to stimulate significant multipliers
and economic growth despite the underutilization of labor and capital.
One cannot say that all small communities are doomed to small indirect and induced employment effects. As one study concludes: "A
small town (with population of 5,000 to 20,000) having certain characteristics may act as the employment center of a sizable labor market.
The functioning of such a town as a labor market center is the prime
mechanism for economic growth in some regions . . ." (Abt Associates, 1968, p. ii). Adequate development planning depends upon the
discovery of what those "certain characteristics" are and where they
exist.

Industry Characteristics and Multipliers

Aside from the characteristics of the community or area, the
other major component of the multiplier equation is the nature of the
industry which locates within it. As stated previously, the two are
related, though not in a simple, mechanistic way, and different combinations of each appear to produce different results. The basic situation is the following: "Large multipliers can be expected from new
industries having considerable interdependence among existing local
business and industries, because they indirectly create many jobs in
[them]" (Brinkman, 1973, p. 72). Illustrations of this multiplier can
be found in the case studies of Braxton County, West Virginia (1.50),

where the primary raw materials (timber and coal) for the particle board plant are purchased locally (Hoover, n.d.a), and White County, Arkansas (1.71), where the manufacturing firms required a number of local service industries (Davis, 1963).

The employment multipliers which most nonmetropolitan communities can expect to realize are restrained by the backward and forward linkages of the firms which locate in them. Unlike the Braxton County and White County experiences many communities find that new industry is linked into external networks both with respect to inputs to the local production process (backward linkages) as well as outputs from the local plant (forward linkages). The degree of external backward and forward linkages is variable across types of industry, of course, and is conditioned in part by the range of services available locally as noted above. Klimasewski's 1974 analysis of manufacturing activity in eastern Tennessee is one of the clearest and most detailed presentations of backward and forward linkages we have observed. He shows how both inputs and outputs feed into networks which extend throughout the nation.

In the extreme the local community may become little more than a labor source for the plant work force with virtually no indirect or induced employment. This situation is clearly illustrated by the rocket fuel and missile fuel development in Box Elder County, Utah, wherein the authors concluded that "when the manufacturing sector is heavily oriented to space- and defense-type manufacturing, and when nearly all the raw materials are imported and the product is either tested or exported, there is little interaction of the county level" (McArthur and Coppedge, 1969, p. 6). Because of the nature of the product, all the aluminum plants studied exhibit this tendency toward external rather than internal employment multipliers (Garth, 1953; Johnson, 1960; Andrews and Bauder, 1968; Gray, 1969). The following statement by Gray (1969, p. 280) concerning Ravenswood, West Virginia, is indicative: "While the increase in indirect employment caused by the plant's operation could be traced from Ohio (power generating plant) to Louisiana (production of alumina from bauxite), this has not helped Ravenswood."

UNEMPLOYMENT

Of the many expectations associated with rural industrial development reduction in local unemployment is one of the most fervently held. There is considerable evidence of the hoped for result but given the apparent soundness of the logic behind such a hope, it is surprising how often experience contradicts it.

Table 5.5 lists the changes in the unemployment rate, before and after the location of manufacturing plants where both rates were reported in the documents. It can be seen that in approximately two-thirds of the cases the unemployment rate declined. Among those showing an increase none was as large as 2 percent. However, the smallness of the decreases relative to the magnitude of the unemployment rates must be noted. It is quite probable the residents of the study areas had hoped for more.

Other analyses discuss the impacts of industries on unemployment without providing comparable overall rates. In these studies one finds a less favorable report regarding reductions in unemployment. For example, Crecink (1970) found that total employment in his county decreased by 190 workers and unemployment rose by 20 workers. In the eight-county area studied by Jordan (1967), unemployment was 34 percent greater two years after the establishment of the shirt plant, and it was 60 percent greater in the two counties most directly affected by the plant. And Searcy (White County, Arkansas), which had the highest employment multiplier, continued to have serious unemployment problems; there were more people unemployed in 1959 than were reported in the total labor force in 1956 (Davis, 1963; Yantis, 1972).

Walraven (1962), Brann (1964), and Stevens and Wallace (1964) also found that industrial development can be accompanied by increases in unemployment. They suggest the following reasons:

1. The possibility of employment in the home town slows outmigration.
2. Participation in the labor market increases.
3. The opening of job opportunities in one community often brings an influx of workers from the surrounding area.
4. The employment situation becomes more dynamic and some workers may be laid off as new jobs are created elsewhere.

Another reason, which they neglect, is the frequent hiring of women in rural plants (as discussed above).

Two major lessons can be drawn from these findings on unemployment. First, they illustrate the need for the establishment of several firms or other employment activities rather than relying on any one to provide enough employment. Although it is difficult to make comparisons on the basis of the information provided in the case studies, it appears that one factor which distinguishes Yantis's counties from some of the others, and might help to explain the higher frequency of reduced unemployment rates, is that all of them gained a number of plants, not just one (Table 5.5). Second, the findings suggest that a community must try to look beyond its own, immediate

TABLE 5.5

Unemployment Rates Before and After Industrial Development

Study Area	Number of Employees	Dates		Rates (percent)		Change
		Before	After	Before	After	
Jackson Co., Iowa[a]	1,900	1950	1960	1.8	3.7	+1.9
Cross Co., Ark.[b]	1,900	1960	1970	5.2	4.6	-0.6
Washington Co., Miss.[c]	2,202	1950	1963	10.1	4.2	-5.9
Box Elder Co., Utah[d]	3,149	1955	1965	6.7	7.0	+0.3
Putnam, LaSalle, and Bureau counties, Ill.[e]	1,039	1966	1973	3.6	5.0	+1.4
Adair Co., Okla.[f]	--	1960	1970	16.4	17.5	+1.1
Cherokee Co., Okla.[f]	--	1960	1970	16.2	10.0	-6.2
Muskogee Co., Okla.[f]	--	1960	1970	8.9	7.4	-1.5
Hot Springs Co., Ark.[g]	2,263	1958	1970	11.9	7.0	-4.9
Baxter Co., Ark.[g]	1,018	1964	1970	8.2	4.7	-3.5
Howard Co., Ark.[g]	781	1960	1970	4.3	3.9	-0.4
Logan Co., Ark.[g]	690	1958	1970	15.6	6.8	-8.8
Randolph Co., Ark.[g]	1,123	1964	1970	9.4	9.3	-0.1
Benton Co., Ark.[g]	1,827	1960	1970	5.5	4.5	-1.0
White Co., Ark.[g]	1,394	1960	1970	12.1	12.1	0.0
Laurel Co., Ky.[h]	--	1960	1963	12.6	7.1	-5.5

Sources: Funk (1964)[a]; Brady (1972)[b]; Pray (1965)[c]; McArthur and Coppedge (1969)[d]; Summers (unpublished data)[e]; Shaffer (1972)[f]; Yantis (1972)[g]; Garrison (1967)[h].

problems and carry out broader, long-range area development programs. The diffusion of economic effects over wide areas, which we
have repeatedly come across, accentuates the integrated character of
local economies and reaffirms the necessity for integrated development efforts.

IMPACT OF DEVELOPMENT UPON INCOME

As we stated previously, the supporters of rural development
are enthusiastic about the prospects of incoming industry because it
is expected to have positive economic benefits for the residents of
the developing community. While these effects can be assessed along
a variety of dimensions, expected increases in real individual and
family income are benefits of immediate concern to the local residents.

It is anticipated that development will increase the demand for
labor, both through direct employment and the stimulation of other
sectors of the local economy, which will reduce unemployment and
underemployment. These changes will, in turn, tend to increase the
average income among the community's residents. For the most
part, available data tend to support the assumption that development
will result in an increase over time in average income (for both individuals and families), but as we shall argue below, these findings
should not be accepted uncritically for the purposes of policy-making.

The most frequently reported type of income measures are per
capita and median family income. They provide a basic, albeit gross,
indication of the income trends associated with rural industrial development. Tables 5.6 and 5.7 present the figures from before and
after the location of manufacturing plants, and the percent changes
which occurred. Unless noted otherwise, these data were adjusted
to represent constant purchasing power (real income).

As with the employment effects, we find striking amounts of
variation in income changes. In Table 5.6 it is found that the increases in per capita income range from 5.3 percent to 183.0 percent, but in over half of these studies the increase was less than 50
percent. The data in Table 5.7 on median family income show a
similar large variation: from an increase of 25.6 percent to 178.4
percent, but with about a third of the studies showing changes less
than 50 percent. Not surprisingly, many of the largest percentage
increases are found in those locations with the lowest per capita or
median family incomes. In such areas even small increases in absolute dollars can generate dramatic percentage increases. As a
result we might anticipate large percentage increases in those areas
which have the lowest average incomes prior to development.

Since economic stagnation is one of the primary reasons for trying to entice industry into rural areas, small income effects which may result from development constitute a very real and common problem (Hansen, 1970, p. 237). Some analysts have hoped that wages would rise with industrial development, but, as Dietz (1971, p. 69) found, "the low pay scales which attract new manufacturing plants to rural areas do not apparently reach urban center rates after the plant has developed." It is important to note, however, that in economically depressed areas even small absolute increases in annual income may have socially significant effects (Garrison, 1972). In particular, positive changes in income may tend to inhibit the out-migration of marginally successful families.

A number of factors appear to account for the cases with the smaller (percent) increases in income. First, they often involve the lower-wage industries, such as wood, textiles, and apparel, which do not add as much to the local income stream as other types of industries. The examples include a particle board plant in Braxton County, West Virginia (Hoover, n.d.a), a woolen goods plant in Charlotte County, Virginia (Bureau of Population and Economic Research, 1956), a shirt plant in the Ozark area of Arkansas (Jordan, 1967), and a yarn plant in Laurel County, Kentucky (Garrison, 1967).

Second, the industries which import raw materials into the area and export products to outside areas tend to create smaller income effects (for reasons which were discussed previously in regard to employment). Here we can point to plants producing aluminum in Flathead County, Montana (Johnson, 1960), chemicals in Baxter County, Arkansas (Yantis, 1972), and steel in Putnam County, Illinois (Summers, 1973). It should be noted that these cases involved relatively high wages and large numbers of employees.

Third, the existence of a substantial amount of commuting, of both nonresidents into the county for work and residents out of the county for purchases, is another factor which reduces the size of income growth generated by a new industrial plant. A clear example of this is the steel mill in rural Illinois where 82 percent of the workers lived outside the county (Summers, 1973).

The review of the available research, then, provides an apparent empirical base for the argument that industrial growth stimulates the average income of residents in nonmetropolitan areas. There are, however, conceptual as well as measurement limitations to be considered.

Earnings and Cash Transfers

At the very least, money income can be divided into earnings and cash transfers (Merriam, 1968). The latter category includes

TABLE 5.6

Per Capita Income Before and After Industrial Development

Study Area	Number of Employees	Product	Dates Before	Dates After	Per Capita Income Before	Per Capita Income After	Percent Increase
Braxton Co., W. Va.[a]	77	particle board	1958	1963	$1,398	$1,472	5.3
Flathead Co., Mont.[b]	686	aluminum	1951	1956	1,504	1,614	7.3
Charlotte Co., Va.[c]	484	woolen goods	1949	1954	654	755	15.4
Baxter Co., Ark.[d]	1,018	chemicals	1964	1969	1,930	2,396	20.2
Ozark area, Ark.[e]	750	apparel	1960	1963	989	1,243	25.7
Howard Co., Ind.[f]	4,006	printing, publishing, and other nondurable goods; primary metals; machinery and equipment	1944	1959	1,309	1,671	27.7
Laurel Co., Ky.[g]	107	yarn	1958	1963	858	1,109	29.2
Randolph Co., Ark.[d]	1,072	electrical equipment, wood, leather	1964	1969	1,423	1,869	31.2
Keith Co., Neb.[h]	1,000	capacitors	1954	1968	1,858	2,603	34.7
Dawson Co., Neb.[h]	600	shock absorbers	1961	1968	1,623	2,252	38.8
Fleming Co., Ky.[g]	228	auto trim, shoes	1958	1963	995	1,404	41.1
Choctaw Co., Okla.[i]	200	apparel, furniture, chemicals	1950	1958	470	674	43.4
Marion Co., Ky.[g]	496	barrels, electrical equipment, apparel	1958	1963	901	1,309	45.3
Lawrence Co., Tenn.[j]	2,000	bicycles	1955	1960	834	1,213	45.4
Russell Co., Ky.[g]	206	apparel	1958	1963	596	891	49.5

County		Products					
Putnam Co., Ill.[k]	1,039	steel	1965	1972	1,941	2,926	50.8
Lincoln Co., Ky.[g]	380	apparel	1958	1963	825	1,273	54.3
Sargent Co., N.D.[h]	400	machinery	1954	1968	1,050	1,698	61.7
Custer Co., Neb.[h]	360	medical supplies	1961	1968	1,523	2,053	64.4
Hot Springs Co., Ark.[d]	2,175	metal, SC&G, wood	1958	1969	1,489	2,581	73.3
Rolette Co., N.Dak.[g]	160	watch bearings	1953	1968	800	1,391	73.9
White Co., Ark.[l]	590	leather, wood, rubber and plastic, SC&G, metal, machinery					
Muskogee Co., Okla.[m]	200	furniture, air conditioning, metal	1949	1959	611	1,070	75.1
Logan Co., Ark.[d]	690	chemicals, SC&G, transportation equipment, metal	1960	1970	1,716	2,100	81.7
Adair Co., Okla.[m]	80	apparel	1958	1969	909	1,743	91.7
Howard Co., Ark.[d]	781	communication components	1960	1970	739	1,432	93.8
White Co., Ark.[d]	1,263	paper, apparel, metal, SC&G, wood	1960	1969	1,373	2,825	105.8
Benton Co., Ark.[d]	1,827	machinery, metal, electrical equipment, rubber and plastic, SC&G	1955	1969	890	2,233	150.9
		machinery, textiles, metal	1954	1969	938	2,663	183.9

Note: SC&G is stone, clay, and glass.

Sources: Hoover (n.d.a)[a]; Johnson (1960)[b]; Bureau of Population and Economic Research, University of Virginia (1956)[c]; Yantis (1972)[d]; Jordan (1967)[e]; Stevens and Wallace (1964)[f]; Garrison (1967)[g]; Dietz (1971)[h]; Klein (1959)[i]; Wilson (1965)[j]; Summers (unpublished data)[k]; Davis (1963)[l]; Shaffer (1974)[m].

TABLE 5.7

Median Family Income Before and After Industrial Development

Study Area	Number Employees	Product	Dates Before	Dates After	Median Income Before	Median Income After	Percent Increase
Putnam Co. area, Ill.[a]	1,039	steel	1965	1970	$6,204	$7,790	25.6
Muskogee Co., Okla.[b]	200	furniture, air conditioning, metal	1960	1970	4,505	5,669	25.8
Cherokee Co., Okla.[b]	10	upholstery and carpet	1960	1970	3,044	4,435	46.0
Howard Co., Ind.[c]	4,006	printing, publishing, and other nondurable goods, primary metals, machinery and equipment	1949	1959	3,175	4,901	54.5
Adair Co., Okla.[b]	80	communication components	1960	1970	2,198	3,640	65.6
Hot Springs Co., Ark.[d]	2,175	metal, SC&G, wood	1959	1969	3,492	4,535	66.5
Malvern Co., Ark.[d]	2,175	--	--	--	3,799	4,227	42.6
Baxter Co., Ark.[d]	1,018	chemicals	--	--	2,468	3,466	80.0
White Co., Ark.[d]	1,263	machinery, metal, electrical equipment, rubber and plastic, SC&G	--	--	2,312	3,167	81.1

Searcy, Ark.[d]	1,263	--	--	--	2,937	3,076	34.3
Douglas Co., Mo.[e]	403	athletic equipment, wood	1949	1959	1,084	2,050	89.0
Randolph Co., Ark.[d]	1,072	electrical equipment, wood, leather	1959	1969	2,112	3,162	92.0
Pocahontas, Ark.[d]	1,072	--	--	--	2,905	3,216	41.9
Howard Co., Ark.[d]	781	paper, apparel, metal, SC&G, wood	1959	1969	2,670	4,057	94.8
Nashville, Ark.[d]	781	--	--	--	2,869	3,598	60.8
Benton Co., Ark.[d]	1,827	machinery, textiles, metals	1959	1969	2,661	4,185	101.6
Rogers, Ark.[d]	1,827	--	--	--	3,569	4,736	70.6
Logan Co., Ark.[d]	690	chemicals, transportation equipment, apparel, SC&G	1959	1969	1,847	3,214	123.1
Paris, Ark.[d]	690	--	--	--	2,578	3,185	58.4
Lawrence Co., Tenn.[f]	2,000	bicycles	1949	1959	1,245	3,178	155.0

Note: SC&G is stone, clay, and glass; dashes indicate data not provided.

Sources: Summers and Clemente (1973)[a]; Shaffer (1974)[b]; Stevens and Wallace (1964)[c]; Yantis (1972)[d]; Hagerman and Braschler (1966)[e]; Wilson (1965)[f].

public assistance (such as unemployment and aid payments to dependent children, retirement and social security benefits, dividends and interest on savings, alimony, and so on). Clearly variations in average income levels could be caused by changes in earnings, or cash transfers, or both. Areas characterized by low wage rates, which are attractive to industry, are the same economically depressed regions which may be candidates for a disproportionate share of direct governmental aid. Changes in county per capita income, for example, may reflect increases in federal and state cash transfers, and not changes due to industrial development in the county.

Life Cycle and Temporal Variation

The importance of per capita income, or median family income, as a criterion for economic gain is linked to the demographic composition of the area being investigated. For example, the benefit of additional income to a family is somewhat determined by the size of the family and the ages of its members; in short, a family's position in the family cycle is a crucial factor to be considered when assessing the possible impact of industrial development (Kuznets, 1955; Merriam, 1968; Miller, 1970).

Further, as Kuznets (1955) has pointed out, using annual average income as a criterion has an inherent problem: it ignores interannual variation which may be substantial in areas where there is large temporal variation in employment. It appears that lower-income groups are especially susceptible to such variation (Merriam, 1968, pp. 732-33). This is particularly important since industry migrates to low-income regions; we might expect that developing regions will exhibit this tendency toward pronounced temporal variation in annual income. Beck (1975) estimated that over a five-year period in one nonmetropolitan area not undergoing development (Iroquois County, Illinois) 28.1 percent of the population increased their annual earnings, 33.3 percent lost earnings, and only 38.6 percent were stationary. There is some evidence, therefore, that considering annual income may disguise (with either an upward or downward bias) the true economic position of the family.

Distribution of Income Gains

While there is evidence that the average income may increase during industrial development, there is still the question of whose income increases. Most of the research findings are directed at the average income and there has been much less attention to how increases are distributed throughout the population (Shaffer, 1974; Beck and Madans, 1975). The few studies which have undertaken to investigate this question of distribution strongly suggest that some groups in the population receive negligible economic benefits from industrial development. Clemente and Summers (1973), for example, found that the construction of a large steel mill in rural Illinois actually had a negative effect on the relative income status of the elderly residents of the area. Similarly, Till (1972) in a study of four nonmetropolitan areas in the South concluded that blacks benefited less from industrial development than did whites. Merrill and his colleagues (Abt Associates, 1968) reach the same conclusions from their investigations in the South. However, both Till (1972) and Shaffer (1974) presented data which indicate that the poor benefit from development. Yet, in a reconsideration of the Summers (1973) data, Beck (1975) found that industrial growth had no significant impact on the percentage of families below the poverty level.

Although there are a few studies which do consider the question of distribution, we feel that it is fair to argue that insufficient attention has been given to the distributional aspects of the gains, as well as the costs, of rural development. It is inadequate to contend simply that development is a desirable community goal because it may marginally increase average income. Indeed, development may raise aggregate or average income while simultaneously depressing the relative economic position of certain segments of the population in the developing community; the elderly or minority groups for example (cf. Abt Associates, 1968; Summers and Clemente, 1973). The basic issue is whether we can afford growth in community well-being if it is purchased at the expense of the disadvantaged.

Social Equity

The next issue to be considered is one of social equity, and it revolves around the role of inmigration in altering the developing region's social and economic composition. To some degree the development of a rural area may induce a flow of labor into that region, and some of the income generated by development will be absorbed by these newcomers. It is quite possible that those studies based on two or more cross-sections which demonstrated an increase in either per capita or median family income may be misleading in the sense that there is no assurance that the people originally living in the developing area will share in any of the economic benefits deriving from industrial growth. Shaffer (1974) reports that in several studies (for example, Bender, Green, and Campbell, 1971) inmigration had large mitigating effects on the impact of industrial development on the residents of the study communities. In a reanalysis of data from Summers (1973), investigating a rural steel plant, Beck and Madans (1975) found that much of the apparent benefit of this development accrued to persons who moved into the area after development began. The inmigrants controlled 12.2 percent more of the aggregate annual earnings than would be expected on the basis of their numbers in the population whereas the long-term residents controlled 3.4 percent less of the earnings than expected. Further they found that the inmigrants were younger and better educated than the original residents. This may imply that the newcomers will have an additional advantage in the competition for any future jobs created in the area.

This suggests that the people who bear the cost of the development (by increased taxes for land development, for example) may not be the same people who will capture the benefits, and in fact they may find themselves in a worse relative position after development than before. Although from the point of view of the aggregate community, it is possible that development may represent a net economic gain, this is little consolation to those who have not shared in this benefit.

Level of Consumption

It has been suggested (for example, Kuznets, 1960; Merriam, 1968, p. 726) that an appropriate measure of individual or family economic status would be based on the level of consumption of goods and services. If such a measure were available, we feel that it is likely that the view of industrial development as producer of economic gain may be too optimistic. This is especially apparent if the distinction were made between essential consumption (food, shelter, clothes, transportation, etc.) and nonessential consumption. Given that industry tends to locate in economically depressed areas, it could be found that development tends to stimulate essential consumption while leaving nonessential consumption unaffected (cf. Maitland and Friend, 1961). It may be increases in the latter category which should be used as the indicator of community economic affluence due to development. Unfortunately, the case studies we reviewed have not grappled with this issue, and it is presented here as a hypothesis for further investigation.

SUMMARY

It is convenient, partially because of its simplicity, to view positive changes in average income as an appropriate criterion for successful industrial development in nonmetropolitan areas, and when this benchmark is employed we found that there is a great deal of evidence to support the allegation that development will increase average income. While simplicity is often a virtue, in this case it may be damning since using changes in average income may mask many problems which should be faced squarely. In particular, the issues surrounding the distribution of purported economic gains begs for further investigation. In this same vein, careful attention needs to be paid to the distributional aspects of the costs of rural development. In short, more detailed analyses of the "winners" and "losers" in development are needed.

6

FISCAL IMPACT IN
THE PUBLIC SECTOR

Manufacturing is sought eagerly by many public officials because they believe industrial development will ease the fiscal crisis in smaller communities (Marshall, 1965; Maxwell, 1965; C. Smith et al., 1971; Hansen and Munsinger, 1972). From Congress to county boards new industry is regarded as a solution to budgetary problems, especially in towns and counties experiencing population losses and declines in business activity. The enthusiasm rests firmly on the notion that new industry will enlarge the existing tax base (Walker, 1956; Hirsch, 1961; Carroll and Sacks, 1962; and Brinkman, 1973), and thereby provide local relief from a growing tax burden. Growth in the aggregate value of real property is seen as the key to the hoped for relief since real property is the major local source of tax revenues in most communities (Maxwell, 1965). But the sources of potential benefits extend beyond real property value. There are additional routes through which increased industrial employment may generate greater public revenues: increased consumable income, greater volume of retail sales, direct payments by industry, and state and federal transfer payments.

It is important to note that virtually all the expected growth in public revenue depends upon growth in the private sector. Therefore, within the prevailing political and economic framework, increases in local public revenues can result from industrial development only when there is growth in the private sector which is converted into public monies. The conversion mechanism usually is taxation in one or another form which may be levied directly by local governments or by state and federal legislatures to be returned to local communities.

But revenue is only one side of the fiscal ledger. Public expenditure is equally important since no relief is gained when increases in revenues are equalled or exceeded by expenditures. Although proponents of industrial development often minimize or even ignore the cost side of the ledger (U.S. Chamber of Commerce, 1960, 1968, 1973) it is nonetheless a reality that new industry has a price tag.

The cost factors involved can be divided into two general categories: locational costs and service costs. Under locational costs are found those concessions to the new industry which are given as an inducement to bring the industry to the community. Included are such items as "tax holidays," site purchase and preparation services, revenue bonds, general purpose bonds, debt services, and loss of previously collected real estate taxes on the plant site. Service costs may be further divided into those provided by local government directly to the new industry and the increase in those provided to the community which are attributable to the presence of the new industry. The latter are closely tied to population growth resulting from increased employment opportunities. Thus, it is clear that both sides of the ledger must be examined if one is to assess the fiscal impact of new industry on the public sector of local communities.

In the previous chapter we reviewed several studies which provided considerable evidence of positive effects in the private sector traceable to the location of new industry in the community. The objective of this chapter is to review the case studies in search of evidence relevant to the public sector costs and benefits. The local public sector encompasses both municipal and county governments as well as local school districts.

EXPANDING FISCAL CAPACITY

From the public sector point of view the value of industrial development lies in its effect on the fiscal capacity--ability-to-pay--of the local government and school district. By increasing fiscal capacity local leaders hope to achieve some degree of opportunity to enhance governmental services without additional taxes on existing residents or alternatively, to maintain existing services while reducing taxes. Legislation in most states creates a situation in which the fiscal capacity of local governments is dependent primarily upon (1) property, real and personal, and (2) business transactions involving items of monetary value, that is, wages and salary paid, retail sales, land transfers, and so on. Therefore, it is in the explanation of how these are affected by industrial development that one discovers the logical paradigm for fiscal gains to the public sector.

The origin of this logical paradigm is traceable to a simple but powerful economic idea, the export base concept (Andrews, 1953-56; Alexander, 1954; Keynes, 1965; Tiebout, 1956a, 1956b, 1962).

According to this formulation, local industries can be usefully divided into those which sell their products within the local market and those which sell outside the local economy. The latter are referred to as export industries and are considered "basic" because of their role in generating a net flow of money into the local economy. They generally are said to include agriculture, mining, and lumbering as well as manufacturing and, more recently, recreation. Nonexport industries supply goods and services to business firms and workers in both the export and nonexport sectors. Thus, growth in nonexport industry is largely limited by expansion of the export sector. One must note that the essential element in the concept is the net flow of funds/income into the local community.

To the export base must be added the multiplier concept according to which new industry generates additional money in the local economy through spending and respending (Isard, 1960; Palmer, 1958; Pfouts, 1960). This circulation of money leads to a cumulative effect that exceeds the dollar value of the initial investment or inflow of funds. The multiplier concept, which often is used to relate investment to income, also has been used to estimate changes in labor force, population, employment, housing demand, and numerous other variables. Perhaps the most widely known application of the multiplier notion is that regularly published by the U.S. Chamber of Commerce (1960, 1968, 1973) wherein estimates of benefits are given for each 100 new industrial jobs in a local community.

While the export base and multiplier ideas are basically a scheme for understanding how income and unemployment in one segment of the private sector flows into other segments of the private sector (Thompson, 1968), analytically the scheme can be extended to the presumed flow of money into public revenues from local industrial employment and income. (While it is possible to consider investment as well as income and employment multipliers, in most instances, investment is not used for small area analysis but rather for national analysis.) Indeed, such an extension underlies virtually all the protagonist arguments for industrial location as a solution to local fiscal problems. It is rather interesting, therefore, that very few authors of case studies have designed their research to assess explicitly how well the realities of costs and benefits of new industry to local communities fit the paradigm. Nevertheless, it has value as a device for organizing case study findings and since it is implicit in most studies we shall employ it as the structure for our review of public sector impacts.

PUBLIC SECTOR COSTS AND BENEFITS

The flow of money, jobs, people, goods, and services implied in the export base and multiplier paradigm are graphically presented in Figure 6.1. The schematic presentation is an adaptation and extension of Hirsch's 1961 regional fiscal impact model which differs primarily by its inclusion of concepts that were less widely recognized at the time. Also it combines the cost and benefit flows into a single schematic. These are the flows which in summation are expected to yield a net fiscal gain to the local public sector. We shall turn attention first to the benefit side.

The Benefit Stream

Industry's Direct Payments

Flowing into the benefit stream are those payments made directly to the local government by new industry: real and personal property tax payments, gross receipt tax payments, and fees for services rendered by the local government to the new industry.

Property Tax Payments. The extent of benefits realized through direct payments by the new industry is variable from community to community and depends in large measure on the local tax structure and upon negotiated agreements between local government officials, development representatives, and industrial management.

The range of variability in direct payments is clearly evident in those case studies which report property tax payments (real and personal) made by the firms to local governments. In four of the seven midwestern communities studied by Bucher (1971) the local government received no tax revenues from firms they had subsidized to encourage their location. Garrison (1967) also reports no revenue collection from new plants in three of the eight Kentucky communities he studied. At the other extreme Uhrich (1974) reports that the Medical Products Division of Minnesota Mining and Manufacturing (3M) paid a total of $163,808.58 in property taxes to the Brookings, South Dakota, city government and school district in 1973. The 3M case is exceptional among those reviewed. Besides those already mentioned none of the remaining ten plants examined in the case studies made payments exceeding $6,000 per year (Merrill and Ryther, 1961; Helgeson and Zink, 1973; Bucher, 1971; Garrison, 1967).

It is important to note that these differences appear to be unrelated to the size of the plant; at least when size is measured in terms of work force. For example, the combined work force of four new plants in Jamestown, North Dakota (Helgeson and Zink, 1973), was 389. Together the four companies paid an estimated $14,366 in taxes to the local government in 1972, an average of just over $3,000 each.

FIGURE 6.1

Flow Chart for Public Sector Costs
and Benefits of New Industry

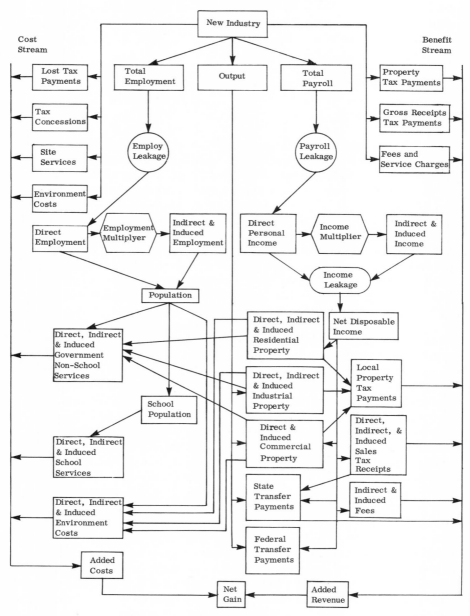

Source: Adapted from Hirsch (1961).

The plant noted by Bucher (1971) as having paid $6,000 in tax revenue had a work force of 420.

Yet, 3M employed only 360 people.

We realize, of course, that property tax assessments are not based on size of work force. But we make note of this lack of correlation because we have observed the tendency of community industrial development enthusiasts to link potential tax benefits to number of workers employed by the plant.

The more crucial determinants of tax payments to local governments relate to the structure of local taxes. The revenue which a community may realize from a given piece of industrial real estate depends upon several factors which local officials control and some which they do not. Under their control are such items as the assessment ratio (assessed value/true market value), frequency of reassessment, and the mill rate. In all states certain restrictions are placed on the taxing powers of local authorities. Thus depending on state legislation a community in one state may realize more potential revenue from a plant than would a community in another state with the same plant. For example, in Kentucky manufacturing equipment and raw materials inventories were exempted from local taxation at the time of the Garrison study, 1958-63. They still are in some states, but not in others. These are factors which impose a determining influence on the amount of tax revenue the local public sector may realize directly from local industry and which are beyond the direct control of local officials.

But there are tax factors which can be manipulated by local authorities so as to reduce the direct payments of industry to local government. This is done primarily through granting "tax holidays" during which the industrial property is exempted from taxation. Such holidays typically are for 5, 10, or 15 years. In places where outright exemption is illegal the practice of low assessment often is substituted. Either of these practices reduces the tax revenue the public sector receives directly from the new industry. Tax concessions are forms of local subsidization of industrial development and, therefore, are a cost to the local government. We shall return to this issue later in this chapter.

Fees and Service Charges. Communities with municipally owned utilities can expect direct payments from industry for those services rendered. In Bucher's (1971) study of seven midwestern communities he reports industrial payments of utilities. Unfortunately, no dollar figures are reported. Rather he calls attention to the fact that utility fees are expected at least to equal the cost of extending utility service to the plant site. Garrison (1967) reports that Stanford, Kentucky, received payment for extending a water line to a new plant. In a number of the other Kentucky communities Garrison implies that local utilities were municipally owned and received fees from the new companies. By far the most precise report of utility revenue is that of Uhrich (1974) in which he indicates a payment of $134,220.95 from 3M to Brookings, South Dakota. However, he also notes a cost to the local government of exactly the same amount. Thus, the revenue received from utility payments represented no net gain to the local community. One suspects that is the case in many communities and, therefore, the revenue is given little attention by researchers.

Two things are striking about the case studies with respect to industry's direct payments to local government. First, there is almost no attention given to new industry as a direct source of revenue. And second, where attention is focused on the issue at all, it appears that much of the potential is bargained away. One thing seems clear. Many local leaders are willing to trade direct revenues from new industry for indirect funds on the apparent assumption that the latter will outweigh the former.

Local Property Tax Payments

New industry has a growth effect on the local property tax revenues through two avenues. The first originates with the plant payroll and the second is initiated by the new industry's output. Both feed into the assessed property valuation which is a primary ingredient in the volume of property tax revenues collected by the local government and school district.

Payroll and Income Leakage. The wages and salaries paid by the new industry contribute to the benefit stream to the extent that the plant's payroll is paid to persons who spend it in the host community. In most communities some amount of payroll leakage may be expected to occur because a part of the wages and salaries are paid to employees living outside the local community. That portion of the plant's total payroll paid to community residents (total payroll minus payroll leakage) is referred to as direct personal income (see Figure 6.2). Through the multiplier effect indirect and induced personal income is generated which combines with direct personal income to increase the aggregate disposable income available for use in local markets.

Some of this gain in aggregate disposable income is lost to local markets however. A certain proportion almost surely will be "exported"--spent for goods and services in neighboring communities, on vacations, through mail order purchases, for nonlocal taxes, or in investments outside the community. Some portion may simply be saved for future use. And to many persons in rural communities the concept of credit buying and long-term debt is abhorrent with the result that increases in disposable income often are used to retire existing debts rather than being spent. These various forms of reduction in the aggregate disposable income constitute an income leakage. Stevens and Wallace (1964) called attention to various "leakages" in their study of Kokomo and Howard County, Indiana. However, Wadsworth and Conrad (1966) were perhaps the first to document the nature and extent of income leakage. In their study of Linton, Indiana, they discovered an average weekly payroll of $6,000 shrunk to $4,779 through (1) exportation of payroll, (2) increased savings, and (3) paying off old debts.

Yet in spite of the clarity and precision of Wadsworth and Conrad's work few researchers in the following years have explicitly incorporated income leakage estimates into assessments of industrial import in the private sector. Notable exceptions are the work of Shaffer (1972), Brady (1974), and Uhrich (1974). Our concern here with leakages is to call attention to their presence. Gains in aggregate disposable income may be more apparent than real for the local market.

Residential Property. Nevertheless, some of the increased income is expected to flow into residential development--new construction and home improvements. Both activities are expected to increase the assessed valuations of residential property which thus expands the flow of local property tax. This anticipated development of residential property is documented in some of the case studies.

In one of the earliest studies Daoust (1954) observed the construction of 14 new homes when Carboloy located in Edmore, Michigan, and created nearly 300 new jobs. The estimated market value of these homes was $360,000. During a similar historic period (1947-58) Merrill and Ryther (1961) report quite extensive residential growth in "Midway," Kansas; 2,068 residential buildings were constructed with further residential property expansion occurring through annexation. Also, during the last half of the 1950s Davis (1963) reports a substantial residential expansion in Searcy, Arkansas; 224 homes valued at $2,995,130. Even vacant lot values rose significantly in Searcy, 300-500 percent according to Davis's estimate. When Aluminum Company of America located a large plant in Rockdale, Texas, in 1952 residential developments occurred quickly and extensively. There were 448 workers at the plant when Garth (1953) summarized development progress and already 353 new homes had been constructed with an aggregate value exceeding $1 million. And Uhrich's study of Brookings, South Dakota, revealed 115 new homes, 9 new mobile homes, and 2 used ones which he attributed directly to the presence of 3M. While not citing specific numbers of residential building projects Andrews and Bauder (1968), Debes

(1973), and Miller (1967) all make reference to new home construction in, respectively, Monroe County, Ohio; Parsons, Kansas; and Tarboro, North Carolina.

On the basis of these studies alone it is quite clear that additional manufacturing jobs in a community mean new home construction. It is equally apparent that the number of new homes a community may expect for a given number of new jobs cannot be predicted with much certainty unless additional characteristics of the community, the work force composition, and local labor supply are considered as well. For example, compare the Edmore, Michigan, and the Rockdale, Texas, experiences. The two communities were comparable in population; 1,971 and 2,311 respectively and the work forces at the two plants were not terribly dissimilar, 285 and 448 respectively. Yet Edmore found itself with only 14 new homes while Rockdale had 353. The difference lies in the commuting habits of workers. Edmore workers were primarily commuters from nearby villages and towns while the Rockdale community had little competition from neighboring communities for provisioning workers with housing (or other goods and services).

Although none of the case studies dealt specifically with availability of housing that factor is also an important one to consider in translating new jobs to residential property growth. Many small towns do have a supply of underutilized or vacant housing. To the extent that new employees and their families occupy these properties, their presence has no direct growth effect on the residential property tax base. However, greater utilization of existing property may prevent a deterioration of the tax base.

As Scott and Summers (1974) have observed the composition of the work force also is a contingent factor. If the new industry hires primarily female workers, as do many of the "cut and sew" firms attracted to rural areas (see Chapter 4), there may be very little new home construction. Women workers become additional wage earners in families already living in the community or nearby. It is quite probable that some of the additional disposable family income will be used for home improvements and for new home construction but such upgrading of quality of housing activity can be extended over several years. Hence, the immediate effect on the residential property tax base may be rather small.

Local labor supply and its relation to the new industry's labor demands also affects the potential for increases in residential property. Many small towns and rural areas have substantial underutilization of available labor. If the skill requirements of the new industry can be met locally, little immediate effect of the new industry on residential development will be felt. By utilizing locally housed unemployed and underemployed persons and stimulating labor market

market participation, the new industry can sometimes fill its labor needs without significantly adding to the local population and thereby minimize the immediate effect on residential additions to the property tax base.

It should be noted that for some communities the goal may be to halt the decline in the tax base with no desire for growth, in which case the minimizing factors may be of little concern. But for communities with a growth goal, these factors deserve careful attention.

Industrial and Commercial Property. The output of the new industry is an important tributary leading into the benefit stream although it is seldom discussed in the studies under review. New construction, as well as improvements in existing property, may be prompted by the output of the new industry (Hirsch, 1961). The extent of indirect and induced growth in industrial and commercial property will depend in large part upon the type and volume of the output of course. But minimally the output may be expected to produce some growth in activities such as banking, transportation, and legal services and of course may be far more extensive if the new industry's output requires further processing which can be done by local firms.

Increases in disposable personal income also may generate indirect and induced growth in the commercial sector, especially in retail business but also in activities such as real estate, insurance, banking, and recreation. These indirect and induced effects presume either an increase in the aggregate disposable personal income, or in the per capita income, or both. They represent another manifestation of the multiplier concept but here involving a transformation of personal income into commercial property expansion.

While it is conceivable that growth in aggregate and/or per capita disposable income may produce someindirect and induced expansion in industrial property, the effect probably is a restrained one at the local level. Perhaps food manufacturing and processing for the local market is a logical first area of expansion. And other nondurable manufacturing activities are more likely to undergo expansion before durables since the latter generally have a larger minimal scale of operations.

There are, then, several logically potential avenues through which new industry may generate an expansion of the commercial and industrial sectors of the property tax base. Yet few of the case studies have focused attention on their physical expansion. In only five studies is there any discussion of commercial property expansion.

In their study of six small Wisconsin cities (5,000-10,000 population) Andrews et al. (1959) report that all three of the more industrialized cities showed substantial growth in number of retail establishments (13.4 percent, 27.1 percent, and 51.3 percent) while none of the three less industrial communities experienced growth greater than 10 percent. In Edmore, Michigan, several new businesses were noted by Daoust (1954) although he is not specific with respect to either their number or type of business activity. According to Davis (1963), Searcy, Arkansas, had nearly $3 million in commercial construction between 1951 and 1959 adding nearly one-half million square feet of floor space to the business sector. The number of parcels was quite as impressive as the total volume. From 1956 to 1959 the city issued 50 building permits for commercial construction valued at $1,407,200. This growth paralleled the addition of seven new plants with a combined work force of approximately 1,200 employees. In contrast to this level of expansion Rockdale, Texas (Garth, 1953), and Linton, Indiana (Wadsworth and Conrad, 1966), experienced little commercial development. However, in the case of Rockdale it seems highly probable that business expansion must have occurred subsequent to Garth's report in view of the housing development (353 new homes) and the absence of nearby service centers.

Excess capacity of local commercial establishments probably explains some of the minimizing effect of new industry on commercial growth. At least three of the case study authors called attention to excess business capacity in discussing the minimal employment multipliers they observed (Wadsworth and Conrad, 1966; Garrison, 1972; Helgeson and Zink, 1973). Thus, the amount of local property tax growth via commercial development may be easily overestimated if the business capacity of existing establishments is not carefully calculated.

Indirect and induced industrial property expansion is even less in evidence than commercial growth among the case studies. Only two reports give precise figures. Davis (1963) notes the addition of 96,000 square feet of manufacturing floor space between 1956 and 1959 in Searcy, Arkansas. No indication of the use of the space is given. He did comment that industrial sites had increased approximately 500 percent in value during the same time period. Miller (1967) reported that between 1958 and 1966 Tarboro, North Carolina, had issued 28 industrial building permits but no further indication of square footage, value, or use was reported.

In spite of the lack of attention to indirect and induced industrial property expansion, one can note in Appendix A that multiple plant locations over a span of five to ten years are quite common. It is impossible, of course, to determine the extent to which second, third, and subsequent plant locations are prompted by payroll and output at the initial plant location. However, it seems rather likely that in their totality the multiple plant sites expand the industrial property

tax base of the local community. The probability is less than certainty, however, because of the potential for various types of concessions which may have been granted by the local community.

Assessed Property Valuation. The assessed value of real property in
a community is the aggregated value of all parcels of real estate in
that community. For any specific parcel the assessed value is some
fraction of its considered market value. The assessed value divided
by the market value is the assessment ratio which is determined by
the local tax levying body; for example, the county board or city
council. It varies greatly among communities but is generally less
than .50 and sometimes is as low as .10. In the latter instance a
parcel judged by the tax asssessor to have a market value of $10,000
would be placed on the tax roll at a $1,000 assessed value.

Obviously, the assessed property valuation which a community
has at its disposal can be increased in any one of three ways. Since
the aggregate valuation is a function of (1) true market value of parcels of real estate, (2) the assessment ratio, and (3) the number of
parcels on the tax roll, an increase in any one (or more) of these
factors will produce an increase in the assessed valuation of property
assuming there is no decrease in the others. It is the increase in
number of parcels and true market value of existing parcels that is
expected to result from new industry. True market value may be
increased either through improvements to the property, or through
an expansion of its potential alternative uses, or through a more
rapid rise in demand for its existing use than occurs in supply. We
noted already that the case study documents give some support to the
expectation of increases in the number of residential, commercial,
and industrial property parcels, although we noted the growth often
was less than anticipated.

The case studies leave little doubt that assessed valuation of
property increased in the years following new industrial plant location
or expansion. No less than 11 studies report increases while there
are no reports of decreases. Debes's (1973) analysis of real estate
in Parsons, Kansas, from 1960 to 1970 is the most thorough and revealing of the studies reviewed. He reports that "the direct and indirect effects (of industrial development) together caused an increase
of approximately 7.2 to 7.8 million dollars in total residential real
estate valuations over the ten year study period" (Debes, 1973, p.
71). Furthermore, he shows that about 18 percent of the increased
residential valuation was attributable to direct effects of industrial
development. Obviously the indirect effects were very important to
residential property assessments in Parsons, Kansas.

One of the largest percentage increases was reported in Monroe
County, Ohio, where Andrews and Bauder (1968) note that real

property valuations rose from $25.3 million in 1958 to $85.2 million in 1959 (237 percent) and to $124.8 million in 1960 (393 percent over the two-year period). In Ava, Missouri, the school district property valuations rose nearly as much according to Hagerman and Braschler (1966); over the period 1959 to 1964 there was a 235 percent increase. However the city of Ava realized only a 62 percent increase from $1.138 million in 1959 to $1.844 million in 1964. Merrill and Ryther (1961) report an increase of $38 million in "Midway," Kansas, while the school district increased its assessed valuation from $19.1 million to $31.8 million. Smaller percentage increases were reported by Brady (1974), Daoust (1954), Miller (1967), Stevens and Wallace (1964), Tennessee Town and City (1957), and Wilson (1965).

In comparing three small industrial cities in Wisconsin with three nonindustrial cities of similar size, Andrews et al. (1959) found the industrialized cities had higher property valuations (with one exception). The differences were due mainly to the presence of manufacturing and mercantile property, particularly mercantile. Even so, residential property accounted for 50 to 60 percent of the total property valuation.

These reports are uniformly favorable toward industrial development as a means of increasing assessed valuation of property. Yet one should exercise some caution in interpretation because there are several ways in which assessed valuations may be increased, which we noted above, and little insight is provided in these case studies as to the precise sources of the increased property valuations.

Tax Rates. Between the assessed valuation of real property and local property tax revenue stands the property tax rate (or mill rate). Along with the assessment ratio the tax rate is determined by the local tax levying authority. Obviously, a local governmental fiscal body may increase the amount of property tax revenue from a fixed property base by merely altering either the assessment ratio or the tax rate or both. Since both of these coefficients are determined by local politicians changes in them are subject to community influences in addition to the strictly market factors. Consequently, it is difficult to interpret changes in tax rates (or assessment ratios) as consequences of industrial invasion. Nevertheless, tax rates are reported by several authors. In discussing tax rates these researchers clearly imply a normative position to the effect that reducing tax rates is a desirable outcome of industrial development. However, for the reasons just noted it is our contention that change in tax rates, per se, is essentially uninterpretable as an indicator of fiscal consequences of industrial development.

The case studies provide empirical evidence which supports our view. Nine studies comment on tax rate changes. Two indicate reductions in tax rates (Andrews et al., 1959; Wadsworth and Conrad, 1966). Another reported a decrease in the general revenue tax rate of the city and the school tax rate but these were accompanied by an increase in the interest and sinking fund rate of the city and the general revenue rate of the county (Hagerman and Braschler, 1966).

Brady (1974) reported no change of tax rates for Wynn, Arkansas, as did Miller (1967) for Tarboro, North Carolina. In Lawrenceburg, Tennessee, the city tax rate was unchanged while the county had an increase (Wilson, 1965). And finally three studies reported increases in tax rates (Daoust, 1954; Merrill and Ryther, 1961; Stevens and Wallace, 1964).

It appears quite clear that new industry in a community has virtually no predictive value with respect to tax rates.

Local Property Tax Revenue. We have noted above the unanimity among the case studies with respect to the point that industrial development in a community is accompanied by increases in assessed valuation of property. The fiscal reservoir provided by this expanded tax base apparently is drawn upon immediately by local officials. In every study dealing with local property tax revenue an increase is reported (Andrews et al., 1959; Andrews and Bauder, 1968; Brady, 1974; Daoust, 1954; Dietz, 1971; Merrill and Ryther, 1961; Shaffer, 1972; Stevens and Wallace, 1964; Uhrich, 1974; Wadsworth and Conrad, 1966; Wilson, 1965).

Local property tax revenues increase consistently across the communities as do assessed valuations of real property. On the basis of these case study findings one is inclined to conclude that industrial plant location is a guarantee for increased property tax revenue. We believe there is a serious need to observe restraint in accepting such a conclusion at face value, for two reasons. First, these case studies report increasing revenue figures during a period when virtually all communities were experiencing growing property tax revenue. This reflects the real increases in costs of government and the inflationary increases. Second, because these case studies generally made no comparisons of local increases with state, regional, or national trends it is not logically safe to attribute the observed increases solely to local industrial development.

Retail Sales. The growth in disposable income also should generate greater retail sales and thereby add to the local sales tax receipts. This may be expected to be an input to the benefit stream directly only in those communities having a local sales tax levy. In many nonmetropolitan communities the local government does not have this taxing authority under existing state statutes. But it is important to examine the evidence of growth in retail sales in communities with industrial development to assess the extent to which there is an increase. Whether the potential for revenue via local sales tax is realized is secondary in importance since it is the potential, or fiscal capacity, which is of primary concern.

There were nine case studies in which the dollar volume of retail sales was examined. In every case there was an increase in sales. In the six small Wisconsin cities studied by Andrews et al. (1959) the three with industrial growth experienced an increase of 34.4 to 40.6 percent while the three nonindustrial cities showed increases of 16.7 to 28.8 percent. Similarly, Andrews and Bauder (1968) found in their study of Monroe and Noble counties that Monroe, where the aluminum plant located, had an increase of 43 percent compared to nonindustrial Noble County which had an 11 percent increase.

These two comparisons, which incorporate control (or comparison) communities, strongly suggest that one should not hastily attribute all retail sales growth in a community to the presence of new industry. Nevertheless, both studies show rather substantially larger increases in the industrially developing community. Significant increases were also reported in most cases which only examined a single community over a period of several years.

Hagerman and Braschler (1966) reported that retail sales in Douglas County, Missouri, increased from $2,955,000 in 1953 to $4,277,000 (constant dollars) in 1964, an increase of 145 percent. Similarly, Merrill and Ryther (1961) found that volume of sales rose by 38 percent in "Midway," Kansas, from 1947 to 1958. For Center County in which the city is located the sales tax receipts rose 114 percent over the same years. In Edgecombe County, North Carolina, Miller (1967) found an increase of $30,505,240 in retail sales from 1959-60 to 1965-66, an increase of 71.9 percent. Wilson (1965) reported that retail sales in Lawrence County, Tennessee, increased 67 percent while Lawrenceburg, Tennessee, had an increase of 48 percent. From 1950 to 1953, the village of Edmore, Michigan, had an increase of 18.6 percent in sales tax receipts (Daoust, 1954).

In two separate studies of Indiana communities the increases reported were quite small by comparison. Stevens and Wallace (1964) found that total retail sales in Howard County (including Kokomo) rose 19.1 percent from 1948 to 1958 while total sales in Indiana increased 25.0 percent. During the same period per capita sales in Indiana rose 8.3 percent while they increased only 2.1 percent in Howard County. Similarly, Wadsworth and Conrad (1966) found that retail sales in Linton, Indiana, increased only 1.7 percent from 1963 to 1964. Incidentally, it is interesting to note that these

two Indiana studies were pioneering efforts in introducing the concept
of income leakage as an explanation of the limited local effects of industrial development.

While these studies clearly indicated increases in retail sales
were associated with industrial invasion of the local communities,
they do not identify precisely what portion of the increase one should
attribute to the new industry. That is to say, direct, indirect, and induced sales are not clearly disaggregated to permit a careful assessment of the effect of new industry. Moreover, in several instances
the authors failed to note whether or not the dollar volume comparisons across time were in constant or current dollars. If the latter
were the case, some unknown part of the increase may be attributable
to inflation. These are methodological weaknesses, but there is the
further substantive limitation in that none of the studies indicate
clearly whether or not the communities levied local retail sales taxes
on the increased fiscal resource. Nevertheless, one may tentatively
conclude that industrial development does result in some expansion
of the fiscal capacity of local communities through increases in retail
sales which have the potential for contributing to the benefit stream
either through local retail sales tax receipts or through state sales
taxes returned to the local community in transfer payments.

Fees for Services. User fees and charges vary profusely with respect to the services to which they are attached. For example, they
may include a wide variety of licenses and permits wherein the fee
presumably helps offset regulatory costs such as building permits and
business licenses. Or they may involve a fee charged on the assumption that the user of a service benefits directly by the activity or use
over and beyond those benefits received by the general public. Vehicle stickers, admission fees to publicly owned and operated recreation facilities, rental fees for use of publicly owned land, facilities,
or equipment, or the service charges made by a public hospital,
clinic, or ambulance service are all illustrative of this type of user
fee. Both these types may increase either in total volume or per
capita (or both) as a result of increases in disposable income (total
or per capita) or consumption patterns of residents. Furthermore,
they may be increased by expanded activity in the nonretail commercial sector of the local economy.

There is yet another category of user fee which may contribute
significantly to local revenue. However, its collection requires direct public participation in local business activity through ownership,
especially of those enterprises with a profit potential. But given the
capitalistic origins of our economy institutionalization of this practice
has been and continues to be controversial. Although public ownership of utilities and transportation enterprises has become fairly

widely accepted, acceptance even in these areas of public participation is not universal. But regardless of public opinion as to the appropriateness of public ownership of potential money-making enterprises, such direct participation in the private sector expansion generated by industrial development remains a logically viable mechanism by which industrial invasion may contribute to the public sector benefit stream.

Brady (1974, p. 9) reports that in Wynne, Arkansas, "Total permits, fees and licenses, which accounted for 28.3 percent of municipal income in 1970, increased by a total of 251.6 percent from 1960 to 1970, and 158.4 percent per capita; court fines and auto licenses accounted for the majority of this increase." The publicly owned water and sewer utilities in Wynne also showed increases over this decade. Total revenue in the water department increased 97.0 percent while the per capita increase was 22.3 percent. Increases in the sewer department were somewhat smaller; 2.2 percent for total revenue and a 5.5 percent per capita increase.

Daoust (1954) found the water utility revenue of Edmore, Michigan, also increased, largely because of new consumers. From 1950 to 1953 revenues rose from $4,349.59 to $5,647.53 (29.8 percent).

In Ava, Missouri, the municipally owned water, sewer, and electrical utilities all showed increased revenue over the period from 1953 to 1964. Combined water and sewer receipts averaged $22,000 per year from 1953 to 1959, then rose to $35,466 in 1964, an increase of 61.2 percent. However, Hagerman and Braschler (1966) attribute most of this increase to raises in the price of water rather than to increased usage. From 1954 to 1964 sales of electrical current to residential and commercial customers increased 92.4 percent from $65,672 to $126,359. Even more important for our concerns is their finding that net income (receipts less expenses) of the electrical department increased 186.1 percent ($19,366 in 1954 to $55,413 in 1964).

Uhrich's (1974) analysis of the impact of a new industry on municipal revenue in Brookings, South Dakota, does not provide a longitudinal comparison but rather identifies the revenues directly and indirectly attributable to new residents. Utility revenue from new residents was $92,958.30 and other revenues (excluding property taxes) were $7,970.40. Secondary municipal revenue impact was estimated to be $163,694.97.

These studies provide consistent evidence that user fees and charges provide increased revenue in communities with new industry. While only two studies reported evidence regarding nonutility revenues (Brady, 1974; Uhrich, 1974), in both cases the evidence indicated substantial increases. These findings are consistent with the logical paradigm which argues that a portion of the increases in total and per capita disposable income will flow into the benefit stream via user fees

and charges (see figure 6.1). The evidence regarding utility revenues is also supportive of this logic. But one must be cautious because the studies do not consistently and clearly discern whether the
increases in utility revenue are due to (1) rate increases, (2) number
of new customers, or (3) increased per capita consumption. But
given the evidence of population and per capita income growth in communities with new industry (see Chapters 4 and 5), we are inclined to
infer that utility revenue increases are the product of all three components. The evidence available in so few case studies is inadequate
to support a firm conclusion regarding the relative influence of the
three immediate causes of the increased revenue. A guarded optimism would be more appropriate.

In view of the revenue gains from utilities, one must raise the
possibility of more extensive public ownership of local business enterprises and/or public investment in business activity through part-
nership or purchase of stock. None of the case studies explored the
extent to which these techniques are already being used by local officials as a means of converting private sector gains into public sector
gains.

Intergovernmental Transfer Payments. All local governments are
restricted by state statutes in the manner and extent to which they
may raise revenues. For example, few municipalities are permitted
to levy an income tax or wage tax, especially smaller cities and towns.
Partially because of the legislative constraints placed upon them
many municipalities appeal to state and federal governments for
transfers of funds back to the local level. Questions of efficiency
and equity notwithstanding, both state and federal governments have
responded to these appeals with a profusion of intergovernmental
transfer payment schemes.

Industrial invasion may be expected to affect the volume of these
transfer payments through several cash flow streams which ultimately
contribute to public sector benefits at the local level. Two of the most
important are personal income and industrial output. Direct, indirect,
and induced income generates both state and federal income taxes,
some of which finds its way back to local communities through intergovernmental transfer payments. A similar circuitous route can be
traced from personal income into the local benefit stream through retail sales, state sales taxes, and transfer payments, or through motor
vehicle registrations and gasoline taxes and transfer payments. Thus,
income resulting from industrial invasion flows into the benefit stream
simultaneously through several routes which converge as transfer payments to the local community.

The output of new industry in most states also generates revenue
collections by state and federal governments which contribute to funds
for transfer payments to local municipalities. For example, many

states levy a gross receipts tax directly on the output of industry or collect corporate income taxes. In many instances the turnback procedures rebate a larger projection of such revenues directly to the local municipalities in which they originate rather than adding them to the general fund.

New industry may indirectly generate revenue for its host community by adding to the cost of local government or school district operations and thereby increase the local unit's legitimate claim to additional transfer payments. The extent to which this process operates and its net benefit to the local unit depends largely on the formulas by which transfer payment demands are calculated.

While analytically these money flows are quite comprehendible, isolating and measuring that portion of the total flow originating from industrial invasion is very difficult. Thus, it is no surprise to find in the case studies that rather primitive research procedures were used to relate industrial invasion and intergovernmental transfer payments.

Among the seven case studies focusing on intergovernmental transfer payments there is unanimous support for the expectation that industrial invasion is associated with an increase in transfer payments. Andrews et al. (1959) studied both corporate and individual income taxes returned to six small Wisconsin cities over the period from 1949 to 1956. Two of the three more industrial cities fared better than the state as a whole in both corporate and individual taxes returned. At the same time all three less industrial cities were below the state average. Moreover, the more industrialized cities had a larger percentage of change between 1949 and 1956.

For Wynne, Arkansas, state aid as a source of municipal income became more important over the period from 1960 to 1970 (Brady, 1974). The increase was 157.5 percent in total and 89.2 percent per capita. According to Brady the largest component of the increase was in turnback highway funds. Sales tax turnback was also a major component of the increase in state aid. Not only was there a sizable change in state aid over time, it also became an increasingly large portion of total municipal income. In 1960 state aid made up 31.1 percent of Wynne's total income but by 1970 it was 41.9 percent. Even more dramatically, federal and state contributions to the Wynne Public School System increased respectively 1,138.0 percent and 116.5 percent in total amount. On a per capita basis the federal increase was 755.4 percent while the state support increased 49.6 percent. As with municipal income, transfer payments became an increasingly larger share of total receipts. In 1960 federal funds made up less than 1 percent of the school income but by 1970 were accounting for 6.38 percent. State aid increased from 26.9 percent of the 1960 total to 31.68 percent in 1970.

Similar results were reported for Ava, Missouri (Hagerman and Braschler, 1966). In 1952-53 the local school district received $96,224 in state and federal aid. By 1963-64 their combined contribution had climbed to $349,556, an increase of 263.3 percent. During that same period the total receipts of the school district increased 406.9 percent. Thus, the large increase in state and federal aid was much below the overall increase in school district receipts. In this respect the Ava, Missouri, experience differs from that of Wynne, Arkansas. It would appear that both are growing but Wynne is shifting more of the cost of schooling to transfer funds while Ava is shouldering more of it locally. However, Hagerman and Braschler note that only part of the Ava increase can be attributed to industrial invasion because some redistricting and modification of state aid programs occurred during the study decade.

In Howard County, Indiana, state support to the local schools through distribution of gross income tax increased 38.4 percent from 1950-52 to 1958-60. State "shared" revenues to Kokomo (city in Howard County) increased 179.1 percent due largely to gasoline taxes and motor vehicle registration fees. Transfer payments to the county government increased much less, only 3.5 percent. This was due largely to a notable decline (-36.3 percent) in federal and state welfare payments.

Wilson (1965) reports that in Lawrence County, Tennessee, state aid made up 66.7 percent of receipts ($1,511,910) in 1956 and 70.8 percent in 1963 ($2,048,243). In the small city of Lawrenceburg municipal receipts increased 77.9 percent from 1956 to 1963 ($240,106 to $427,221). State aid made up 26.7 percent in 1956 but had declined slightly to 23.8 percent in 1963.

In their report on Linton, Indiana, Wadsworth and Conrad (1966) note that increases in state transfer payments made possible a reduction in the property tax rate. However, no specific dollar amounts were reported.

These studies would lead one to believe that industrial invasion is associated with an increase in the amounts of transfer payments. They also suggest that with industrial invasion communities may come to depend on state and federal payments for a larger share of their total receipts. There are, at least, two possible reasons for such a shift.

First, the local officials may not be able to extract revenues from the private sector in proportion to its economic growth because of statutory limitations. Property tax is the primary mechanism available to local officials and it is heavily used already. State and federal agencies do have freedom to apply other taxing mechanisms on the economic activity locally.

Second, the shift may be a temporary one which will regress after a period of adjustment. For example, gasoline tax and motor vehicle registrations which were noted as important revenue sources in the case studies are more immediately responsive to growth in economic activity than assessed valuation of property. Property assessments often are not done annually and even when they are taxes are not paid until the following year. Hence, property taxes inevitably lag behind expansion of economic activity. Costs, on the other hand, often appear quickly and local officials may be temporarily relying more on transfer payments.

We have now examined the evidence of revenue benefits to the public sector which may be attributed to new industry. The studies are very consistent in reporting increases in local revenue. The assessed valuation of property clearly is expanded and property tax receipts were increased in every community. Retail sales consistently increased resulting in added revenue from sales tax receipts. Intergovernmental transfer payments increased in absolute dollar amounts and the studies appeared to reveal a tendency for communities to become more dependent on federal and state "shared" revenues, to shift the distribution from local toward nonlocal revenue sources. While most new industries made some contribution directly to local revenue the studies suggest a tendency of local officials to rely primarily on indirect means of extracting public sector benefits from industry.

If one considers only the benefit stream, the conclusion must be that new industry produces added revenue for the local public sector. But ending the examination of how industrial invasion affects the fiscal domain in the public sector would be a gross error. There remain questions about the wisdom of relying primarily on indirect methods of transforming private sector gains into public sector benefits, the efficiency of current extraction procedures, structural constraints imposed by state and federal legislation on local officials, and the equity of the taxation among current and potential sources of revenue. But these must remain unanswered questions for the moment since they are issues raised by the case studies rather than resolved by them.

However, the studies do provide evidence regarding public sector costs of industrial invasion. Since added revenue may be equalled or even exceeded by added costs, it is extremely important to examine the evidence of how new industry contributes to the cost stream.

The Cost Stream

Industry's Direct Costs

On the cost side new industry may affect the local community even before it actually arrives. In many instances it is necessary for the community to incur some costs in order to attract new industry. These most frequently involve land acquisition and site preparation which usually includes extension and improvement of access roads, utility connection, and modification of the landscape of the site. Site preparation also may include the construction of one or more buildings. There are almost always some advertising expenses necessary to attract attention to the community's assets. If the site is on land purchased by the municipality from private ownership, which it often is, one must consider as a cost those previously collected taxes which are no longer collectable. Cost, in the same sense, can occur also when the site remains in private ownership but is taxed at a lower rate than its previous usage allowed. Not infrequently the site is owned by the new industry but taxed at a nominal rate or even exempted from taxes for a specified time. In other words, the new industry is given a "tax holiday." All these development efforts by the local community are forms of local subsidization of industry and must be regarded as costs to the local community. Some protagonists of industrial development, such as Moes (1962), argue that local subsidization is wise and is a short-term cost offset by long-term gains, but the evidence available makes that a debatable point. However, there is no disagreement that subsidies are a cost which must be entered into the calculation of net gains.

Once located the new industry will require various services of the local government. These include items such as police and fire protection, water and sewerage, electrical and/or gas service, and access road maintenance. In most instances, the new industry makes payments for services rendered by the local government but the payment is not always equal to the cost of provision. When that occurs the local community has engaged in another form of subsidy to industry. The point here is that provision of services is a cost to the community for which it may, or may not, be fully reimbursed by the new industry.

In addition there are environmental costs associated with the location and operation of new industry (Moore, 1973). The potential cost attribution includes ecological disturbances as a direct result of site clearing and modification. For example, water runoff may be increased substantially by covering large areas of land surface with buildings, roads, and parking lots leading to an immediate cost requirement for a new or expanded storm sewerage system. There is the potential also of affecting the local wildlife ecology through site preparation. In addition there are costs associated with the long-term operation of the new industry, particularly in regard to water, air, and noise pollution. Clearly, the extent of such environmental costs depends upon the size and type of facility involved. Moreover, it is difficult to translate such costs into precise dollar values. Yet, it is equally clear that environmental degradation does represent a cost factor.

Among the case studies only two dealt in detail with the direct costs of new industry to the public sector (Garrison, 1967, 1970; and Bucher, 1971). Four others considered direct public sector costs of new industry but did not focus primarily on this issue (Hagerman and Braschler, 1966; Shaffer, 1972; Uhrich, 1974; and Wadsworth and Conrad, 1966). Inasmuch as so little attention has been given to this area of public cost it will be instructive to report both the Garrison and Bucher results in some detail.

The Garrison study involved five towns in Kentucky located outside standard metropolitan statistical areas, with 1960 populations between 1,000 and 5,000 and which had hosted between 1958 and 1963 at least one new manufacturing plant employing at least 100 workers. In four of the five towns there were local financial inducements used to attract industry. In Flemingsburg the city issued $250,000 worth of industrial revenue bonds to finance land acquisition and building construction for a shoe factory. Since the land and building were city owned they were exempt from real property tax. In addition the city granted the company a five-year exemption from personal property taxes.

London purchased property for an industrial park outside the city through proceeds from a bond issue supported by a tax levy. Since the industrial park was outside the city it generated no tax revenue for the city even though 16 acres were deeded to a spinning company and thus returned to private ownership. In addition the city issued industrial revenue bonds to finance construction of the plant and purchase part of the company's equipment. Moreover, the city constructed a sewerage plant and an elevated water tank on the plant site.

In Stanford the plant was financed by a privately owned nonprofit development corporation which raised inducement funds by selling stock to local residents and borrowing from the local bank. As privately owned land the plant property was subject to local taxes. However, the development corporation received a favorable assessment since the property was appraised at about 1 percent of its market value.

The city of Lebanon provided financial inducements to three companies. For one firm the city issued a $650,000 revenue bond and held title to the land, building, and part of the equipment of the plant making them nontaxable. The city also extended a water line to the plant at a cost of $10,000 to the city. The only inducements for the other two firms involved extension of water lines at a cost of $9,200 to the city.

The Bucher study involved eight communities which had industrial development programs. Presumably they were all in Missouri
since the study was sponsored by the Missouri Division of Commerce
and Industrial Development although their exact identity is not dis-
closed in the report. All eight communities had less than 10,000
population and were located at least 50 miles from a metropolitan
area.

In all eight communities land sites were purchased through
local financial inducements. And additionally, all eight communities
financed all or part of the plant construction and/or the purchase of
equipment. The communities also incurred costs for the installation
of roads, water, sewerage, and electric facilities.

In city A studied by Bucher the new firm was given financial
assistance through two general obligation bond issues ($150,000), the
proceeds of which were used to purchase a five-acre site and construct a building for the plant. The city also incurred utility installation costs of $27,000.

City B issued a $3.5 million municipal industrial bond, the pro-
ceeds of which were used to purchase a 98-acre site, construct a
building, and provide $500,000 in equipment. In addition the city in-
curred costs ($50,000) in improving the plant site and providing com-
munity services. These costs were absorbed through various operating budgets of city departments.

Although the firm locating in city C was financially able to absorb all construction costs, the management insisted the city make
an investment in the facilities as a preventive measure against future
labor problems. The city investment was financed through a $100,000
industrial development bond issue. Since the site was located outside
the city, there were no tax revenues.

Land, building, and major equipment purchase was provided as
inducement by city D through $475,000 in municipal industrial bonds,
$200,000 in revenue bonds, and $275,000 in general obligation bonds.
The local industrial development corporation also provided $15,000
over a three-year period. Community services and utilities also cost
the city $15,000.

City E provided, as an inducement, a $525,000 general obliga-
tion municipal industrial bond issue to cover operating expenses, construction of a building, and purchase of equipment. Land was purchased by the local development corporation and donated to the city,
thus removing the property from the tax roll. Moreover, improvements in the city water and sewerage facilities were required, $5,000
for the former and $75,000 for the latter.

In city F the purchase of a plant site, construction of a building,
and provision of equipment were provided through a $260,000 general

obligation municipal industrial bond issue. An access road was constructed at a cost of $5,000 and paid for through the street maintenance fund. Sewer, water, and electrical utilities costs ($20,300) were borne by the utilities operating accounts.

An industrial revenue bond issue of $550,000 was used by city G to construct a $538,000 building for the new firm in that city. Costs for the construction of an access road were absorbed by the city's street department. To absorb the costs of extending municipally owned utilities to the plant site the city issued bonds totalling $430,000.

Finally, city H purchased three parcels of land at a cost of $50,000 paid for from various city accounts containing a surplus balance. Beyond that the city issued a $425,000 general obligation municipal industrial development bond the proceeds of which were used to construct a building, pave a parking lot, and provide equipment. Additionally, the municipally purchased land was transferred, free of charge, to the firm.

Similar inducement costs were involved in the acquisition by Linton, Indiana, of an aluminum chair factory. The city residents carried a $50,000 bond over a 20-year term at 3.5 percent interest (Wadsworth and Conrad, 1966). The major incentive was a "practically free" 300-acre plant site. However, the city also spent $23,428 to extend electric, water, sewer, and gas lines to the plant site.

Hagerman and Braschler (1966) indicate that public costs of locating and expanding two plants in Douglas County, Missouri, totalled $400,893. However, they included sale of stock in the local industrial development corporation which may be questionable as a public cost. Yet, the costs in land and buildings is a small portion of what Hagerman and Braschler regard as public costs. A water and sewer system expansion was necessary which was financed by a $225,000 general property obligation bond issue. Also included is the $2,278,400 cost of rebuilding a highway. Since there is no explanation of the purpose of the highway one must merely assume the construction was a direct consequence of the industrial plant location and expansion.

In assessing costs and benefits of new industry to the public sector of several eastern Oklahoma communities Shaffer (1972) developed a precise but rather elaborate accounting system which clarifies the cash flow on both sides of the ledger. Unfortunately for our purposes the aggregation of cost figures combines costs assignable directly to the firm with the direct, indirect, and induced costs of community services to residents and public school operations. However, he does indicate, without providing dollar amounts, that the industrial development programs in these Oklahoma communities included financial inducements through low interest financing, or low rent, or at cost, plant sites, building construction, market information, training of the labor force, providing of transportation facilities, special utility rates, and tax considerations such as favorable rates, favorable assessments, or outright exemption.

The Shaffer accounting model was also applied by Uhrich (1974) to assess the industrial development in Brookings, South Dakota. Although the development there involved a plant investment of $2.8 million in real estate and personal property (equipment) and a $40,000 sewer expansion, Uhrich asserts that "the City of Brookings did not incur any known expenses" (p. 66).

From these studies it is obvious that local financial inducements may be extensive both in their dollar value and the manner in which they are given to the new or expanding firms. But of course one does not need to rely on these case studies to observe the degree to which local financial inducements are an integral part of the competition among communities for new industries. Local subsidization is not an unexplored topic even though it has been generally ignored by the authors of these case studies. (See Abt Associates [1968] for a succinct summary.)

Our purpose in calling attention to local subsidization activities is to emphasize the fact that such activities represent costs to the community and specifically to the public sector. It appears from the comments of researchers such as Garrison, Bucher, and others, that local public officials often underestimate the extent to which community services and utilities needed by the new industry will require public sector financial subsidy beyond the initial commitment to land, building, and equipment.

Having made that point one cannot avoid asking whether communities are able to effectively recover these costs over some specified period of time. There are several ways a community's public sector has of doing so: taxes, utility charges, rental or lease payments, purchase agreements, increased value of real estate, intergovernmental transfer payments. These are the revenue or benefit stream sources discussed previously. It appears that in some instances part of the subsidy cost is recovered, but in other instances only a partial recovery is achieved. Moreover, direct costs of subsidization are not the only costs incurred by the public sector. There are also government services, school, and environmental costs which the public sector must recover as well in order to realize a net gain from new industry.

Direct, Indirect, and Induced
Governmental Services

Increased demand for basic services by the local population represents a major potential cost factor of most new industry. This is generated primarily by an increase in population brought about through direct, indirect, and induced employment attributable to the new industry.

However, it is also possible that demand for quantity of services per capita and/or quality of services may be increased even while population size remains unchanged. This is what one might regard as induced demand since it refers to changes in demand resulting from altered patterns of behavior among the existing population.

This flow is represented in Figure 6.1 by the total employment of the new industry minus that portion of the plant work force residing outside the community and commuting to work. The commuters are represented as the employment leakage. Application of the multiplier concept presumes that for each community resident employed by the new industry some number of additional resident workers will be employed in other local businesses. Some of these new employment opportunities will be filled by persons already living in the community but who were contemplating outmigration. Thus, direct, indirect, and induced employment may reduce outmigration and thereby slow population losses. It is also highly probable that some of the new employment opportunities will be seized by persons moving into the community who by their presence produce a growth in population. And since inmigrants are generally younger than the average age of ' residents they alter the age structure in such a way that future growth may be more likely to occur. Where population growth occurs it is virtually inevitable that the community will experience an increased demand for health, recreational, and general services which represent additional costs to the local government.

While we have represented growth in real property as a factor contributing to the benefit side, such growth may also represent a cost to the local government. The number of parcels of property affect the demand for government services such as police and fire protection, water and sewerage, and street and road maintenance just as surely as does population size. Indeed, it would be possible for a local government to incur increased demand for services because of growth in industrial and/or commercial property in the absence of increased residential parcels or population. Presumably, the demand factors covary but it should be noted that population is not the only demand factor affecting the direct, indirect, and induced government services resulting from new industry.

New industry clearly is associated with an increase in the public sector costs of delivering basic services to residents. Twelve studies report data revealing community service costs (Andrews et al. , 1959; Andrews and Bauder, 1968; Brady, 1974; Daoust, 1954; Garrison, 1967, 1971; Garth, 1953; Hagerman and Braschler, 1966;

Miller, 1967; Shaffer, 1972; Shaffer and Tweeten, 1974; Stevens and
Wallace, 1964; Uhrich, 1974; and Wadsworth and Conrad, 1966).
Eleven show substantial increases, Linton, Indiana, being the excep-
tion (Wadsworth and Conrad, 1966).

Utilities, especially water and sewerage, appear to be a primary source of increased costs. This was dramatically illustrated
in Edmore, Michigan (Daoust, 1954), where development overloaded
the town water system, resulting in bacterial contamination which
necessitated the construction of a new system. Similarly, Rockdale,
Texas, was forced to drill a new city well to halt a water shortage
(Garth, 1953). Rockdale also found it necessary to issue a bond for
sewerage line extension as a result of development. Brady (1974)
reported that Wynne, Arkansas, needed expansion of its sewerage
facilities resulting in a 267 percent increase in expenses with less
than 1 percent increase in user income. Ava, Missouri, also found
it necessary to install a new water and sewerage disposal system
(Hagerman and Braschler, 1966). Similarly, in the early years of
development in Ava there were large outlays necessary for street
repairs and the acquisition and operation of an electrical distribution
system.

One inference which may be drawn from these studies is that
officials often miscalculate the extent of underutilization of existing
facilities. An argument often heard regarding benefits to the public
sector is to the effect that public facilities are used at less than their
full capacity without there being a proportional reduction in cost of
operation. Development which brings a fuller utilization should be
welcomed because of its positive effect on per capita operating costs.
These studies lead to the conclusion that development frequently over-
loads existing systems and results in major public sector outlays of
funds which may increase the per capita, as well as total, cost of
services.

The amount and cost of additional public services generated by
new industry depends largely on population growth of the community.
This conclusion, reached by Garrison (1971, p. 494), is consistent
with the logical flow of effects represented in Figure 6.1 and appears
to be corroborated by other case studies. Support is particularly
clear in the Shaffer study of 12 eastern Oklahoma communties (1972)
and the Uhrich (1974) analysis of Brookings, South Dakota. In both
cases the researchers interviewed plant employees to determine their
place of residence and with this knowledge were able to allocate quite
precisely the additional public sector costs attributable to direct and
indirect effects of new industry. While the remaining studies are
less precise in accounting for the additional public service costs,
the authors' descriptions of local conditions leave little doubt that
such things as additional police and fire protection, water, sewerage,

electrical facilities, recreational equipment, and street paving are prompted by the growth of population associated with new industry.

Residential patterns, plant site, and political boundaries combine to produce an uneven distribution of public service costs among local governmental units. As we noted in Chapter 4 sizable segments of the work force in nonmetropolitan industrial plants live outside the town or village in which the plant is located. There is considerable employment leakage which has a minimizing effect on the public service costs to the host community. However, it may result in population growth in surrounding communities who do not have the plant within their boundaries. When this happens the host community may find itself in a favored cost-revenue situation relative to neighboring communities. This appears to have been the situation in Edmore, Michigan (Daoust, 1954), Putnam County, Illinois (Summers, 1973), and Ava, Missouri (Hagerman and Braschler, 1966). However, the advantages of externalizing public sector costs in this way must be weighted against reductions in internalized payroll and income. Since population growth (a cost) and income (a benefit) are positively related, minimizing population growth almost certainly constrains the flow of revenue into the benefit stream.

Direct, Indirect, and Induced School Services

School population is a direct consequence of population size and generates direct, indirect, and induced costs in the provision of school services through an increase in average daily attendance. These costs occur both in capital expansion required to accommodate the additional enrollment and in the increased demands for services which affect the operational budgets of local schools.

The evidence is quite consistent that new industry brings additions to the public school enrollments. Of the seven studies reporting enrollments, all show increases (Brady, 1974; Davis, 1963; Daoust, 1954; Garrison, 1967; Merrill and Ryther, 1961; Miller, 1967; and Uhrich, 1974). However, only three studies make a positive identification between new residents brought to the community by the industry and school enrollments. Uhrich (1974) identified 50 new students directly associated with the presence of new industry. These students added an estimated $40,040 to the capital outlay of the school district and $4,660.50 to the operating budget. Garrison (1967) found in the five Kentucky towns that new students varied from zero to 25 (0, 2, 4, 11, 25). Additional direct costs associated with these students were $0, $224, $511, $1,320, and $2,400 respectively. Daoust (1954) also indicated 30 additional families in Erdmore, Michigan, associated with the new industry. The number of students was not reported but it is somewhat moot since they generated no additional costs. With the exception of Erdmore and one Kentucky town, these studies support the logical expectation of direct cost effects of new industry on public schools.

Indirect and induced effects can be seen in total enrollment figures and in total budget allocations. Where these figures are higher than the direct effect figures one may infer the existence of secondary effects but cannot disaggregate the indirect from the induced effects. Considering enrollments it appears that there are substantial indirect and induced effects. The total enrollment in "Midway," Kansas (Merrill and Ryther, 1961), increased 64.1 percent. In Searcy, Arkansas, enrollment rose 55.8 percent (Davis, 1963) and in Wynne, Arkansas, the average daily attendance increased 44.7 percent. Tarboro, North Carolina, had an enrollment increase of 14.3 percent (Miller, 1967). These increases are greater than those noted in the examination of direct effects, thus implying the existence of secondary enrollment effects.

From the standpoint of concern with cost of public school services, expenditures by school districts are more revealing than enrollment statistics even though examination of the latter is instructive for its clarification of the paradigm represented in Figure 6.1. In discussing the direct effects above, we noted that additional students consistently resulted in increased operating budgets and sometimes higher capital outlay budgets as well.

But beyond that, the evidence of increased costs appears consistently in all the studies. In Howard County, Indiana, Stevens and Wallace (1964) found an 81.4 percent increase in the total yearly expenditures of the county's five school districts over the years from 1947-49 to 1956-58. In Ada, Missouri, school expenditures rose 301 percent from 1952-53 to 1963-64. However, only part of this increase should be attributed to development since a district consolidation occurred during the study period. Unfortunately, Hagerman and Braschler (1966) give no indication of an appropriate separation of the increase. School expenditures rose 88.4 percent in Wynne, Arkansas (Brady, 1974).

Two studies report primary and secondary effects separately (Shaffer and Tweeten, 1974; and Uhrich, 1974). In studying 13 eastern Oklahoma school districts Shaffer and Tweeten (1974) found that secondary costs exceeded primary costs in six instances. And in Brookings, South Dakota, secondary costs were slightly greater than primary costs (Uhrich, 1974).

Clearly, additional school services are demanded in most communities with industrial invasion and thus contribute to the cost stream in the public sector. Some of these additional costs are recovered through increased taxes and intergovernmental transfer

payments, especially where states have equalization programs. However, the data in these case studies do not permit an assessment of
the extent to which costs were recovered as a direct consequence of
the increased enrollments.

Environmental Costs

Population growth may be expected to generate direct, indirect,
and induced environmental costs to the local community. The presence of more people living in a delimited area increases air, water,
and noise pollution which creates added public health costs as well as
the costs of programmatic efforts to maintain environmental quality.
In addition to the immediate and tangible costs of maintaining environmental quality one may also consider the long-term alterations of the
environment involved in loss of open space, land development, and
road construction as well as the esthetic nature of the environment
which is modified by increased man-land density and land use patterns.

Given the plausibility of the argument that population growth has
adverse effects on the local environment and thus adds to the public
sector costs, it is rather startling to discover that virtually none of
the case studies contain an analysis of the issue of environmental
costs associated with industrial invasion. Yet one should not be alto-
gether surprised by the authors' lack of attention to the environment
since more of these studies were completed prior to the emergence of
an aroused public concern for environmental pollution.

But even in the absence of careful analysis there are passing
references made to environmental degradation. As we noted above,
Daoust (1954) reported a rather dramatic environmental impact in
Edmore, Michigan, where the town water system became so con-
taminated with bacteria that a new system had to be installed.

Without providing supporting evidence Abt Associates (1968,
p. 103) comment as follows regarding water pollution: "The most
striking social cost to the town imposed by industry is water pollution,
which in most of the towns studied has reached serious proportions.
The concern for this problem shown by town governments is after the
fact. Since industry is primarily responsible, the weak position taken
by local government suggests that the absence of water pollution control is one form of industrial incentive."

Investigation of the public sector costs of environmental degradation is one of the most pressing of research needs in the matter of
fiscal impact of industrial invasion. To be sure, it will be a most
difficult issue to assess precisely because of the variable lag factors
involved with the several types of pollution. Yet, the overall assessment of public sector fiscal impact cannot ignore this critical cost
factor.

Net Gains

The net gain of new industry to the local public sector is the difference between its direct, indirect, and induced costs and its direct, indirect, and induced benefits--the balance of added costs and added revenue. In most discussions of the potential public sector gains resulting from new industry, emphasis is placed on the benefit side of the ledger with little attention to the complexities of the potential cost of industrial invasion. Our review of case studies revealed only a few researchers who gave explicit attention to both sets of factors.

Garrison's analysis of local government impact in five Kentucky towns (1967, 1971) considered both primary and secondary costs and benefits. The primary effects included, on the benefit side, expenditures by new industry for local taxes and, on the cost side, expenditures or changes in local government services for the express benefit of, or directly attributable to, the new industry. The secondary effect considered the impact of the plant's nontax expenditures on local government revenue, expenditures, and services.

Among the five towns there were eight new plants. Only two of the plants produced revenue in excess of that yielded by the property prior to the plant location. In six of the eight cases cost to the local government of additional services exceeded additional revenue; the net primary benefits were negative. Analysis of secondary impacts, where one might expect positive net benefits due to operation of the multiplier effect, corroborates the negative impact of new industry. In attempting to explain these negative benefits Garrison reasoned that they resulted when a large nontax inducement (for example, provision of utilities or donation of land) was combined with property tax avoidance and availability of local labor minimized the addition of new residents (and disposable income) to the communities.

The most extensive and careful assessment of net gains of new industry to the local community, both private and public sector, is the analysis of 12 eastern Oklahoma communities by Shaffer (Shaffer, 1972, 1973, 1974; Shaffer and Tweeten, 1972, 1974a, 1974b). His assessment technique involves (as noted previously) a rather elaborate accounting system which identifies both primary and secondary benefits and costs to the private and public sectors.

Primary and secondary effects are defined by Shaffer in a fashion similar to the definitions used by Garrison. The primary revenues for government are property taxes, sales taxes, and municipal utility revenues generated by the plant and new residents. Primary costs to the local municipality are expenditures for services provided the plant and new residents. Secondary benefits are based on changes in tax revenues from former residents and secondary costs included additional services provided former residents. In considering school districts, which Shaffer analyzes separately from local government, secondary effects are those changes in revenue and additional educational services provided former pupils. Data from which estimates of these effects are made were collected from several sources including government records, worker questionnaires, and management questionnaires. Several estimates for each effect were calculated under varying sets of assumptions with respect to the time span over which effects accrue, and to resource utilization and resource mobility.

Case I (in Shaffer's study) represents a short-run situation and because of the short time lag involved no secondary effects. Under these assumptions the annual impact on the municipal government was small--from a net loss of $3,553 to a net gain of $1,510 with an average per plant loss of $265. The school district impact was slightly higher: $422.

Case II represents a short-to-intermediate-run situation in which no local secondary effects are assumed to occur but only partial loss of previous jobs and income is assumed. Under these conditions the estimated effect on local government averaged a positive $259 per year with a range from a loss of $2,851 to a gain of $2,132. There were no changes in the school district net gain estimates between Case I and Case II.

Case III represents the intermediate-to-long-run time perspective wherein secondary effects are allowed to occur because of resource mobility and local underemployment. Some loss of previous labor income is assumed also. Shaffer indicates that the assumptions of this model most closely approximate the conditions observed in the 12 communities. It is enlightening, therefore, to note that the municipal government net gain averaged $521 with annual net gains ranging from a minus $2,621 to a positive $3,246. The average school district impact was $401 with a range from a negative $815 to a positive $2,617.

Case IV incorporates assumptions which allow all components of the model to operate in a way most favorable to the community. Since this set of assumptions is highly improbable the estimates may be viewed as an upper limit of net benefits. Under these conditions the community impact averages $176,850 and ranges from $40,924 to $384,493 per plant.

Each of the cases involved estimates of net gains to the private sector also. We will not review those results, but it is instructive to note that in every case the private sector net benefit was dramatically larger than those for the local government and school district. For example, in Case III the private sector net gain averaged $152,981. In the same case public sector gains averaged only $521 and the school district net impact averaged $401.

The negative or small positive public sector impact led Shaffer to conclude (1972, p. 94) that the analysis "did not support the view held by many that new industry greatly increased the fiscal base of a rural community."

Uhrich (1974) used the Shaffer system to make an analysis of Brookings, South Dakota, using data from 1973. He found that the municipal government realized a net gain of $51,252.68. The school district showed a net gain of $92,797.74. As in the Oklahoma communities these net gains appear small when compared to the private sector net gain of $2,982,138.

These three studies provide clear evidence that in spite of the sizable contributions of new industry to the public sector the net gain is relatively small and in several communities is actually negative. This is in sharp contrast to the generally large, positive net gains to the private sector. Therefore, one must seriously question the commonly held belief that new industry will substantially improve the fiscal burden of many nonmetropolitan communities. However, the strong positive effects in the private sector appear to be quite consistent. Were the public sector more assertive or more effective in channeling some of these gains into the public sector, it is possible that industrial invasion could be made to contribute more positively to its fiscal well-being.

7

ON THE
HUMAN SIDE

While it is important to study the effects of rural industrial development in demographic and economic terms, the overall analysis is incomplete without reference to the social impacts. Social trends may be slow-moving as well as difficult to record and analyze, but their effects are far-reaching and must be considered by planners.

Opinions and attitudes about the whole process of industrial invasion and its impacts, solicited from residents, employees, and employers in affected communities, constitute another important area of investigation. If social planning is to be responsive to people's needs, this type of information is required.

Chapter 7 discusses the human side of nonmetropolitan industrial invasion by describing changes in social participation, community expectations and satisfactions, and acceptance of development.

SOCIAL PARTICIPATION

Participation in formal and informal social groups is an important part of the lives of many people in rural areas. Patterns of activity in social, religious, civic, and fraternal organizations may be influenced in several ways by the establishment of industry in the community. On the individual level, local residents' participation may be altered when they take jobs at the plant, while inmigrants face a change in social milieu, and possibly also a change of occupation. Newcomers may differ from oldtimers in their perceptions of the value and purpose of existing institutions. Changes in the amount and type of social involvement, brought about by an altered balance of these two groups in the population, in turn may influence the leadership and activities of community organizations.

Twelve studies discuss industrial invasion and social participation in varying depth.   Maitland and Friend (1961) and the five studies they summarize look at various aspects of the differences in type and amount of participation between plant employees and area residents. Andrews and Bauder (1968) document changes in formal and informal participation, leadership, and community identification.   Other authors look at social costs and impacts on churches and social organization.

Formal Social Participation

Three of the case histories summarized by Maitland and Friend (1961) provide details of the type of membership in formal organizations of plant employees and a sample of heads of households in each area.   Table 7.1 shows the proportion of each group at different levels of participation.

TABLE 7.1

Type of Social Participation Among Plant Employees
and Area Heads of Households
(percentages)

	Type of Participation		
	None or Inactive	One Type Only, Secular or Religious	Both Types
Mississippi			
Plant employees	33	55	10
Area sample	40	45	10
Louisiana			
Plant employees	19	62	19
Area sample	20	51	29
Central Utah			
Plant employees	22	52	24
Area sample	30	48	22

Sources: Mississippi data are from Maitland and Wilber, 1958; Louisiana data are from Bertrand and Osborne, 1959; central Utah data are from Christiansen, Maitland, and Payne, 1959.

Nonparticipation

Within each study approximately the same percentage of plant workers as area residents had no memberships in secular or religious organizations. In central Utah (Christiansen, Maitland, and Payne, 1959) all the workers belonged and only 2 percent of the area heads of households did not hold any membership. In Chickasaw County, Mississippi (Maitland and Wilber, 1958), and in central Utah, a greater proportion of the area sample were nonparticipants, but in Lousiana (Bertrand and Osborne, 1959) there was little difference. Christiansen, Maitland, and Payne (1959) also studied the participation of wives of the workers and those in the area sample, concluding that wives of farmers and nonfarm heads were more active in formal social groups than workers' wives. In all groups, the same percentage of wives and husbands held no memberships. The workers and their wives were equally inactive, while area sample wives were more active socially than their husbands, a not unexpected result. The low proportion of nonmembers may have been due to the influence of the Mormon Church in this Utah community, where most people belonged to the church even if they did not participate.

Participation in One Type of Organization Only

The great majority of all who participated in formal social organizations were active in one type only. In each study more workers than area heads of households followed this pattern, and in all cases the heavily favored type was a religious organization. Only in central Utah (Christiansen, Maitland, and Payne, 1959) was there an appreciable proportion active only in secular groups; 15 percent of the plant workers were in this category, which possibly represented inmigrants who were not Mormons, and therefore, less likely to be active in religious affairs. Similar proportions of husbands and wives belonged only to one type of organization in central Utah.

Participation in Both Types

In each study there was little difference between the proportions of plant employees and open-country heads of households active in both types of organization. In central Utah (Christiansen, Maitland, and Payne, 1959) the plant workers and their wives showed a similar percentage taking part in both types, but a much greater proportion of open-country wives were involved in both types. In Louisiana (Bertrand and Osborne, 1959) more open-country heads of households participated in both types of organization than did plant workers.

Religious activity was the type of formal participation most favored by all groups in these three studies. People who were involved in secular organizations only were in a minority. In central Utah, and in Mississippi (Maitland and Wilber, 1958), plant employees and area heads of households were, in general, similar in their patterns of membership in formal organizations.

Amount of Participation

All five studies in the summary (Maitland and Friend, 1961) discuss the amount of individuals' activity in formal social groups, mostly in terms of the number of memberships held and participation indexes. Maitland and Wilber (1958) find the overall differences between plant workers and open-country heads to be slight. Workers belonged to at least two organizations more often than open-country heads. There was residence-related variation in the latter group, in that those living on farms were more likely to belong to more groups than nonfarm residents. Among workers, membership was positively associated with income, but the relationship was less clear for open-country heads. Bertrand and Osborne's (1959) index of social participation shows the plant employees to be slightly more active than the average rural person, but the authors concede that this may be due to the age, racial, and religious characteristics of the samples. Christiansen, Maitland, and Payne (1959) find no significant differences in the proportion of plant employees and area residents having high and low participation scores. Inmigrant workers and their wives scored lower than local workers. As was the case above, it is suggested that many of these were not Mormons and hence not connected with one of the community's most important social institutions. In central Utah the wives of workers and open-country residents were more active participants than their husbands, while the plant employees were as active as the area heads of households. Kaldor, Bauder, and Trautwein (1964) find the area residents to be much more active than plant workers; they held an average of 6.4 memberships per household to the workers' 2.5. Contrary to Maitland and Wilber's (1958) findings, the nonfarm residents in the area sample had higher participation levels than area farmers. With some minor exceptions it appears that there was little difference in levels of participation between plant workers and open-country heads of households. Looking at the whole community in the Hennepin study area in Illinois, Erickson (1969) finds much variability in the amount of participation, including little involvement in power-oriented organizations, and only slightly more in norm-oriented groups.

Changes in Participation

In the five summarized studies (Maitland and Friend, 1961) plant employees and area residents were asked about changes over the previous five years in the number and type of social activities in which they took part. In each instance, most of them felt there had been little change. In Louisiana (Bertrand and Osborne, 1959), the workers reported increased participation more often than open-country residents, suggesting that industrial employment may have been associated with this. More blacks reported greater participation. Those who said they were more involved attributed this to more interest in and more time for outside activities. The reasons for greater involvement elicited by Kaldor, Bauder, and Trautwein (1964) were the joining of new organizations or the more frequent attendance at those already patronized. With only 23 percent of these Iowa workers reporting any change, there is no great amount of support for the hypothesis that nonfarm employment may change the amount of time available for nonoccupational activities, or may change the kinds of interest central to social participation through exposure to different people and attitudes.

Using a different research design, Andrews and Bauder (1968) discuss changes in social participation in experimental and control counties in Ohio. They hypothesize that industrial invasion will cause an increased range of social contacts for individuals, and shifts in locality identification. They find that identification with the home county while away from it increased in the experimental county and decreased in the control. There was little change when people were away from home but still within the county. Industrial expansion "put the county on the map" but did not bring greater identification with the county seat.

There were two trends in formal social participation in Monroe, the experimental county. There were changes in the characteristics of the members of organizations and in the type of organization. Newcomers belonged to fewer groups and held fewer offices. They made up a large proportion of the population; thus there was an overall lessening in social involvement. However, the newcomers had a higher participation score, that is, they belonged to fewer organizations but were much more active in them than the oldtimers. In Monroe County the oldtimers reduced their number of memberships and total participation substantially during industrialization, whereas there was a slight increase in the control county. Andrews and Bauder conclude that industrial development reduced organization activities in Monroe by changing the occupational distribution of the labor force. There was an increase in the proportion of blue-collar workers, who are thought to have low participation rates, and a reduction in the percentage of white-collar workers who have high levels. However, during the industrialization period the participation rates of blue-collar employees increased, which may reflect an association between improving socioeconomic status and increasing social responsibility. Thirty percent of the formal social groups had been organized since the establishment of the plant. At the end of the industrialization period there were more groups concerned with industrial or business affairs than there were church, school, and fraternal organizations, and the former types of groups experienced greater membership increases than the latter. Newcomers to the county were much more active than local residents in business, professional, and labor organizations. The plant workers' additional memberships were in groups concerned with occupational roles, especially in labor unions.

Leadership

Andrews and Bauder (1968) hypothesize that "leadership in formal organizations will become less concentrated" with industrial development. Their data only partially support this. They find some increase in the variety of persons represented but also a definite concentration of leadership. There was an increase in the number of organizations taking the lead in the community, and a change in the persons thought to be leaders. Before the plant was established in Monroe County, those interviewed identified people in elective positions--for example, county superintendents--as pace-setters, while five years later it was thought that businessmen, extension agents, and county officials were the leaders. The shift in the control county was similar but not as marked. In Monroe, the ministers took the lead in the early part of industrial invasion, perhaps creating awareness of social problems, but later gave way to community development groups, which had the power to act to find solutions. There was an increase in the number of different organizations taking the lead. These shifts in leadership support the Andrews and Bauder (1968) hypothesis that "more power groups will evolve and leadership functions will shift to new groups." At the end of the study period 45 percent of the voluntary associations in Monroe County had at least one officer who was employed at the factory. The Andrews and Bauder (1968) hypothesis that "newcomers will assume leadership positions formerly held by old-timers" was only partly confirmed, possibly because most of the plant's managerial and professional employees did not live in the county. With most of their workers living in the county, Black, Fredrickson, and Maitland (1960) find that a significantly larger proportion of them held one or more leadership positions in community organizations than did area residents. This may be partially explained by the higher education levels of the workers, a characteristic which is often positively correlated with leadership. The inmigrants in this study held fewer leadership positions than native plant employees, perhaps due to their newness and non-Mormon affiliation.

In their study done 14 years after the first factory went in, Merrill and Ryther (1961) find that the newcomers were vigorous men who used their managerial abilities and leadership qualities in civic, social, and religious organizations. Their employers encouraged this level of participation, but not the holding of political office at the municipal level.

Using data from their Illinois study area, Summers, Seiler, and Wiley (1970) illustrate the use and validation of the reputational method of assessing leadership. They asked heads of households to identify leaders in decision-making about business and economic development, educational matters, and local government affairs. They show that the leadership in all three areas was not monolithic, that is, it was not in the hands of the same people in each case.

Seiler (1974) extends this analysis to study the influence of representatives of the absentee corporation on local leadership and decision-making. Although finding that most community leaders did not think there were people outside the area who were important in influencing decisions, he rejects the possibility that there was no corporate influence. Instead, he suggests that influence was exerted through a selected few community leaders. He sees the link as being between the plant manager and the single most powerful local leader in the spheres of government and business. He speculates that the corporation was motivated to act in this way because of the presence of a stable leadership group and a desire to influence unobtrusively.

Informal Social Participation

Andrews and Bauder (1968) hypothesize that with industrial invasion the geographical range of informal visiting will increase and that informal social participation with family and kin will decrease, to be replaced by more participation in formal and nonkin associations. They find that there was change in both counties they studied, but more in the experimental. As predicted, there was more informal visiting over a wide area, but contrary to their expectations, no decline in interaction with family and kin.

Other Impacts

Saltzman (1964) does not discuss changes in individual participation but mentions two instances where the firms that established new factories contributed financially to formal social organizations, in one case to a youth foundation, and in the other to a church.

Merrill and Ryther (1961) studied the changes in the organizations themselves. They find that all the churches in the study area grew, although only about 50 percent of that increase may have been due to industrial development. The growth produced problems of crowded buildings, and the integration of newcomers into church offices and positions generated differences of opinion which some ministers thought healthy. Half the churches had changed traditional programs and patterns of worship at the instigation of newcomers, and two-thirds of the ministers reported increasing counseling duties. Reasons given for this included population increase; more female employment which created some family problems and lack of child supervision; higher incomes, which led to more debt; and greater emotional tensions induced by a faster pace of life. Nearly all the churches reported financial gains, due to larger donations--a trend initiated by the newcomers. Membership in the community's social and service clubs grew 10 percent during the industrial invasion period and plant employees held a disproportionately high percentage of the offices. These organizations capitalized on the talents and sense of responsibility of the employees, who brought new ideas and were willing to participate.

Ramana (1968) reports similar changes in the churches in the central Illinois study area. The various denominations sought unity among themselves, and organized meetings with law officers and other leaders to discuss social situations in their communities. One such problem was the apparent increase in crime, especially juvenile delinquency, liquor violations, and gambling, although this was not necessarily attributable to industrial invasion. The community response was to strengthen and improve existing social control agencies, especially police forces.

Merrill and Ryther (1961) discuss the social costs of the integration of newcomers. They point out that there was dissension in social groups as new ideas were introduced, and factions formed. The social structure of the community changed and there was a diminution in the influence of the previous leaders, the middle class. Reduced community cohesion is attributed to increasing size.

Matz's (1957) study of an anonymous small town, while falling outside the time frame of this review, documents the relationships between oldtimers and newcomers. When the plant was built, the residents buried their differences and presented a united front to the newcomers. There were social gulfs between the two groups as well as between managers and blue-collar workers. The overall effect of industrial invasion was to atomize the clear-cut social structure.

Recreation and Spare Time

Andrews and Bauder (1968) expected that industrial invasion would bring increasing separation of work and leisure. However, they find that while there was no change in the proportion taking vacations among the experimental county residents, fewer vacations were taken away from home. In the control county, fewer people took vacations, but those who did spent more time away from home. Also contrary to expectation was the increase in local hunting and fishing activities in the experimental county. There was little change in hobby activities, and differences in sports and movie attendance could not be imputed to industrial invasion.

Farm residents in Kaldor, Bauder, and Trautwein's study (1964) reported a decline in leisure activities once they began nonfarm work. They attributed this to greater absence from home and the physical demands of the job.

Bertrand and Osborne (1959) report that industrial employment did not greatly affect leisure time activities of plant workers. Changes that did occur were increased radio and television use, and more visiting, resting, reading, and working around the house. At the same time there was less participation in sports, movie attendance, and sewing. The leisure activities of black workers were altered more than those of whites, possibly due to a differential gain in income.

Conclusions

In these studies, industrial development did not appear to have dramatic effects, a result which may be due in some cases to the short time period between the advent of industry and gathering of these data. However, some patterns and trends emerge. Those plant workers and open-country residents who do belong to secular and religious groups are likely to be involved in one only, and the two groups of people participate approximately equally. Many rural residents saw little change in participation during the industrial invasion period. In one case, decreasing involvement is seen as a result of a changing occupational structure rather than change in individuals. Contrary to expectation, leadership is thought to have become more concentrated with industrial invasion, with little displacement of established power groups. Leisure activities of workers do not seem greatly affected by their industrial employment.

ATTITUDES AND OPINIONS

In 37 of the studies, opinions were solicited from groups within industrializing communities--plant employees, open-country heads of households, factory managers, parents of school children--and their attitudes on a wide range of subjects were documented. Some questions were asked often, for example, "Has the community benefited from the plant?", while some were used only by one author to shed some light on a particular area of interest. Such was Sizer and Clifford's (1966) query about the quality of lunches provided at the schools. The attitudinal information is summarized below in three general categories: matters relating to the community, those of concern to the individual, and opinions of employers.

Opinions About the Community

Expectations and Outcomes

Several studies set out to discover what expectations rural people had had of industrial invasion and to what extent these had been filfilled. Opinions were sought concerning changes in the community, and the level of community satisfaction after the introduction of industry.

Before the aluminum plant in Monroe County, Ohio (Andrews and Bauder, 1968), began operating, the researchers asked residents whether they thought the community or the factory would benefit more from the change, and opinions were evenly divided. Five years later the community was thought to have come out ahead. In both the experimental and control counties, expectations of personal benefit generally exceeded actual outcome, perhaps because fewer people than were expecting benefits actually obtained them. The groups expected to benefit most were young people, those with a high school education, and townspeople. Those not predicting any personal benefit were old, not looking for industrial employment, or unqualified for that type of work. Five years later, respondents in both counties thought these predictions had been borne out. Initially, people in both counties thought skilled workers and long-time residents would also benefit. In the experimental county five years later, it was thought that the businessmen and newcomers had been more fortunate. The authors estimate that 22 percent of Monroe County households received some benefit from the plant's operation, compared with 2 percent in Noble, the adjacent control county. In the Hennepin study area Hough and Clark (1969) find different types of benefits expected by different types of people. Personal benefit was anticipated more by men than by women, and by those in high community positions. Conversely, group benefit was foreseen by women more than men, by those aged 30 to 70 years, but not by those in high positions. In five studies, respondents were asked if the community had benefited from the plant and opinion was strongly positive. The plants were seen to have provided work, bought and sold goods on the local market, increased business, boosted incomes and population, and brought about civic improvements and better housing. A minority in some studies thought their communities had suffered due to an unstable labor market, the large proportion of outsiders hired by the factory, overextension of credit, advent of "undesirables," increased crime, and higher living costs. Although a majority of open-country residents had not benefited personally, most of them felt their communities were better off, and said they would like to see more manufacturing activity. Not surprisingly, plant employees were more likely to perceive factory-induced benefits than open-country residents.

Black, Fredrickson, and Maitland (1960) asked residents of Box Elder County, Utah, whether or not they thought the plant had caused changes in the community. More nonfarmers than farmers and more plant workers than nonplant workers thought so. These people thought their community had become more urban, that the non-Mormon newcomers might lower moral standards, and they saw a change in status symbols from the ascriptive type (family name) to the achieved (social position, material possessions).

Community Satisfaction

In discussing community satisfaction as a social indicator, Rojek, Clemente, and Summers (1974) point out that it has many dimensions. Interviews with residents of the north central Illinois study area showed that these people assessed their overall satisfaction with their communities with four factors in mind--medical services, public services, educational facilities, and commercial services. It is suggested that the administrative structure of communities may determine the factors people use for analyzing their degree of satisfaction.

Several authors describe the effects of factory-induced changes in terms of community satisfaction with the end-products of industrialization. They asked residents what they liked and disliked about their towns after the plants were established. Only Summers (1973) describes changes in satisfaction, and he finds that people in the study area as a whole had a slightly lower level of satisfaction, in this case with public services, at the end of the industrial invation period than before. Several other authors tell of a variety of specific sources of satisfaction and dissatisfaction. Positive feelings included relief that population had not declined further, and perception of inmigrants as being of good "type and character" and useful in school, church, and cultural organizations. Residents felt the plants had made their communities better places to live, and had boosted morale. Businessmen were satisfied with the economic diversification that had taken place; others felt the plant accounted for the improvement in the local shopping area and had favorably influenced rents, vacancy rates, and real estate values. Farmers were satisfied with the changes brought about by the factories because they included opportunities to increase income with off-farm work, and new markets for agricultural products. Erickson (1969) notes few signs of alienation as measured by personal feelings of powerlessness.

There was also dissatisfaction among community groups. Some businessmen were unhappy that the plant offered higher wages than had previously prevailed. Some wealthy people opposed the introduction of industry because they felt it would change the quiet countryside, and Hough and Clark (1969) report that respondents with higher socioeconomic status were less likely to accept the changes accompanying industrial invasion. A sample of factory managers and employees thought that inmigrants would be dissatisfied because of their difficulty in adjusting to the lack of cultural facilities, limited range of shops, and higher prices of goods. Complaints were voiced by residents about industrial bond issues, the continuing exodus of young people, and the large proportion of plant employees who were inmigrants. In one small town residents felt the building set aside for the factory should have been used for a different purpose. Where a plant had failed there was dissatisfaction with the way the local industrial development corporation had selected and investigated the company. In another area, it was believed that the plant had disturbed the community, made taxes higher, raised property values and prices, and made labor harder to obtain.

In a few cases, cautious optimism was evident. Residents of one town were proud of the plant, but some wondered how long it would last, and if the local industrial development corporation would get its money back. Some farmers initially opposed industrial invasion for fear it might lure away their workers, but became more supportive when they saw that the factory employed mostly women.

Community Pride

Black, Fredrickson, and Maitland (1960), and Bertrand and Osborne (1959), discuss community pride in terms of opinions about changes in roads, facilities, and home maintenance. In the two studies 50 and 40 percent respectively of the respondents saw improvement during industrial invasion in spite of some fears that newcomers might be indifferent to home maintenance. In the Bertrand and Osborne study fewer blacks saw improvement.

Public Facilities

Several authors recorded the opinions of rural residents about the public facilities in their communities, in particular, health facilities, housing, schools, and churches. The bulk of their material is contained in the five studies summarized by Maitland and Friend (1961), and Sizer and Clifford's (1966) investigation of educational attitudes in Jackson County, West Virginia.

Metz's 1968 study of branch plants in Minnesota notes that plant managers felt that communities actively seeking industry were more likely to be active in the provision of good public services. They saw the lack of adequate health facilities as a drawback to attracting industry. Both workers and managers felt that a major disadvantage of rural location was the scarcity of rental housing. Inmigrants were forced immediately to buy or build their houses. Miller (1967) also notes a need for housing in the town where the factory was located, and reports that many residents said they would move into town given the availability of suitable housing. Black, Fredrickson, and Maitland (1960) mention that the inmigrants they interviewed felt there was a housing shortage in the town. In their comparative study, Andrews and Bauder (1968) report that a larger proportion of residents in the experimental county saw improvement in public facilities in the previous five years than did those in the control county.

Schools

In the five studies summarized by Maitland and Friend (1961) the questions asked about the schools were designed to ascertain whether or not plant workers and open-country residents held different opinions. They find that in each study half or more of both groups thought the schools had improved, especially in the areas of facilities, teachers, and curricula. Higher levels of education were associated with a more critical attitude in central Utah (Christiansen, Maitland, and Payne, 1959). There, where the respondents had several more years of schooling than the national average, one-third felt that the schools were worse than previously. Bertrand and Osborne (1959) find that black workers were more likely than their white counterparts to perceive improvement, and Maitland and Wilber (1958) find more optimistic appraisals among the 35-49-year age group, those who had moved less, and those active in community affairs.

In Ohio, Andrews and Bauder (1968) find very little change in opinions about the education system over the industrial invasion period. At both times they were questioned, a majority thought the schools were better than or the same as they were five years previously.

Sizer and Clifford's whole (1966) study is about attitudes toward various aspects of the school system in Jackson County, West Virginia, where a large aluminum plant was built. Their main hypothesis is that inmigrants (those moving in since a time just before the establishment of the plant) brought with them a set of educational values and

norms which were different from those of the native residents; that
there would be a conflict of values and that the inmigrants would seek
to implement theirs by leadership in the PTA, influence on school
board members, and raising school levies. Their questions about the
school system produced apparent differences of opinion between the
two groups of residents. Both groups believed in the value of education, but the newcomers were stronger supporters. Just under half
of each group approved of the teachers' job performance. Approximately twice as many inmigrants as natives thought the teachers were
underpaid, and more so than those elsewhere. Twice as many newcomers also were dissatisfied with the schools, citing buildings,
range of subjects, facilities, and recreation programs. Newcomers
and natives had similar opinions about transportation, school lunches,
and vocational education. A second sample of parents of school children showed a similar attitudinal distribution. Sizer and Clifford
conclude that their hypothesis is confirmed. However, further test-
ing showed that for both natives and inmigrants a rise in the number
of years of education or income yielded increasingly favorable attitudes toward education and schools. The attitudinal differences were
due to differences in the income and education levels of the two groups.
Sizer and Clifford also sought opinions about attitudes toward the
schools. They find the inmigrants to be more critical of others' attitudes than the natives. A majority of inmigrants thought people did
not take enough interest in the schools, and that an additional levy
for the schools would not be supported. Inmigrants often said residents of the area close to the plant would be in favor of more levies
but other county residents would not.

Churches

Data about churches are provided by Maitland and Friend (1961).
Residents of the five areas studied were asked if they thought the local
churches had improved in the previous five years, that is, the period
of industrial invasion. About half of each group (plant workers and
open-country residents) responded affirmatively, mentioning facilities,
people's attitudes, programs, attendance, and leadership. The substantial minorities who saw no change may have been nominal church-
goers. Very few thought the churches were worse. The same question was asked by Andrews and Bauder (1968) in Monroe County, Ohio,
where a majority saw positive change, or none at all.

Johnson (1969), and Johnson and Summers (1971), report clergymen's perceptions of changes associated with industrial development
and their reactions to these changes. A majority of the religious leaders predicted social change in the community, while only a minority
foresaw its occurrence in the churches. These men expected industrial

growth to be beneficial to the community and were optimistic about the effects on the church and the church-community relationship. Johnson (1969) asserts that although clergymen were redefining their role in the light of expected changes, actual alterations in role performance in response to changes associated with industrial development were minimal. Johnson and Summers (1971) hypothesized that ministers who expected industrial invasion to produce significant social change would be more likely to modify the goals of their congregations than those who did not. This hypothesis is only partly confirmed because, while a majority expected change, they anticipated more than actually had taken place in the first years after the plant was established. Where goals had been modified, the action was motivated by expected rather than perceived sociocultural change. Both of the above studies point out that clergymen who expected change and were prepared to alter their role performances and goals were likely to have certain characteristics. These include being Protestant, liberal theologically, well-educated; having had some specialization in secular subjects in their academic careers; and having had short tenure in their present position.

OPINIONS ABOUT SOCIAL PARTICIPATION

Neighborliness

When asked if there had been a change in neighborliness in the previous five years, most plant workers and open-country residents in Maitland and Friend's five studies (1961) replied in the negative. The authors see the response as an indicator of social cohesion. In Chickasaw County, Mississippi, Maitland and Wilber (1958) find more favorable opinions among those aged 35-49 years, plant workers who had not moved in the previous ten years, and those with higher incomes. In Louisiana, Bertrand and Osborne (1959) report 20 percent as saying that neighborliness had declined. Asking the same question, Andrews and Bauder (1968) find a majority in the Ohio experimental county (Monroe) believing there had been either no change or an increase. In the control county (Noble) a majority saw no change.

Leadership

Andrews and Bauder asked residents in both 1967 and 1962 which groups in their county provided leadership in taking action on county and local community matters. At the county level, groups initially mentioned were the chamber of commerce, businessmen's groups, and farm organizations. Later, more groups were seen to be involved. In the experimental county there was a shift away from farm organizations to businessmen's groups, a change that was not reported in the control county. At the community level, businessmen's groups were seen as leaders at both times. These results suggest that most of the changes in the perceived power structure associated with industrial expansion occurred at the county level.

Social Control

Two reports on the Hennepin, Illinois, study area discuss community attitudes toward social control mechanisms. Johnson (1968) finds that both county sheriffs and court officials expected industrialization to cause population growth, bringing more crime, and more work for them. Clark, Summers, and Hough (1968) sampled community opinions about social control in both the experimental and control counties. They report that it was believed that churches and schools played a more dominant role in affecting social control than either the police or neighborhood. Respondents shared the enforcement officials' view that industrialization would bring more crime, but felt that the current network of informal controls would continue to be adequate. Clark, Summers, and Hough find understanding of social control to be influenced by socioeconomic status and class. The higher the social class, the more emphasis the respondents placed on informal control methods, and the more they supported legal enforcement institutions. Much less satisfaction with current services was found among those who had been criminally victimized in the previous year, or who were related to a victim.

OPINIONS ABOUT INDIVIDUAL CONCERNS

Attitudes Toward Industrial Work

Since it was assumed that industrial work would be a new experience for many in the plant labor forces, an important area of inquiry was centered on what the workers thought of their situation. Seven studies provide some answers.

Bertrand and Osborne (1959) find that those with farm experience but currently working at a nonfarm job had a slight preference for industrial work. Its advantages were seen as higher, more regular pay, shorter hours, and more attractive and less difficult work. Those preferring farm work said it was easier, and that they liked working in the open air and being self-employed. Asked about desirable job conditions, workers with nonfarm experience cited steady work and high pay, while farmers wanted a safe, clean place to work and good hours. To Bertrand and Osborne the implication is that the rural person holds a glamorized stereotyped opinion about industrial employment conditions, which may initially induce him to seek such a job.

Questioning the same workers and residents, Osborne (1959) reports that a minority expected plant work to be steady in the future, an attitude that may have been based more on desire than objectivity. When asked what they would do if laid off their present job, most workers replied that they would look for another industrial job, although many women would draw unemployment benefits or retire from the market. The males showed little desire to return to farming--60 percent of open-country residents said they would look for nonfarm work if laid off. However, the majority of them knew of no other industrial work in the area, and said they would be reluctant to leave to look for jobs. Osborne (1959) suggests this reflects the values of rural people-- the preference for country living, fear of moving, and the importance of family ties, in sum, a preference for social location over economic status. He concludes that it is probably better to take industry to such people than to try to induce their migration. Plant employees in Christiansen, Maitland, and Payne's (1959) Utah study expressed similar intentions if laid off work. Three-quarters of the workers thought having a plant job made it easier to get by because they had a higher steady income and were eligible for more credit.

Workers in Jamestown, North Dakota (Helgeson and Zink, 1973), chose manufacturing jobs partly because such employment was thought to offer job training and opportunity for advancement. While most said their job role was compatible with their level of training, 37 percent disagreed, feeling themselves to be capable of more advanced work. While some objected to the loss of independence and degree of time discipline associated with becoming wage workers, most accepted the new job role and were pleased with the resulting higher standard of living.

Chance to Get Ahead

In six studies residents were asked whether their "chance to get ahead" had improved during the industrial invasion period. Responses to this question are probably related to individual interpretation of it. The answers may be concerned with economic, occupational, or social mobility, but it is not possible to separate these in the response categories. In two cases (Christiansen, Maitland, and Payne, 1959; Andrews and Bauder, 1968) the majority replied pessimistically, an opinion which may have been associated with awareness of previous population decline. In Box Elder County, Utah (Black, Fredrickson, and Maitland, 1960), fewer than half saw improvement, while 34 percent perceived no change. Both Bertrand and Osborne (1959), and Maitland and Wilber (1958), find that more plant workers than open-country heads of households thought their chance of getting ahead had increased. They saw more jobs and payrolls as the cause, although 8 percent disagreed, saying that the high cost of living had offset any improvement due to the factory's presence.

Attitudes Toward Industry

In two case histories the attitude of residents toward industry in the abstract sense is explored. Andrews et al. (1959) find that inhabitants of more industrialized and less industrialized cities have similar opinions. These people were aware of the local level of industrial development, and three-quarters thought industry was beneficial to their city, making it more progressive and a better place to live; most wanted more industry and thought inducements should be offered to secure it. They also believe that somebody (person or group) was responsible for failing to attract more manufacturers. The chamber of commerce, city government, and business interests were cited most frequently as being at fault. It was also believed that existing industry was keeping more industry away. Andrews et al. find more interest in these topics in the less industrialized cities, and report that on the whole, public attitudes were very favorable toward industry.

Discussing McMinnville, Oregon, Rathburn (1972) contends that increasing numbers of citizens were beginning to doubt the validity of industrial development as a solution for local problems of housing shortages, pollution, and commercial sprawl. Some felt that industrial development was destroying the town they were trying to preserve.

Many factors play a part in the perception of impacts of industry, and the translation of this into attitudes toward industrial development. Two studies is too small a number from which to make even tentative generalizations.

EMPLOYERS' ATTITUDES

A small number of authors rounded out their study of attitudes by questioning the industrial employers about their workers and the community.

Quality and Supply of Labor

Somers (1958) and Gray (1969) discuss the employee qualifications demanded in the hiring of workers at a large aluminum plant and in the nearby town of Ravenswood, West Virginia. An eighth-grade education was set as the minimum level necessary for simply clerical tasks and mathematical calculations associated with any kind of employment. Gray suggests that as the quality of labor improves, employers' expectations of educational levels of job applicants also rise, leaving the uneducated at an even greater disadvantage. The aluminum plant hired those between 18 and 65 years of age, and used an application form designed to test comprehension and accuracy. Hiring policy gave preference to applicants whose commuting time would be less than 30 minutes, and who were experienced in aluminum or light manufacturing work.

Employers in Helena-West Helena, Arkansas (Brann, 1964), described the local labor supply as adequate, but unskilled and having an undesirable attitude. They believed that the lack of skilled workers was preventing the attraction of more industry. A similar lack was seen by employers as the limiting factor of the labor supply in northwestern Arkansas (Walraven, 1962), although they had no difficulty in staffing their plants. They also saw skilled workers as former union members who would make trouble in nonunion plants.

In his study of Indians on a Wisconsin reservation Ritzenthaler (1953) reports the plant supervisor to be satisfied with the quality of the labor. He believed that the Indians had about the same ability to learn a new job as white employees of the company's city plant, and that there was less discontent in the reservation factory. He also felt the quality of the Indians' workmanship to be equal to the best in the city.

Stability of Work Force

Plant managers in two studies held differing views of the stability of rural work forces. In Minnesota, Metz (1968) reports that employers saw their labor forces as more stable and reliable than their urban counterparts. Conversely, in northwestern Arkansas (Peterson, 1974), managers were annoyed by the prevalence of job-hopping among young men. They characterized these workers as unstable because they changed their minds about preferred type of work, and sought higher immediate pay rather than career opportunities. This behavior was seen as a stage in rural work forces becoming industrially oriented in their attitudes, habits, and family work patterns.

Attitudes Toward the Community

Some plant representatives described the type of community suitable for industry. Merrill and Ryther (1961) report that managers wanted their town to be desirable from the employees' point of view, with a pleasant environment and good services. They believed that good living conditions and amenities increased workers' productivity and reduced turnover. In Helena-West Helena, Arkansas (Brann, 1964), plant officials described community facilities as poor, and saw a need for better recreation facilities, schools, hospitals, and general services.

CONCLUSIONS

In general, people believed their community had benefited from industrial development, although plant workers were more likely to hold this opinion than open-country residents. They saw the plant as helping to stabilize population, providing jobs, and giving rise to economic diversification. Several studies report little difference between plant employees and open-country residents, natives, and in-migrants in opinions about local schools and churches. Most thought there had been little change in neighborliness over the industrial invasion period. Overall, plant employees were satisfied with their jobs, although not all thought that their chance to get ahead had improved. Plant representatives praised rural workers' reliability but lamented their lack of skills. In sum, industrial invasion was generally seen as beneficial to rural communities.

INTRODUCTION TO SKETCHES

This section is designed to provide a brief summary of basic information about the case study documents and the plant locations they describe.

Organization of the sketches is by location. Plant sites are grouped by state, where possible. In instances where a case study looks at several plant locations in different states, the sketches are grouped by census regions where possible. If the plants are too widely scattered, the sketches are grouped under "other areas." Listed under "unidentified" are those studies which for confidentiality or other reasons did not indicate precise plant locations.

With the exception of some sites in Arkansas and some which are unidentified each plant location, or group of locations, is discussed in one sketch only. However, one plant may have been studied by more than one researcher, in which case information from all relevant documents is incorporated into one sketch.

The information is grouped into three sets of characteristics-- those of the community where the plant was established; those pertaining to the researchers and their methods; and those describing the manufacturing firm.

Site Characteristics

A. Location. In general the information about location is set out in the following way: the state, states, or region; the town, and the county in which the town is located--for example, Arkansas: Star City, Lincoln County. Where there are several locations within a state the format is the state, town A, county A; town B, county B, etc.; for example, Oklahoma: Stilwell, Adair County; Muskogee, Muskogee County. For all characteristics only data provided by the case studies are included.

Other combinations of locations are reported as clearly as possible under this general format.

B. Community Size. Population data are shown for the area surrounding the plant location. Usually the size of the town is given and then that of the surrounding county or larger area.

Research Characteristics

A. <u>Period of Study</u>. This refers to the year or years in which the research was carried out. It may, but does not necessarily, refer to the date of publication of a study or to the time period under study.

B. <u>Unit of Analysis</u>. This is the impact area chosen by each researcher. Many of the documents describe the effects of industrial development on either the town or county in which the plant was established or both. Some designate larger units such as several counties, a region, or a state.

C. <u>Type of Data Used</u>. All the researchers used secondary sources, for example, federal, state, and local government publications, while the majority supplemented these with primary data, that is, information they collected themselves by means of surveys.

D. <u>Major Variables</u>. This section lists the main subject areas that are discussed in each study. With one exception, the number of variables under each subheading (economic, demographic, social) is limited to three of the most important, although the study may discuss others less fully. Some studies look at one type of impact only, for example, economic; hence "not studied" is indicated beside some of the subheadings.

E. <u>Researchers</u>. The names are those of all authors of documents pertaining to a particular plant location. Collaboration of authors as listed is not necessarily implied.

F. <u>Documents</u>. Each number represents a case study document describing a particular plant location. The numbers correspond to those in the list of case study documents in Appendix B. Conversely, the number in parentheses after each document listed in Appendix B refers to the sketch number in Appendix A.

Firm Characteristics

Where the relevant information is supplied in the case studies each plant is listed separately. Otherwise, grouped data are given. The data are as follows.

<u>Plant Product</u>. The type of output of each manufacturing plant is described as specifically as possible.

<u>Number of Plants</u>. This is shown for each type of plant, where possible.

<u>Number of Employees</u>. This figure represents employment of a plant once it had attained full production. Where two figures are shown, they represent the effects of cutbacks or expansion of the work force.

Date of Location. This represents the year in which a plant began production. It is not the time at which the location decision was made, nor the date of the beginning of plant construction, although many studies discuss the impacts of these phases of industrial development.

CONTENTS

SKETCH NUMBER 1--ARKANSAS

I. SITE CHARACTERISTICS

   A. Location: Arkansas: Malvern, Hot Spring County; Mountain Home, Baxter County; Nashville, Howard County; Paris, Logan County; Pocahontas, Randolph County; Rogers, Benton County; Searcy, White County

   B. Community Size: Malvern, 9,275; Mountain Home, 2,880; Nashville, 3,579; Paris, 3,155; Pocahontas, 4,391; Rogers, 5,250; Searcy, 6,675

II. RESEARCH CHARACTERISTICS

   A. Period of Study: 1971
   B. Unit of Analysis: town and county
   C. Type of Data Used: primary and secondary
   D. Major Variables:
       Economic: private sector, public sector, community services
       Demographic: population size
       Social: not studied
   E. Researchers: Yantis, Davis, Walraven, Opitz, Peterson, Wright
   F. Documents: 186, 51, 118, 119, 178, 179

III. FIRM CHARACTERISTICS

Plant Product	No. of Plants	No. of Employees	Date of Location
Malvern			
fabricated metal products	2	105-130	1958, 1963
metal	2	983-1,183	1963, 1967
stone, clay, and glass products	4	575-665	1958
wood products	2	210-285	1957, 1968

Plant Product	No. of Plants	No. of Employees	Date of Location
Mountain Home			
chemicals	1	1,000	1964
stone, clay, and glass products	1	12	1965
fabricated metal products	1	6	1968
Nashville			
paper	1	11	1960
apparel	1	190	1961
fabricated metal products	3	156–205	1951, 1952, 1962
stone, clay, and glass products	1	175	1963
wood products	2	129–200	1945, 1960
Paris			
stone, clay, and glass products	1	20	1957
chemicals	2	32–60	1957, 1959
transportation equipment	1	110	1963
apparel	1	500	1965
Pocahontas			
leather products	1	425–476	1957
wood products	1	100	1956
electrical equipment	1	416	1960
fabricated metal products	1	9	1958
transportation equipment	1	13	1969
other: unspecified	1	109	1958
Rogers			
machinery	3	109–737	1954, 1960, 1964
paper	1	120	1963
textiles	1	119	1969
fabricated metal products	1	60	1969
other: unspecified	1	791	1958
Searcy			
leather products	1	350–413	1947
wood products	1	98	1951
rubber and plastic products	1	37	1955
stone, clay, and glass products	1	18	1956
machinery	1	500	1957
metal	1	32–100	1959
fabricated metal products	2	44–66	1956, 1961
electrical equipment	1	162	1969

SKETCH NUMBER 2--ARKANSAS

I. SITE CHARACTERISTICS

    A. Location: Arkansas: Benton County, Madison County, Washington County

    B. Community Size: 3 counties, 94,388 (estimated)

II. RESEARCH CHARACTERISTICS

    A. Period of Study: 1960, 1967

    B. Unit of Analysis: region, town, and county

    C. Type of Data Used: primary and secondary

    D. Major Variables:

        Economic: labor supply, employment, public sector
        Demographic: population size, commuting, characteristics of plant employees
      Social: attitudes

    E. Researchers: Peterson, Wright, Walraven, Opitz, Yantis

    F. Documents: 117, 118, 178, 179, 186

III. FIRM CHARACTERISTICS

Plant Product	No. of Plants	No. of Employees	Date of Location
pianos, wood products, electrical equipment, hosiery, synthetic fiber, other: unspecified	total of 25 (approximate)	total of 4,800 (approximate)	1955-66

SKETCH NUMBER 3--ARKANSAS

I. SITE CHARACTERISTICS

    A. Location: Arkansas: Searcy, White County

    B. Community Size: not stated

II. RESEARCH CHARACTERISTICS

    A. Period of Study: 1962

    B. Unit of Analysis: town and county

    C. Type of Data Used: primary and secondary

D. Major Variables:
    Economic: employment, income, banking and finance
    Demographic: population change
    Social: not studied
E. Researchers: Davis, Yantis
F. Documents: 51, 186

III. FIRM CHARACTERISTICS

Plant Product	No. of Plants	No. of Employees	Date of Location
flooring	1	total of 590	1951
shoes	1		1946
food	1		1951
poultry	1		1956
other: unspecified	2		1956

SKETCH NUMBER 4--ARKANSAS

I. SITE CHARACTERISTICS

A. Location: Arkansas: Wynne, Cross County
B. Community Size: Wynne, 6,696

II. RESEARCH CHARACTERISTICS

A. Period of Study: 1973
B. Unit of Analysis: town and county
C. Type of Data Used: primary and secondary
D. Major Variables:
    Economic: employment, income, public services
    Demographic: migration, commuting
    Social: not studied
E. Researchers: Brady, Kuehn, Bender, Green, Hoover
F. Documents: 22, 99

III. FIRM CHARACTERISTICS

Plant Product	No. of Plants	No. of Employees	Date of Location
apparel	1	total of 1,900 (approximate)	1954
shoes	1		1960
copper tubing	1		1964

SKETCH NUMBER 5--ARKANSAS

I. SITE CHARACTERISTICS

A. Location: Arkansas: all rural counties
B. Community Size: Arkansas: 1,900,000 (approximate)

II. RESEARCH CHARACTERISTICS

A. Period of Study: 1969
B. Unit of Analysis: state and county
C. Type of Data Used: secondary
D. Major Variables:
    Economic: employment
    Demographic: population size and change, migration
    Social: not studied
E. Researchers: Stuart
F. Documents: 156

III. FIRM CHARACTERISTICS

Plant Product	No. of Plants	No. of Employees	Date of Location
apparel	total of 7	total of 250-1,494	not stated
wood products	total of 4	total of 300-747	not stated
metal products	1	100-249	not stated

SKETCH NUMBER 6--ARKANSAS

I. SITE CHARACTERISTICS

A. Location: Arkansas: Benton, Bauxite, Saline County
B. Community Size: Saline County, 29,000

II. RESEARCH CHARACTERISTICS

A. Period of Study: 1962
B. Unit of Analysis: town and county
C. Type of Data Used: secondary
D. Major Variables:
    Economic: employment, income
    Demographic: commuting
    Social: not studied
E. Researchers: Gray, R.
F. Documents: 65

III. FIRM CHARACTERISTICS

Plant Product	No. of Plants	No. of Employees	Date of Location
aluminum reduction	1	not stated	1951

SKETCH NUMBER 7--ARKANSAS

I. SITE CHARACTERISTICS

    A. Location: Arkansas: Gassville, Baxter County
    B. Community Size: Gassville, 233

II. RESEARCH CHARACTERISTICS

    A. Period of Study: 1966
    B. Unit of Analysis: town and county
    C. Type of Data Used: primary and secondary
    D. Major Variables:
        Economic: employment, income, public sector
        Demographic: characteristics of labor force
        Social: not studied
    E. Researchers: Jordan, Brinkman
    F. Documents: 86, 24

III. FIRM CHARACTERISTICS

Plant Product	No. of Plants	No. of Employees	Date of Location
apparel	1	750	1960

SKETCH NUMBER 8--ARKANSAS

I. SITE CHARACTERISTICS

    A. Location: Arkansas: Helena-West Helena, Phillips County
    B. Community Size: Helena-West Helena, 19,885; Phillips
        County, 43,997

II. RESEARCH CHARACTERISTICS

    A. Period of Study: 1961
    B. Unit of Analysis: town and county

C. Type of Data Used: primary and secondary
D. Major Variables:
  Economic: employment, agriculture
  Demographic: migration, population size, racial
                composition
  Social: not studied
E. Researchers: Brann
F. Documents: 23

III. FIRM CHARACTERISTICS

Plant Product	No. of Plants	No. of Employees	Date of Location
concrete mats	1	150	1947
fertilizer	1	25	1950
monuments	1	6	1950
apparel	1	592	1951
blinds	1	4	1951
tires	1	450	1955
wood products	1	20	1955
insecticides	1	20	1956
plastics	1	250	1957
luggage	1	25	1957
water skis	1	10	1960

SKETCH NUMBER 9--ARKANSAS

I. SITE CHARACTERISTICS

A. Location: Arkansas: Star City, Lincoln County
B. Community Size: Star City, 1,496

II. RESEARCH CHARACTERISTICS

A. Period of Study: 1958
B. Unit of Analysis: town
C. Type of Data Used: primary and secondary
D. Major Variables:
  Economic: employment, private sector, agriculture
  Demographic: commuting, characteristics of plant workers
  Social: community development
E. Researchers: Arkansas Department of Labor, Employment
                Security Division
F. Documents: 5

III. FIRM CHARACTERISTICS

Plant Product	No. of Plants	No. of Employees	Date of Location
shirts	1	500 (approximate)	1956

SKETCH NUMBER 10--CALIFORNIA

I. SITE CHARACTERISTICS

A. Location: California: Hanford, LeMoore, Corcoran, King's County; Redding, Shasta County, Visalia, Tulare County; Merced, Merced County

B. Community Size: Redding, 12,773; Shasta County, 60,400; King's County, 49,594

II. RESEARCH CHARACTERISTICS

A. Period of Study: 1973

B. Unit of Analysis: town and county

C. Type of Data Used: secondary

D. Major Variables:

Economic: employment, U.S. Economic Development Administration development grants

Demographic: population growth

Social: not studied

E. Researchers: Barnett, Shasta County Economic Development Corporation

F. Documents: 6, 148

III. FIRM CHARACTERISTICS

Plant Product	No. of Plants	No. of Employees	Date of Location
Redding not specified	13	total of 2,222	1957-73
Merced not specified	21	total of 2,000	1961-73
Visalia not specified	21	total of 2,300	not specified

Plant Product	No. of Plants	No. of Employees	Date of Location
Hanford tires	1	not specified	1961 (approximate)
Hanford, LeMoore, and Corcoran not specified	8	total of 1,000	1966-73

SKETCH NUMBER 11--ILLINOIS

I. SITE CHARACTERISTICS

A. Location: Illinois: Hennepin, Putnam County
B. Community Size: Putnam County, 4,570

II. RESEARCH CHARACTERISTICS

A. Period of Study: 1966-1974
B. Unit of Analysis: town and county
C. Type of Data Used: primary and secondary
D. Major Variables:
   Economic: occupational structure, agriculture, labor
      supply, occupational mobility, public sector,
      income, private sector
   Demographic: commuting, social mobility, migration,
      urbanization, human ecology
   Social: social control, community identity, social roles,
      attitudes, alienation, religion, status attainment,
      community satisfaction, leadership
E. Researchers: Summers, Beck, Dotson, Chen, Scott, Clark,
      Hough, Clemente, Rojek, Darroch, DeMartini,
      Durant, Erickson, Haga, Folse, O'Meara,
      Johnson, Kayser, Ramana, Schneiderman,
      Wahi, Seiler, Burke, Saltiel, Veatch, Holley,
      Stengel, Wiley, Shaffer, Moore, Wanner,
      Wheaton, Alwin
F. Documents: 7, 8, 9, 10, 11, 12, 13, 33, 34, 36, 37, 38,
      39, 40, 41, 42, 43, 44, 45, 46, 49, 50, 53,
      56, 57, 67, 70, 73, 74, 75, 76, 77, 78, 81,
      82, 83, 84, 90, 91, 92, 93, 94, 95, 96, 123,
      127, 128, 131, 132, 133, 134, 135, 136, 137,
      138, 139, 140, 153, 157, 158, 159, 160, 161,
      162, 163, 164, 165, 166, 167, 175, 180, 181

III. FIRM CHARACTERISTICS

Plant Product	No. of Plants	No. of Employees	Date of Location
steel	1	1,039	1967

SKETCH NUMBER 12--INDIANA

I. SITE CHARACTERISTICS

A. Location: Indiana: Linton, Greene County
B. Community Size: Linton, 6,000

II. RESEARCH CHARACTERISTICS

A. Period of Study: 1964
B. Unit of Analysis: town and county
C. Type of Data Used: primary and secondary
D. Major Variables:
     Economic: employment, private sector, public sector
     Demographic: population size
     Social: attitudes
E. Researchers: Wadsworth, Conrad, Brinkman
F. Documents: 172, 173, 174, 24

III. FIRM CHARACTERISTICS

Plant Product	No. of Plants	No. of Employees	Date of Location
metal chairs	1	100	1964

SKETCH NUMBER 13--INDIANA

I. SITE CHARACTERISTICS

A. Location: Indiana: Kokomo, Howard County
B. Community Size: Kokomo, 38,670; Howard County, 54,498

II. RESEARCH CHARACTERISTICS

A. Period of Study: 1963
B. Unit of Analysis: town and county

    C. Type of Data Used: primary and secondary
    D. Major Variables:
        Economic: income, public sector, employment
        Demographic: population size, composition
        Social: not studied
    E. Researchers: Stevens, Wallace, Brinkman
    F. Documents: 155, 24

III. FIRM CHARACTERISTICS

Plant Product	No. of Plants	No. of Employees	Date of Location
not stated	not stated	not stated	1947-60

SKETCH NUMBER 14--IOWA

I. SITE CHARACTERISTICS

    A. Location: Iowa: Maquoketa, Jackson County
    B. Community Size: Maquoketa, 4,307; Jackson County, 18,622

II. RESEARCH CHARACTERISTICS

    A. Period of Study: 1960
    B. Unit of Analysis: town and county
    C. Type of Data Used: primary and secondary
    D. Major Variables:
        Economic: private sector, employment, agriculture
        Demographic: population size
        Social: attitudes, social participation, family organization
    E. Researchers: Funk, Kaldor, Bauder, Trautwein, Maitland,
                Cowhig, Friend, Miernyk
    F. Documents: 58, 87, 88, 103, 104, 111, 170

III. FIRM CHARACTERISTICS

Plant Product	No. of Plants	No. of Employees	Date of Location
small engines	1	100-1,900 (approximate)	1950

SKETCH NUMBER 15--IOWA

I. SITE CHARACTERISTICS

    A. Location: Iowa: Jefferson, Greene County; Centerville, Appanoose County; Creston, Union County; Orange City, Sioux County; Lake Mills, Winnebago County; Grinnell, Poweshiek County; Decorah, Winneshiek County; 115 unnamed rural towns and cities

    B. Community Size: Jefferson, 4,735; Centerville, 6,531; Creston, 8,234; Orange City, 3,572; Lake Mills, 2,124; Grinnell, 8,402; Decorah, 7,458; unnamed towns, 1,600-8,500

II. RESEARCH CHARACTERISTICS

    A. Period of Study: 1971, 1972
    B. Unit of Analysis: town and county
    C. Type of Data Used: primary and secondary
    D. Major Variables:
        Economic: employment, income
        Demographic: population change, migration
        Social: attitudes, leadership
    E. Researchers: Kaldor, Dahlke, Paden, Krist, Seaton
    F. Documents: 86, 117

III. FIRM CHARACTERISTICS

Plant Product	No. of Plants	No. of Employees	Date of Location
Jefferson			
metal products	1	total of 390+	1959
athletic equipment	1		1960
other: unspecified	10		1960
Centerville			
electrical equipment	1	total of 800+	1960
other: unspecified	5		1962-1972
Creston			
kitchen equipment	1	total of 403	1958
chemicals	1		1966
other: unspecified	2		1964

Plant Product	No. of Plants	No. of Employees	Date of Location
Orange City			
not specified	not stated	total of 195+	1962-1970
Lake Mills			
auto parts	1	350	1958
doors, windows	1	50	1962
farm equipment	1	14	1971
metal products	1	not stated	not stated
Grinnell			
farm machinery	1	total of 105+	not stated
stadium bleachers	1		not stated
other: unspecified	1		not stated
Decorah			
screws	1	80	not stated
other: unspecified	1	190	not stated
Unnamed towns			
not stated	not stated	total of 4,600 (approximate)	1968-1970

SKETCH NUMBER 16--KANSAS

I. SITE CHARACTERISTICS

    A. Location: Kansas: Parsons
    B. Community Size: Parsons, 13,000 (approximate)

II. RESEARCH CHARACTERISTICS

    A. Period of Study: 1970
    B. Unit of Analysis: town
    C. Type of Data Used: primary and secondary
    D. Major Variables:
        Economic: property values, housing supply and demand
        Demographic: not studied
        Social: not studied
    E. Researchers: Debes
    F. Documents: 52

III. FIRM CHARACTERISTICS

Plant Product	No. of Plants	No. of Employees	Date of Location
plastic products, fabricated metal products, metal equipment and instruments, transportation equipment	total of 8	total of 434	1960-70

SKETCH NUMBER 17--KANSAS

I. SITE CHARACTERISTICS

    A. Location: Kansas: unnamed town
    B. Community Size: town, 16,632

II. RESEARCH CHARACTERISTICS

    A. Period of Study: 1960
    B. Unit of Analysis: town
    C. Type of Data Used: primary and secondary
    D. Major Variables:
        Economic: public sector
        Demographic: characteristics of plant employees, commuting
        Social: social participation, attitudes
    E. Researchers: Merrill, Ryther
    F. Documents: 108, 109

III. FIRM CHARACTERISTICS

Plant Product	No. of Plants	No. of Employees	Date of Location
fertilizers	2	100, 270	1951, 1955
stationery	1	200	1958

SKETCH NUMBER 18--KENTUCKY

I. SITE CHARACTERISTICS

A. Location: Kentucky: 4 unnamed towns
B. Community Size: 9,000; 2,600; 4,500; 2,600

II. RESEARCH CHARACTERISTICS

A. Period of Study: 1965
B. Unit of Analysis: town
C. Type of Data Used: primary and secondary
D. Major Variables:
   Economic: role of banks in rural industrial development
   Demographic: not studied
   Social: not studied
E. Researchers: Irwin
F. Documents: 80

III. FIRM CHARACTERISTICS

Plant Product	No. of Plants	No. of Employees	Date of Location
not stated	not stated	not stated	1956-1964

SKETCH NUMBER 19--KENTUCKY

I. SITE CHARACTERISTICS

A. Location: Kentucky: Flemingsburg, Fleming County; London, Laurel County; Stanford, Lincoln County; Lebanon, Marion County; Russell Springs, Russell County
B. Community Size: Flemingsburg, 2,067; London, 4,035; Stanford, 2,019; Lebanon, 4,813; Russell Springs, 1,125

II. RESEARCH CHARACTERISTICS

A. Period of Study: 1966
B. Unit of Analysis: town and county
C. Type of Data Used: primary and secondary

D. Major Variables:
   Economic: income, employment, local government
   Demographic: not studied
   Social: not studied
E. Researchers: Garrison
F. Documents: 59, 60, 61, 62

III. FIRM CHARACTERISTICS

Plant Product	No. of Plants	No. of Employees	Date of Location
Flemingsburg			
auto trim	1	125–180	1959
shoes	1	150	1962
London			
yarn	1	107	1962
Stanford			
apparel	1	380	1959
Lebanon			
whisky barrels	1	131	1961
electronic equipment	1	144	1959
apparel	2	223	1958, 1960
Russell Springs			
apparel	1	206	1959

SKETCH NUMBER 20--KENTUCKY

I. SITE CHARACTERISTICS

A. Location: Kentucky: Munfordville, Hart County
B. Community Size: Munfordville, 2,500; Hart County, 13,700

II. RESEARCH CHARACTERISTICS

A. Period of Study: 1963
B. Unit of Analysis: county
C. Type of Data Used: primary and secondary
D. Major Variables:
   Economic: employment, housing, private sector
   Demographic: population size, age composition
   Social: not studied

E. Researchers: Hoover, Brinkman
F. Documents: 72, 24

III. FIRM CHARACTERISTICS

Plant Product	No. of Plants	No. of Employees	Date of Location
bedding	1	111	1963

SKETCH NUMBER 21--LOUISIANA

I. SITE CHARACTERISTICS

A. Location: Louisiana: Roseland, Tangipahoa Parish
B. Community Size: 43,730 within 25 miles of plant

II. RESEARCH CHARACTERISTICS

A. Period of Study: 1957
B. Unit of Analysis: town and parish
C. Type of Data Used: primary and secondary
D. Major Variables:
    Economic: employment, levels of living, agriculture
    Demographic: residential mobility, characteristics of
            plant employees
    Social: attitudes, social participation
E. Researchers: Bertrand, Osborne, Price, Maitland,
            Cowhig, Friend, Miernyk
F. Documents: 16, 17, 18, 19, 103, 111, 116

III. FIRM CHARACTERISTICS

Plant Product	No. of Plants	No. of Employees	Date of Location
wirebound boxes	1	500 (approximate)	1951

SKETCH NUMBER 22--MICHIGAN

I. SITE CHARACTERISTICS

A. Location: Michigan: Edmore, Montcalm County
B. Community Size: Edmore, 971; Montcalm County, 31,013

II. RESEARCH CHARACTERISTICS

    A. Period of Study: 1953
    B. Unit of Analysis: town and county
    C. Type of Data Used: primary and secondary
    D. Major Variables:
        Economic: housing, public services, private sector
        Demographic: population size, commuting
        Social: not studied
    E. Researchers: Calef, Daoust
    F. Documents: 28, 48

III. FIRM CHARACTERISTICS

Plant Product	No. of Plants	No. of Employees	Date of Location
cutting tools, magnets	1	285	1952

SKETCH NUMBER 23--MINNESOTA

I. SITE CHARACTERISTICS

    A. Location: Minnesota: Rochester, Olmstead County
    B. Community Size: Rochester, 30,000

II. RESEARCH CHARACTERISTICS

    A. Period of Study: 1960
    B. Unit of Analysis: town
    C. Type of Data Used: primary and secondary
    D. Major Variables:
        Economic: employment, housing, private sector
        Demographic: not studied
        Social: not studied
    E. Researchers: Morris
    F. Documents: 113

III. FIRM CHARACTERISTICS

Plant Product	No. of Plants	No. of Employees	Date of Location
business machines	1	1,862	1956

SKETCH NUMBER 24--MINNESOTA

I. SITE CHARACTERISTICS

    A. Location: Minnesota: 27 towns
    B. Community Size: 331-17,731

II. RESEARCH CHARACTERISTICS

    A. Period of Study: 1967
    B. Unit of Analysis: town
    C. Type of Data Used: primary and secondary
    D. Major Variables:
        Economic: labor supply, housing, transportation
        Demographic: commuting
        Social: attitudes
    E. Researchers: Metz
    F. Documents: 110

III. FIRM CHARACTERISTICS

Plant Product	No. of Plants	No. of Employees	Date of Location
containers, plastic products, apparel, communications equipment, motors, batteries, toys, fiberglass products, other: unspecified	total of 31	not stated	not stated

SKETCH NUMBER 25--MISSISSIPPI

I. SITE CHARACTERISTICS

    A. Location: Mississippi: Washington County
    B. Community Size: Washington County, 76,638

II. RESEARCH CHARACTERISTICS

    A. Period of Study: 1964
    B. Unit of Analysis: county
    C. Type of Data Used: secondary

D. Major Variables:
   Economic: employment, agriculture
   Demographic: composition of labor force
   Social: not studied
E. Researchers: Pray
F. Documents: 122

III. FIRM CHARACTERISTICS

Plant Product	No. of Plants	No. of Employees	Date of Location
carpets	1	1,017	1952
fabricated metal products	3	150, 360, 500	1958, 1959, 1961
furniture	1	75	1961
boilers and furnaces	1	100	1963

SKETCH NUMBER 26--MISSISSIPPI

I. SITE CHARACTERISTICS

A. Location: Mississippi: Leflore County
B. Community Size: Leflore County, 37,142

II. RESEARCH CHARACTERISTICS

A. Period of Study: 1964
B. Unit of Analysis: county
C. Type of Data Used: primary and secondary
D. Major Variables:
   Economic: employment, private sector
   Demographic: population size, composition
   Social: not studied
E. Researchers: Pittman
F. Documents: 120

III. FIRM CHARACTERISTICS

Plant Product	No. of Plants	No. of Employees	Date of Location
not specified	not stated	1,220-2,650	1959-1964

SKETCH NUMBER 27--MISSISSIPPI

I. SITE CHARACTERISTICS

   A. Location: Mississippi: Pickens, Holmes County
   B. Community Size: Pickens, 727

II. RESEARCH CHARACTERISTICS

   A. Period of Study: not stated
   B. Unit of Analysis: 4 counties
   C. Type of Data Used: secondary
   D. Major Variables:
        Economic: employment, housing, public facilities.
        Demographic: population composition, education,
                     migration
        Social: leadership
   E. Researchers: Crecink
   F. Documents: 47

III. FIRM CHARACTERISTICS

Plant Product	No. of Plants	No. of Employees	Date of Location
tissue paper	1	57	1962

SKETCH NUMBER 28--MISSISSIPPI

I. SITE CHARACTERISTICS

   A. Location: Mississippi: Houston, Chickasaw County
   B. Community Size: Chickasaw County, 18, 951

II. RESEARCH CHARACTERISTICS

   A. Period of Study: 1956
   B. Unit of Analysis: county
   C. Type of Data Used: primary and secondary
   D. Major Variables:
        Economic: income, agriculture, levels of living
        Demographic: characteristics of plant employees,
                     residential mobility
        Social: attitudes, social participation

E. Researchers: Maitland, Wilber, Cowhig, Friend, Miernyk
F. Documents: 103, 104, 105, 111, 182, 183

III. FIRM CHARACTERISTICS

Plant Product	No. of Plants	No. of Employees	Date of Location
furniture	1	130	1954

SKETCH NUMBER 29--MISSOURI

I. SITE CHARACTERISTICS

A. Location: Missouri: Ava, Douglas County
B. Community Size: Ava, 1,581; Douglas County, 9,653

II. RESEARCH CHARACTERISTICS

A. Period of Study: 1965
B. Unit of Analysis: town and county
C. Type of Data Used: primary and secondary
D. Major Variables:
   Economic: government services, employment, income
   Demographic: population growth
   Social: not studied
E. Researchers: Hagerman, Braschler, Brinkman
F. Documents: 68, 24

III. FIRM CHARACTERISTICS

Plant Product	No. of Plants	No. of Employees	Date of Location
treated wood	1	13	1959
sporting goods	2	115-240, 150	1960, 1964

SKETCH NUMBER 30--MISSOURI

I. SITE CHARACTERISTICS

A. Location: Missouri: Lebanon, Laclede County
B. Community Size: Lebanon, 8,616

II. RESEARCH CHARACTERISTICS

    A. Period of Study: 1971
    B. Unit of Analysis: town and county
    C. Type of Data Used: secondary
    D. Major Variables:
        Economic: employment, income, private sector
        Demographic: population growth
        Social: not studied
    E. Researchers: Borgmeyer
    F. Documents: 21

III. FIRM CHARACTERISTICS

Plant Product	No. of Plants	No. of Employees	Date of Location
storm windows	1	5	1965
metal stampings	1	25	1970
custom tools	1	2	1970
not specified	1	not specified	1963
not specified	1	10	1964
not specified	1	15	1967

SKETCH NUMBER 31--MONTANA

I. SITE CHARACTERISTICS

    A. Location: Montana: Columbia Falls, Flathead County
    B. Community Size: Columbia Falls, 1,232; Flathead
        County, 31,495

II. RESEARCH CHARACTERISTICS

    A. Period of Study: 1959
    B. Unit of Analysis: town and county
    C. Type of Data Used: secondary
    D. Major Variables:
        Economic: employment, income, public sector
        Demographic: population change, migration, commuting
        Social: not studied
    E. Researchers: Johnson
    F. Documents: 85

III. FIRM CHARACTERISTICS

Plant Product	No. of Plants	No. of Employees	Date of Location
aluminum reduction	1	512-1,353	1955

SKETCH NUMBER 32--NEW YORK

I. SITE CHARACTERISTICS

    A. Location: New York: all counties, cities, villages, towns
    B. Community Size: not stated

II. RESEARCH CHARACTERISTICS

    A. Period of Study: 1961
    B. Unit of Analysis: village, town, city, and county
    C. Type of Data Used: secondary
    D. Major Variables:
        Economic: tax rates, municipal revenues, expenditures
        Demographic: urbanization
        Social: not studied
    E. Researchers: Carroll, Sacks
    F. Documents: 29

III. FIRM CHARACTERISTICS

Plant Product	No. of Plants	No. of Employees	Date of Location
not specified	not specified	not specified	not specified

SKETCH NUMBER 33--NEW YORK

I. SITE CHARACTERISTICS

    A. Location: New York: Honeoye
    B. Community Size: Honeoye, 800

II. RESEARCH CHARACTERISTICS

    A. Period of Study: 1967
    B. Unit of Analysis: town

C. Type of Data Used: primary and secondary
D. Major Variables:
    Economic: public sector, housing, linkages
    Demographic: not studied
    Social: social participation, attitudes
E. Researchers: Niagara Mohawk Power Corporation
F. Documents: 114

III. FIRM CHARACTERISTICS

Plant Product	No. of Plants	No. of Employees	Date of Location
machinery	1	155	1953
photographic paper	1	not stated	1962

SKETCH NUMBER 34--NORTH CAROLINA

I. SITE CHARACTERISTICS

A. Location: North Carolina: Kinston, Lenoir County
B. Community Size: Kinston, 30,000 (approximate); Lenoir
    County, 60,000 (approximate)

II. RESEARCH CHARACTERISTICS

A. Period of Study: 1964
B. Unit of Analysis: town and county
C. Type of Data Used: primary and secondary
D. Major Variables:
    Economic: not studied
    Demographic: commuting
    Social: not studied
E. Researchers: Lonsdale
F. Documents: 100

III. FIRM CHARACTERISTICS

Plant Product	No. of Plants	No. of Employees	Date of Location
synthetic fiber	1	2,200	1953

SKETCH NUMBER 35--NORTH CAROLINA

I. SITE CHARACTERISTICS

    A. Location: North Carolina: Tarboro, Edgecombe County
    B. Community Size: Tarboro, 8,400

II. RESEARCH CHARACTERISTICS

    A. Period of Study: 1967
    B. Unit of Analysis: town and county
    C. Type of Data Used: primary and secondary
    D. Major Variables:
        Economic: employees' spending patterns, employment, public sector
        Demographic: migration
        Social: not studied
    E. Researchers: Miller
    F. Documents: 112

III. FIRM CHARACTERISTICS

Plant Product	No. of Plants	No. of Employees	Date of Location
not specified	total of 4	total of 1,039	1960, 1961, 1964

SKETCH NUMBER 36--NORTH DAKOTA

I. SITE CHARACTERISTICS

    A. Location: North Dakota: Jamestown, Stutsman County
    B. Community Size: Jamestown, 15,385; Stutsman County, 23,550

II. RESEARCH CHARACTERISTICS

    A. Period of Study: 1972-73
    B. Unit of Analysis: town and 9 counties
    C. Type of Data Used: primary and secondary
    D. Major Variables:
        Economic: employment, regional economy, private sector
        Demographic: population size, migration, characteristics of plant employees
        Social: attitudes

E. Researchers: Helgeson, Zink
F. Documents: 69

III. FIRM CHARACTERISTICS

Plant Product	No. of Plants	No. of Employees	Date of Location
bread dough	1	total of 389	all late 1960s
aerospace components	1		
farm machinery	1		
mobile homes	1		

SKETCH NUMBER 37--OHIO

I. SITE CHARACTERISTICS

A. Location: Ohio: Monroe County
B. Community Size: Monroe County, 14,590

II. RESEARCH CHARACTERISTICS

A. Period of Study: 1957 and 1962
B. Unit of Analysis: county
C. Type of Data Used: primary and secondary
D. Major Variables:
   Economic: employment, income, agriculture
   Demographic: population size, composition, migration
   Social: attitudes, social organization, leisure activities
E. Researchers: Andrews, Bauder, Rogers, Maitland, Cowhig
F. Documents: 3, 4, 103

III. FIRM CHARACTERISTICS

Plant Product	No. of Plants	No. of Employees	Date of Location
aluminum reduction	1	2,600	1959
ferro-alloy products	1	150	1959

SKETCH NUMBER 38--OKLAHOMA

I. SITE CHARACTERISTICS

A. Location: Oklahoma: 18 unnamed communities
B. Community Size: 18 communities, 1,500-13,000

II. RESEARCH CHARACTERISTICS

A. Period of Study: 1962-64
B. Unit of Analysis: town
C. Type of Data Used: primary and secondary
D. Major Variables:
   Economic: employment, community costs and benefits,
        public sector
   Demographic: population size
   Social: not studied
E. Researchers: Saltzman
F. Documents: 130

III. FIRM CHARACTERISTICS

Plant Product	No. of Plants	No. of Employees	Date of Location
textiles	6	937-1,333	1952-61
apparel	7	742-765	1949-61
other: unspecified	21	1,398-1,712	1949-61

SKETCH NUMBER 39--OKLAHOMA

I. SITE CHARACTERISTICS

A. Location: Oklahoma: Choctaw County
B. Community Size: Choctaw County, 20,406

II. RESEARCH CHARACTERISTICS

A. Period of Study: 1955, 1958
B. Unit of Analysis: county
C. Type of Data Used: primary and secondary
D. Major Variables:
   Economic: agriculture, income, private sector
   Demographic: population distribution, migration
   Social: not studied

E. Researchers: Klein
F. Documents: 97

III. FIRM CHARACTERISTICS

Plant Product	No. of Plants	No. of Employees	Date of Location
apparel	1	total of 200+	1954
furniture	1		1954-58
rodénticide	1		1940-47

SKETCH NUMBER 40--OKLAHOMA

I. SITE CHARACTERISTICS

A. Location: Oklahoma: Stilwell, Adair County; Muskogee,
Muskogee County
B. Community Size: Stilwell, 1,916; Muskogee, 38,059

II. RESEARCH CHARACTERISTICS

A. Period of Study: 1970-71
B. Unit of Analysis: town and county
C. Type of Data Used: primary and secondary
D. Major Variables:
Economic: private sector, public sector, school district
sector
Demographic: migration
Social: not studied
E. Researchers: Shaffer, Tweeten, Brinkman
F. Documents: 141, 142, 143, 144, 145, 146, 147, 24

III. FIRM CHARACTERISTICS

Plant Product	No. of Plants	No. of Employees	Date of Location
electrical equipment	1	80	all between 1960
air conditioning and			and 1970
heating	1	80	
furniture	1	25	
machinery	1	80	

SKETCH NUMBER 41--OREGON

I. SITE CHARACTERISTICS

    A. Location: Oregon: McMinnville, Yamhill County
    B. Community Size: McMinnville, 7,649

II. RESEARCH CHARACTERISTICS

    A. Period of Study: 1971
    B. Unit of Analysis: town
    C. Type of Data Used: primary and secondary
    D. Major Variables:
        Economic: not studied
        Demographic: not studied
        Social: attitudes
    E. Researchers: Rathburn
    F. Documents: 124

III. FIRM CHARACTERISTICS

Plant Product	No. of Plants	No. of Employees	Date of Location
not specified	total of 20+	total of 1,100+	1954-71

SKETCH NUMBER 42--SOUTH CAROLINA

I. SITE CHARACTERISTICS

    A. Location: South Carolina: McCormick, McCormick County
    B. Community Size: McCormick, 1,456; McCormick County,
                10,367

II. RESEARCH CHARACTERISTICS

    A. Period of Study: 1947
    B. Unit of Analysis: town
    C. Type of Data Used: primary and secondary
    D. Major Variables:
        Economic: employment, agriculture, private sector
        Demographic: migration, commuting, characteristics of
                plant employees
        Social: attitudes

E. Researchers: Plaxico, Stepp
F. Documents: 121, 154

III. FIRM CHARACTERISTICS

Plant Product	No. of Plants	No. of Employees	Date of Location
woolen yarn	1	313	1946

SKETCH NUMBER 43--SOUTH CAROLINA

I. SITE CHARACTERISTICS

A. Location: South Carolina: Summerville, Dorchester County
B. Unit of Analysis: town and county
C. Type of Data Used: primary and secondary
D. Major Variables:
    Economic: employment
    Demographic: population size, characteristics of plant
                employees, commuting
    Social: leadership
E. Researchers: McElveen, Brinkman
F. Documents: 102, 24

III. FIRM CHARACTERISTICS

Plant Product	No. of Plants	No. of Employees	Date of Location
bricks	1	40	1963

SKETCH NUMBER 44--SOUTH DAKOTA

I. SITE CHARACTERISTICS

A. Location: South Dakota: Brookings, Brookings County
B. Community Size: not stated

II. RESEARCH CHARACTERISTICS

A. Period of Study: 1973
B. Unit of Analysis: town and county
C. Type of Data Used: primary and secondary

D. Major Variables:
    Economic: employment, private sector, public sector
    Demographic: characteristics of plant employees,
            commuting, migration
    Social: not studied
E. Researchers: Uhrich
F. Documents: 171

III. FIRM CHARACTERISTICS

Plant Product	No. of Plants	No. of Employees	Date of Location
medical supplies	1	360	1970

SKETCH NUMBER 45--TENNESSEE

I. SITE CHARACTERISTICS

A. Location: Tennessee: 14 towns in Campbell, Claiborne,
                           Cumberland, Fentress, Grainger,
                           Morgan, Scott, and Union counties
B. Community Size: 70-6,902

II. RESEARCH CHARACTERISTICS

A. Period of Study: 1973
B. Unit of Analysis: town and county
C. Type of Data Used: primary and secondary
D. Major Variables:
    Economic: forward and backward linkages, spending
            patterns
    Demographic: not studied
    Social: not studied
E. Researchers: Klimasewski
F. Documents: 98

III. FIRM CHARACTERISTICS

Plant Product	No. of Plants	No. of Employees	Date of Location
apparel, other: unspecified	total of 49	total of 8,121	not stated

SKETCH NUMBER 46--TENNESSEE

I. SITE CHARACTERISTICS

A. Location: Tennessee: Lawrence County
B. Community Size: Lawrence County, 28,818

II. RESEARCH CHARACTERISTICS

A. Period of Study: 1957, 1958, 1963
B. Unit of Analysis: county
C. Type of Data Used: primary and secondary
D. Major Variables:
   Economic: employment, local government, agriculture
   Demographic: population size, migration
   Social: not studied
E. Researchers: Martin, Tennessee Town and City, Wilson
F. Documents: 106, 168, 185

III. FIRM CHARACTERISTICS

Plant Product	No. of Plants	No. of Employees	Date of Location
bicycles	1	950-2,000	1956
not specified	1	100	1956

SKETCH NUMBER 47--TEXAS

I. SITE CHARACTERISTICS

A. Location: Texas: Rockdale
B. Community Size: Rockdale, 2,311

II. RESEARCH CHARACTERISTICS

A. Period of Study: 1953
B. Unit of Analysis: town
C. Type of Data Used: primary and secondary
D. Major Variables:
   Economic: housing, business, local government
   Demographic: commuting
   Social: leadership

E. Researchers: Garth
F. Documents: 63

III. FIRM CHARACTERISTICS

Plant Product	No. of Plants	No. of Employees	Date of Location
aluminum reduction	1	448	1952

SKETCH NUMBER 48--TEXAS

I. SITE CHARACTERISTICS

A. Location: Texas: Paris, Lamar County
B. Community Size: Paris, 21,643; Lamar County, 43,033

II. RESEARCH CHARACTERISTICS

A. Period of Study: 1963
B. Unit of Analysis: town and county
C. Type of Data Used: primary and secondary
D. Major Variables:
   Economic: employment, agriculture, public sector
   Demographic: population change, composition
   Social: not studied
E. Researchers: Ryan, Clark, Schkade
F. Documents: 129

III. FIRM CHARACTERISTICS

Plant Product	No. of Plants	No. of Employees	Date of Location
machinery	1	350	late 1940s
lamp parts	1	300 (approximate)	1952
fabricated metal products	1	100	not stated
rubber products	1	25	1959
glass beads	1	32	1959
apparel	2	70, 265	1947, 1955
paper products	3	56, 77, 131	1954, 1957, 1956
not specified	10 (approximate)	not stated	1953-1963

SKETCH NUMBER 49--UTAH

I. SITE CHARACTERISTICS

A. Location: Utah: Juab County, Sanpete County
B. Community Size: Juab County, 5,400; Sanpete County, 11,600

II. RESEARCH CHARACTERISTICS

A. Period of Study: 1958
B. Unit of Analysis: county
C. Type of Data Used: primary and secondary
D. Major Variables:
   Economic: agriculture, employment, levels of living
   Demographic: population trends
   Social: social participation, attitudes
E. Researchers: Christiansen, Maitland, Payne, Cowhig,
                 Friend, Miernyk
F. Documents: 35, 103, 104, 111

III. FIRM CHARACTERISTICS

Plant Product	No. of Plants	No. of Employees	Date of Location
rubber products	1	283	1958

SKETCH NUMBER 50--UTAH

I. SITE CHARACTERISTICS

A. Location: Utah: Box Elder County
B. Community Size: 20,000 (approximate)

II. RESEARCH CHARACTERISTICS

A. Period of Study: 1958, 1968
B. Unit of Analysis: county
C. Type of Data Used: primary and secondary
D. Major Variables:
   Economic: agriculture, levels of living, employment
   Demographic: characteristics of local and inmigrant
                plant employees
   Social: attitudes, social participation

E. Researchers: Black, Frederickson, Maitland, McArthur,
            Coppedge, Cowhig, Friend, Miernyk
F. Documents: 20, 101, 103, 104, 111

III. FIRM CHARACTERISTICS

Plant Product	No. of Plants	No. of Employees	Date of Location
rocket fuel	1	3,149	1957

SKETCH NUMBER 51--VIRGINIA

I. SITE CHARACTERISTICS

A. Location: Virginia: Charlotte County
B. Community Size: Charlotte County, 14,057

II. RESEARCH CHARACTERISTICS

A. Period of Study: 1949, 1954
B. Unit of Analysis: county
C. Type of Data Used: primary and secondary
D. Major Variables:
      Economic: agriculture, income, employment
      Demographic: population size, change
      Social: road use, travel habits
E. Researchers: Bureau of Population and Economic Research,
            University of Virginia
F. Documents: 27

III. FIRM CHARACTERISTICS

Plant Product	No. of Plants	No. of Employees	Date of Location
woolen goods	1	293-484	1949

SKETCH NUMBER 52--WEST VIRGINIA

I. SITE CHARACTERISTICS

A. Location: West Virginia: Braxton County
B. Community Size: Braxton County, 15,152

II. RESEARCH CHARACTERISTICS

   A. Period of Study: not stated
   B. Unit of Analysis: county
   C. Type of Data Used: primary and secondary
   D. Major Variables:
        Economic: employment, housing, private sector
        Demographic: population size, age composition
        Social: not studied
   E. Researchers: Hoover
   F. Documents: 71

III. FIRM CHARACTERISTICS

Plant Product	No. of Plants	No. of Employees	Date of Location
particle board	1	77	1963

SKETCH NUMBER 53--WEST VIRGINIA

   I. SITE CHARACTERISTICS

   A. Location: West Virginia: Ravenswood, Jackson County
   B. Community Size: Ravenswood, 1,100; Jackson County, 15,299

II. RESEARCH CHARACTERISTICS

   A. Period of Study: 1964, 1965, 1967
   B. Unit of Analysis: town and county
   C. Type of Data Used: primary and secondary
   D. Major Variables:
        Economic: employment, labor recruitment
        Demographic: commuting, education, migration
        Social: attitudes, social participation
   E. Researchers: Gray, I., Miernyk, Sizer, Clifford, Smith,
                    Somers
   F. Documents: 65, 111, 149, 150, 151

III. FIRM CHARACTERISTICS

Plant Product	No. of Plants	No. of Employees	Date of Location
aluminum reduction	1	3,405	1956

SKETCH NUMBER 54--WISCONSIN

I. SITE CHARACTERISTICS

A. Location: Wisconsin: Lac du Flambeau Indian Reservation, Vilas County
B. Community Size: Lac du Flambeau Reservation, 1,200

II. RESEARCH CHARACTERISTICS

A. Period of Study: 1952
B. Unit of Analysis: Indian Reservation
C. Type of Data Used: primary and secondary
D. Major Variables:
   Economic: employment, level of living, private sector
   Demographic: not studied
   Social: adaptation to wage-work system
E. Researchers: Ritzenthaler
F. Documents: 126

III. FIRM CHARACTERISTICS

Plant Product	No. of Plants	No. of Employees	Date of Location
electric meters	1	64	1946

SKETCH NUMBER 55--WISCONSIN

I. SITE CHARACTERISTICS

A. Location: Wisconsin: Fort Atkinson, Jefferson County; Hartford, Washington County; Monroe, Green County; Prairie du Chien, Crawford County; Richland Center, Richland County; West Bend, Washington County
B. Community Size: Fort Atkinson, 7,005; Hartford, 5,186; Monroe, 7,690; Prairie du Chien, 5,568; Richland Center, 4,786; West Bend, 7,901

II. RESEARCH CHARACTERISTICS

A. Period of Study: 1959
B. Unit of Analysis: town

C. Type of Data Used: primary and secondary
D. Major Variables:
    Economic: employment, taxes, public services
    Demographic: population size, community
    Social: attitudes
E. Researchers: Andrews, Fine, Johnson, Werner
F. Documents: 2

III. FIRM CHARACTERISTICS

Plant Product	No. of Plants	No. of Employees	Date of Location
Fort Atkinson farm equipment, food processing equip- ment, refrigeration equipment, knitted goods, lighting fix- tures, fishing lures, food, electronic equipment, photo- graphic equipment	total of 30+	total of 1,716	not stated
Hartford outboard motors, kitchen utensils, food, leather products, metal stampings		total of 1,123	not stated
Monroe food, electronic parts		total of 394	not stated
Prairie du Chien chemical plant food, cellulose sponges, con- crete blocks, aluminum products, furniture, food		total of 354	not stated
Richland Center bowling pins, food, boxes, cylinder sleeves		total of 184	not stated
West Bend farm machinery, leather products, food, auto accessories		total of 3,433	not stated

SKETCH NUMBER 56--SOUTHERN CENSUS REGION

I. SITE CHARACTERISTICS

    A. Location: Mississippi, South Carolina: 4 unnamed towns and cities

    B. Community Size: 2 towns, each 5,000-20,000; 2 cities, size not stated

II. RESEARCH CHARACTERISTICS

    A. Period of Study: 1967-68

    B. Unit of Analysis: town and county

    C. Type of Data Used: primary and secondary

    D. Major Variables:
       Economic: employment, public services
       Demographic: migration, commuting
       Social: leadership

    E. Researchers: Abt Associates

    F. Documents: 1

III. FIRM CHARACTERISTICS

Plant Product	No. of Plants	No. of Employees	Date of Location
electronic components, chemicals, pharmaceuticals, metal and steel fabricating, textiles, draperies, "cut and sew," timber products, metal working	total of 28+	not stated separately for firms locating in the previous decade	not stated, but assumed to be within the decade 1957-67

SKETCH NUMBER 57--SOUTHERN CENSUS REGION

I. SITE CHARACTERISTICS

    A. Location: Deep South: 244 nonmetropolitan counties in Alabama, Arkansas, Georgia, Louisiana, Mississippi, South Carolina

    B. Community Size: Deep South, 7,303,886

II. RESEARCH CHARACTERISTICS

    A. Period of Study: 1973
    B. Unit of Analysis: region
    C. Type of Data Used: primary and secondary
    D. Major Variables:
        Economic: employment, occupational distribution,
                poverty
        Demographic: racial composition, migration
        Social: not studied
    E. Researchers: Walker, J. L.
    F. Documents: 176

III. FIRM CHARACTERISTICS

Plant Product	No. of Plants	No. of Employees	Date of Location
textiles, apparel, wood products, paper products, chemicals, fabricated metal products	total of 15	between 57 and 1,000	not stated
others: unspecified	not stated	not stated	not stated

SKETCH NUMBER 58--SOUTHERN CENSUS REGION

I. SITE CHARACTERISTICS

    A. Location: The South: Texas, Oklahoma, Arkansas,
                         Louisiana, Mississippi, Tennessee,
                         Alabama, Georgia, Florida, South
                         Carolina, North Carolina, Virginia,
                         Kentucky
    B. Community Size: not stated

II. RESEARCH CHARACTERISTICS

    A. Period of Study: 1972
    B. Unit of Analysis: region
    C. Type of Data Used: primary and secondary
    D. Major Variables:
        Economic: labor demand, poverty
        Demographic: population size
        Social: not studied

    E. Researchers: Till

    F. 169

III. FIRM CHARACTERISTICS

Plant Product	No. of Plants	No. of Employees	Date of Location
not specified	not stated	not stated	not stated

SKETCH NUMBER 59--SOUTHERN CENSUS REGION

I. SITE CHARACTERISTICS

    A. Location: The South: 10 unnamed localities

    B. Community Size: not specified, but less than 10,000

II. RESEARCH CHARACTERISTICS

    A. Period of Study: 1962

    B. Unit of Analysis: not stated

    C. Type of Data Used: primary and secondary

    D. Major Variables:

        Economic: municipal industrial subsidies, income

        Demographic: not studied

        Social: not studied

    E. Researchers: Rinehart

    F. Documents: 125

III. FIRM CHARACTERISTICS

Plant Product	No. of Plants	No. of Employees	Date of Location
not specified	total of 22	not stated	after 1950

SKETCH NUMBER 60--NORTH CENTRAL CENSUS REGION

I. SITE CHARACTERISTICS

    A. Location: North Dakota, Nebraska, Kansas: 13 towns and counties

    B. Community Size: 5 counties, 7,000-19,000 (approximate); 8 counties, not stated

II. RESEARCH CHARACTERISTICS

    A. Period of Study: 1967-68
    B. Unit of Analysis: town and county
    C. Type of Data Used: primary and secondary
    D. Major Variables:
        Economic: employment, agriculture, tertiary sector
        Demographic: population size, composition
        Social: not studied
    E. Researchers: Dietz
    F. Documents: 54, 55

III. FIRM CHARACTERISTICS

Plant Product	No. of Plants	No. of Employees	Date of Location
watch bearings	1	160	1954
farm machinery	1	400	1954
electronic components	2	1,000, not stated	1954, 1959
medical supplies	1	360	1961
auto parts	1	600	1961
mobile homes	1	not stated	1959
aircraft	1	not stated	1954
oil refinery	3	not stated	1937, 1940, 1954
gypsum	1	not stated	1938

SKETCH NUMBER 61--NORTH CENTRAL CENSUS REGION

I. SITE CHARACTERISTICS

    A. Location: Midwest: 7 unnamed towns
    B. Community Size: 2,100; 2,500; 5,000; 5,300; 5,600; 8,200;
            8,600

II. RESEARCH CHARACTERISTICS

    A. Period of Study: 1970
    B. Unit of Analysis: town
    C. Type of Data Used: primary and secondary
    D. Major Variables:
        Economic: employment, public services, consumer
              expenditures

Demographic: residential mobility, characteristics of
plant employees
Social: attitudes
E. Researchers: Bucher
F. Documents: 25, 26

III. FIRM CHARACTERISTICS

Plant Product	No. of Plants	No. of Employees	Date of Location
City A metalworking	1	110	1963
City C aluminum products	1	160	1965
City D metalworking	1	85	1964
City E metalworking	1	53	1964
City F wooden chairs	1	20–50	1965
City G "cut and sew"	1	630	1961
City H metalworking	1	129	1962

SKETCH NUMBER 62--OTHER AREAS

I. SITE CHARACTERISTICS

A. Location: Michigan: town not stated; North Carolina:
Mt. Airy; U.S.: 33 unnamed locations
B. Community Size: not stated

II. RESEARCH CHARACTERISTICS

A. Period of Study: 1963
B. Unit of Analysis: town
C. Type of Data Used: primary and secondary
D. Major Variables:
Economic: employment, income
Demographic: worker characteristics
Social: not studied

E. Researchers: Miernyk
F. Documents: 111

III. FIRM CHARACTERISTICS

Plant Product	No. of Plants	No. of Employees	Date of Location
Michigan auto parts	1	466	1955
North Carolina appliances	1	435	1957
U.S. unspecified	33	total of 2,140	not stated

SKETCH NUMBER 63--OTHER AREAS

I. SITE CHARACTERISTICS

A. Location: Arizona: Navajo County, Apache County; New
Mexico: San Juan County; Mississippi: Alcorn
County, Tippah County; Arkansas: Benton County,
Lee County, St. Francis County, Washington
County
B. Community Size: 15,000-77,000

II. RESEARCH CHARACTERISTICS

A. Period of Study: 1967, 1971
B. Unit of Analysis: region
C. Type of Data Used: primary and secondary
D. Major Variables:
    Economic: poverty, income, employment
    Demographic: migration, commuting, characteristics of
            plant employees
    Social: attitudes
E. Researchers: Kuehn, Bender, Green, Hoover, Olsen,
            Peterson, Wright
F. Documents: 99, 115, 118, 119

III. FIRM CHARACTERISTICS

Plant Product	No. of Plants	No. of Employees	Date of Location
apparel, shoes, electrical equipment, plastic products, fabricated steel, machinery, food products	total of 26	total of 6,729	not stated

SKETCH NUMBER 64--OTHER AREAS

I. SITE CHARACTERISTICS

A. Location: New Mexico: Shiprock (Navajo Reservation);
   Arizona: Fort Defiance (Navajo Reservation);
   Mississippi: Fayette
B. Community Size: Navajo Reservation, 118,925; Fayette,
   1,800

II. RESEARCH CHARACTERISTICS

A. Period of Study: 1972
B. Unit of Analysis: town and reservation
C. Type of Data Used: primary and secondary
D. Major Variables:
   Economic: employment, poverty
   Demographic: characteristics of racial minorities
   Social: community pride
E. Researchers: Graham
F. Documents: 64

III. FIRM CHARACTERISTICS

Plant Product	No. of Plants	No. of Employees	Date of Location
Shiprock semiconductors	1	431-1,148	1965
Fort Defiance electronic components	1	140-244	1968
Fayette auto parts	1	34-60	1970

SKETCH NUMBER 65--OTHER AREAS

I. SITE CHARACTERISTICS

A. Location: Ozark Region: parts of Arkansas, Missouri, Kansas, Oklahoma (134 contiguous counties)

B. Community Size: villages with population of less than 2,500

II. RESEARCH CHARACTERISTICS

A. Period of Study: 1966-67
B. Unit of Analysis: region
C. Type of Data Used: primary and secondary
D. Major Variables:
    Economic: trickle-down and leakage of jobs, income, poverty
    Demographic: migration
    Social: poverty status
E. Researchers: Bender, Campbell, Green
F. Documents: 14, 15

III. FIRM CHARACTERISTICS

Plant Product	No. of Plants	Employees	Date of Location
not specified	not specified	not specified	not specified

SKETCH NUMBER 66--OTHER AREAS

I. SITE CHARACTERISTICS

A. Location: West Virginia: Morgantown; Illinois: Tuscola, Kankakee, 1 unnamed town; Missouri: 1 unnamed town

B. Community Size: Morgantown, 25,000; Tuscola, 3,000; Kankakee, 26,000; unnamed town, Illinois: 5,000; unnamed town, Missouri: 1,000

II. RESEARCH CHARACTERISTICS

A. Period of Study: 1954
B. Unit of Analysis: town and county
C. Type of Data Used: secondary

D. Major Variables:
    Economic: labor supply, labor force participation
    Demographic: migration
    Social: not studied
E. Researchers: Wilcock
F. Documents: 184

III. FIRM CHARACTERISTICS

Plant Product	No. of Plants	No. of Employees	Date of Location
chemicals	1	1,000 (approximate)	1951
petrochemicals	1	500 (approximate)	1953
shoes	2	400, 200	1950, 1952

SKETCH NUMBER 67--OTHER AREAS

I. SITE CHARACTERISTICS

A. Location: Alabama, Arkansas, Georgia, Idaho, Illinois,
    Kentucky, Louisiana, Michigan, Minnesota,
    Mississippi, Missouri, Nebraska, North Carolina,
    Pennsylvania, South Carolina, Tennessee, Texas:
    30 counties
B. Community Size: not stated

II. RESEARCH CHARACTERISTICS

A. Period of Study: 1954, 1962, 1973
B. Unit of Analysis: county
C. Type of Data Used: secondary
D. Major Variables:
    Economic: employment, private sector, income
    Demographic: population size
    Social: not studied
E. Researchers: Chamber of Commerce of the United States
F. Documents: 30, 31, 32

III. FIRM CHARACTERISTICS

Plant Product	No. of Plants	No. of Employees	Date of Location
not stated	not stated	not stated	not stated

SKETCH NUMBER 68--UNIDENTIFIED

I. SITE CHARACTERISTICS

   A. Location: A Middle Atlantic state: an unnamed town
   B. Community Size: town, 2,735 (approximate)

II. RESEARCH CHARACTERISTICS

   A. Period of Study: 1957
   B. Unit of Analysis: town
   C. Type of Data Used: primary and secondary
   D. Major Variables:
      Economic: housing, employment, private sector
      Demographic: population composition
      Social: social participation, social stratification, attitudes
   E. Researchers: Matz
   F. Documents: 107

III. FIRM CHARACTERISTICS

Plant Product	No. of Plants	No. of Employees	Date of Location
not specified	1	2,498	1939

SKETCH NUMBER 69--UNIDENTIFIED

I. SITE CHARACTERISTICS

   A. Location: not stated
   B. Community Size: town, 8,000; county, 13,000

II. RESEARCH CHARACTERISTICS

   A. Period of Study: 1971
   B. Unit of Analysis: town and county
   C. Type of Data Used: primary and secondary
   D. Major Variables:
      Economic: not studied
      Demographic: characteristics of job applicants,
                   commuting
      Social: not studied

    E. Researchers: Howard
    F. Documents: 79

III. FIRM CHARACTERISTICS

Plant Product	No. of Plants	No. of Employees	Date of Location
not specified	1	312	1970

SKETCH NUMBER 70--UNIDENTIFIED

I. SITE CHARACTERISTICS

    A. Location: U.S.: locations not specified
    B. Community Size: not stated

II. RESEARCH CHARACTERISTICS

    A. Period of Study: 1955
    B. Unit of Analysis: nation
    C. Type of Data Used: primary and secondary
    D. Major Variables:
        Economic: government revenues and expenditures
        Demographic: urban decentralization
        Social: not studied
    E. Researchers: Walker, M.
    F. Documents: 177

III. FIRM CHARACTERISTICS

Plant Product	No. of Plants	No. of Employees	Date of Location
not stated	not stated	not stated	not stated

SKETCH NUMBER 71--UNIDENTIFIED

I. SITE CHARACTERISTICS

    A. Location: 23 states: unspecified number of Indian
                      reservations
    B. Community Size: not stated

II. RESEARCH CHARACTERISTICS

    A. Period of Study: 1968
    B. Unit of Analysis: Indian reservation
    C. Type of Data Used: primary and secondary
    D. Major Variables:
        Economic: employment
        Demographic: characteristics of plant employees
        Social: not studied
    E. Researchers: Sorkin
    F. Documents: 152

III. FIRM CHARACTERISTICS

Plant Product	No. of Plants	No. of Employees	Date of Location
furniture, apparel, fishing equipment, wood products, costume jewelry, baskets, Indian artifacts, electronic components	total of 110	total of 8,487 (approximate)	1960–68

1. Abt Associates, Inc.
    1968 "The Industrialization of Southern Rural Areas: A
          Study of Industry and Federal Assistance in Small Towns
          with Recommendations for Future Policy." Washington,
          D.C.: U.S. Department of Commerce, Economic De-
          velopment Administration, Office of Economic Re-
          search. (56)

2. Andrews, R. B., I. V. Fine, A. C. Johnson, and E. E. Werner
    1959 "The Effects of Industrialization on Six Small Wisconsin
          Cities." Wisconsin Commerce Papers, vol. 2, no. 3.
          Madison, Wis.: Wisconsin Business Research Council
          Committee for Economic Development; University of
          Wisconsin, School of Commerce, Bureau of Business
          Research and Service.   (55)

3. Andrews, Wade H. and Ward W. Bauder
    1968 "The Effects of Industrialization on a Rural County:
          Comparisons of Social Change in Monroe and Noble
          Counties of Ohio." Department Series A.E. 407.
          Wooster, Ohio: Ohio Agricultural Research and Devel-
          opment Center. (37)

4. Andrews, Wade H., Ward W. Bauder, and Everett M. Rogers
    1960 "Benchmarks for Rural Industrialization . . . A Study
          of Rural Development in Monroe County, Ohio." Re-
          search Bulletin 870. Wooster, Ohio: Ohio Agricultural
          Experiment Station.   (37)

5. Arkansas Department of Labor, Employment Security Division
    1958 "The Effect of an Industry on a Small Rural Community:
          Byrd Manufacturing Corporation and Star City, Arkansas."
          Little Rock, Ark.: Reports and Analysis Section, Em-
          ployment Security Division, Arkansas Department of
          Labor.   (9)

6. Barnett, Donald C.
    1973 "Keeping the Folks Down on the Farm." Pacific
          Business (March/April): 39-40. Sacramento, Calif.:
          California Chamber of Commerce. (10)

7. Beck, Elwood M.
    1972 "A Study of Rural Industrial Development and Occupa-
          tional Mobility." Ph.D. dissertation, University of
          Tennessee. (11)

8. Beck, Elwood M.
    1972 "Industrial Development and Occupational Movers and
          Stayers." Working paper RID 72.17. Madison, Wis.:
          University of Wisconsin, Department of Rural Sociology,
          Center of Applied Sociology. (11)

9. Beck, Elwood M.
    1973 "A Canonical Approach to Assessing Occupational
          Mobility Matrices." Social Science Research 2: 247-56.
          (11)

10. Beck, Elwood M.
    1973 "Effects of Time on the Relationship Between Status of
          First Occupation and Current Occupational Status."
          Working paper RID 73.2. Madison, Wis.: University
          of Wisconsin, Department of Rural Sociology, Center
          of Applied Sociology. (11)

11. Beck, Elwood M., and Jennifer H. Madans
    1975 "On the Relationship Between Status of First Occupation
          and Current Occupational Status." Work and Sociology
          of Occupations 1, no. 4: 372-95.

12. Beck, Elwood M., Louis Dotson, and Gene F. Summers
    1973 "Effects of Industrial Development on Heads of House-
          holds." Growth and Change 4: 16-19. (11)

13. Beck, Elwood M., and Gene F. Summers
    1973 "Industrial Development and Changes in Occupational
          Structures." Working paper RID 73.11. Madison,
          Wis.: University of Wisconsin, Department of Rural
          Sociology, Center of Applied Sociology. (11)

14. Bender, Lloyd, Bernal L. Green, and Rex R. Campbell
    1973 "Ghettos of Poverty in the Ozarks." Planning 39, no.
          7: 13-15. (65)

15. Bender, Lloyd, Bernal Green, and Rex R. Campbell
    1971 "Trickle-Down and Leakage in the War on Poverty."
          Growth and Change 2, no. 4: 34-41. (65)

16. Bertrand, Alvin L., and Harold W. Osborne
    1959a "Rural Industrialization in a Louisiana Community."
           Bulletin No. 524. Baton Rouge, La.: Louisiana State
           University, Agricultural Experiment Station. (21)

17. Bertrand, Alvin L., and Harold W. Osborne
    1959b "The Impact of Industrialization on a Rural Community."
           Journal of Farm Economics 41, no. 5: 1127-34. (21)

18. Bertrand, Alvin L., and Harold W. Osborne
    1960   "Rural Industrialization: A Situational Analysis."
           Rural Sociology 25, no. 4: 387-93. (21)

19. Bertrand, Alvin L., Paul H. Price, and Harold W. Osborne
    1958   "The Impact of Industrial Development on Rural Levels
           of Living (a Study of Plant Employees in a Sample Area
           in Rural Louisiana)." Mimeographed. Baton Rouge,
           La.: Louisiana State University, Department of Rural
           Sociology. (21)

20. Black, Therel R., Carmen Fredrickson, and Sheridan T. Maitland
    1960   "Industrialization of Box Elder County." Agricultural
           Experiment Station Bulletin 420. Logan, Utah: Utah
           State University. (50)

21. Borgmeyer, William R.
    1971   "A Comparison of Two Non-Metro Growth Centers in
           Missouri." Norman, Okla.: University of Oklahoma,
           Industrial Development Institute (American Industrial
           Development Council thesis). (30)

22. Brady, Guy, Jr.
    1974   "The Economic Impact of Industrialization on a Rural
           Town Economy; Wynne, Arkansas." Master's thesis,
           University of Arkansas. (4)

23. Brann, W. Paul
    1964   "Helena, West Helena, Arkansas: A Case Study in
           Economic Readjustment." In Community Economic
           Development Efforts: Five Case Studies. Supplemen-
           tary paper no. 18. New York: Committee for Eco-
           nomic Development. (8)

24. Brinkman, George
    1973   "Effects of Industrializing Small Communities." Journal

of Community Development Society 4, no. 1: 69-80.
(7, 12, 13, 20, 29, 40, 43)

25. Bucher, Norman J.
    1970 "Spending Habits of Manufacturing Workers." Special
    Report no. 6. Office of Industrial Development Studies,
    University of Missouri. Jefferson City, Mo.: Missouri
    Division of Commerce and Industrial Development. (61)

26. Bucher, Norman J.
    1971 "Impact of New Industrial Plants: Eight Case Studies."
    Office of Industrial Development Studies, University of
    Missouri. Jefferson City, Mo.: Missouri Division of
    Commerce and Industrial Development. (61)

27. Bureau of Population and Economic Research
    1956 "The Impact of Industry in a Southern Rural County:
    Changes in Road Use, Travel Habits and Socioeconomic
    Characteristics in Charlotte County, Virginia, Five
    Years After the Establishment of a New Manufacturing
    Plant." Bureau of Population and Economic Research,
    University of Virginia. Richmond, Va.: Virginia De-
    partment of Highways. (51)

28. Calef, Wesley C., and Charles Daoust
    1955 "A Summary of Two Case Studies on the Impact of New
    Industry on Small Towns: What Will New Industry Mean
    to My Town?" Washington, D.C.: U.S. Chamber of
    Commerce, Office of Technical Services, Area Devel-
    opment Division. (22)

29. Carroll, John J., and Seymour Sacks
    1962 "The Property Tax Base and the Pattern of Local Gov-
    ernment Expenditures: The Influence of Industry."
    In Papers and Proceedings of the Regional Science
    Association, vol. 9. (32)

30. Chamber of Commerce of the United States, Economic Research
    Department
    1960 "What New Industrial Jobs Mean to a Community."
    Washington, D.C.: U.S. Chamber of Commerce. (67)

31. Chamber of Commerce of the United States, Economic Analysis
    and Study.
    1968 "What New Industrial Jobs Mean to a Community."
    Washington, D.C.: U.S. Chamber of Commerce. (67)

32. Chamber of Commerce of the United States, Economic Analysis
     and Study
          1973   "What New Jobs Mean to a Community." Washington,
                   D.C.: U.S. Chamber of Commerce.   (67)

33. Chen, Chong-Tong
          1972   "Impact of Industrialization on Farm Organization in
                   North-Central Illinois." Ph.D. dissertation, Uni-
                   versity of Illinois.   (11)

34. Chen, Chong-Tong, and John T. Scott, Jr.
          1973   "Stochastic Analysis of Occupational Mobility of Labor
                   in a Rural Area." Department of Agricultural Eco-
                   nomics, Report no. AE-4317. Urbana-Champaign,
                   Ill.: University of Illinois.   (11)

35. Christiansen, John R., Sheridan Maitland, and John W. Payne
          1959   "Industrialization and Rural Life in Two Central Utah
                   Counties." Bulletin 416, Utah Agricultural Experi-
                   ment Station. Logan, Utah: Utah State University.
                   (49)

36. Clark, John P., Gene F. Summers, and Richard L. Hough
          1968   "Perceptions of Social Control in a Rural Area."
                   Working paper no. 68.1. Madison, Wis.: University
                   of Wisconsin, Department of Rural Sociology, Center
                   of Applied Sociology.   (11)

37. Clemente, Frank
          1973   "Effects of Industrial Development on Heads of House-
                   holds: Comment." Growth and Change 4: 20-21. (11)

38. Clemente, Frank, Dean Rojek, and E. M. Beck
          1974   "Trade Patterns and Community Identity: Five Years
                   Later." Rural Sociology 39: 92-95.   (11)

39. Clemente, Frank, and Gene F. Summers
          1972   "Rapid Industrial Development and the Relative Status
                   of the Sexes." Working paper RID 72.15. Madison,
                   Wis.: University of Wisconsin, Department of Rural
                   Sociology, Center of Applied Sociology.   (11)

40. Clemente, Frank, and Gene F. Summers
          1973a   "A Comment on Palmore and Whittington's Relative
                   Status of the Aged." Social Forces 51: 494-95.   (11)

41. Clemente, Frank, and Gene F. Summers
    1973b "An Exploratory Note on Family Status and Work-
           Residence Separation." Working paper RID 73.14.
           Madison, Wis.: University of Wisconsin, Department
           of Rural Sociology, Center of Applied Sociology. (11)

42. Clemente, Frank, and Gene F. Summers
    1973c "Industrial Development and the Elderly: A Longi-
           tudinal Analysis." Journal of Gerontology 28, no. 4:
           479-83. (11)

43. Clemente, Frank, and Gene F. Summers
    1973d "Large Industries in Small Towns: Who Benefits?"
           Working paper RID 73.9. Madison, Wis.: University
           of Wisconsin, Department of Rural Sociology, Center
           of Applied Sociology. (11)

44. Clemente, Frank, and Gene F. Summers
    1973e "Rural Industrial Development and Commuting Pat-
           terns." Working paper RID 73.15. Madison, Wis.:
           University of Wisconsin, Department of Rural Soci-
           ology, Center of Applied Sociology. (11)

45. Clemente, Frank, and Gene F. Summers
    1974   "Age and the Journey to Work." The Gerontologist 14.
           (11)

46. Clemente, Frank, and Gene F. Summers
    1975   "The Journey to Work of Rural Industrial Employees:
           A Test of the Metropolitan Model of Commuting."
           Social Forces 54, no. 1: 212-19. (11)

47. Crecink, John C.
    1970   "Rural Industrialization: Case Study of a Tissue Paper
           Mill in Pickens, Miss." Agricultural Economic Report
           no. 189. Washington, D.C.: United States Depart-
           ment of Agriculture, Economic Research Service. (27)

48. Daoust, Charles F.
    1954   "Transition in Central Michigan: Agriculture to In-
           dustry." Master's thesis, University of Chicago. (22)

49. Darroch, Dorothy
    1969   "Some Determinants of Social Distance." Working
           paper no. 69.1. Madison, Wis.: University of

Wisconsin, Department of Rural Sociology, Center of
Applied Sociology.   (11)

50. Darroch, Dorothy, and Gene F. Summers
     1969   "Power and Prejudice." Working paper no. 69.2.
             Madison, Wis.: University of Wisconsin, Department
             of Rural Sociology, Center of Applied Sociology.   (11)

51. Davis, James Nathaniel, Jr.
     1963   "Effects of Industrialization upon the Economy of
             Searcy, Arkansas: A Case Study." Ph.D. disserta-
             tion, University of Arkansas.   (1, 3)

52. Debes, Leroy J.
     1973   "The Impact of Industrialization upon Real Estate in
             Parsons, Kansas." Master's thesis, Kansas State
             University.   (16)

53. DeMartini, Joseph
     1968   "Social Control in Iroquois County." Working paper
             no. 68.2. Madison, Wis.: University of Wisconsin,
             Department of Rural Sociology, Center of Applied
             Sociology.   (11)

54. Dietz, John Leslie
     1971   "Tractors to Capacitors: An Analysis of the Impact
             of New Manufacturing Plants on Small Agricultural
             Communities in the Northern Great Plains." Ph.D.
             dissertation, Syracuse University.   (60)

55. Dietz, John Leslie
     1972   "Rural Area Development: Analysis of the Impact of
             New Factories on Agricultural Towns in the Northern
             Great Plains." Great Plains-Rocky Mountain Geo-
             graphical Journal 1: 19-25.   (60)

56. Durant, Thomas J., Jr.
     1973   "The Impact of Industrial Development on the Farm
             Enterprise." Ph.D. dissertation, University of
             Wisconsin.   (11)

57. Erickson, William L.
     1969   "Alienation, Participation and Environmental Satis-
             faction: A Path Analysis." Master's thesis, Univer-
             sity of Illinois.   (11)

58. Funk, Herbert Joseph
    1964   "Effects of a New Manufacturing Plant on Business
            Firms in an Eastern Iowa Community." Ph.D. dis-
            sertation, Iowa State University.   (14)

59. Garrison, Charles B.
    1967   "Economic Impact of New Industry on Small Towns."
            Ph.D. dissertation, University of Kentucky.   (19)

60. Garrison, Charles B.
    1970   "The Impact of New Industry on Local Government
            Finances in Five Small Towns in Kentucky." Agricul-
            tural Economic Report no. 191. Washington, D.C.:
            U.S. Department of Agriculture, Economic Research
            Service.   (19)

61. Garrison, Charles B.
    1971   "New Industry in Small Towns: The Impact on Local
            Government." National Tax Journal 24, no. 4:
            493-500.   (19)

62. Garrison, Charles B.
    1972   "The Impact of New Industry: An Application of the
            Economic Base Multiplier to Small Rural Areas."
            Land Economics 47, no. 4: 329-37.   (19)

63. Garth, John
    1953   "When Big Business Comes to a Country Town: Why
            Alcoa Spent $80,000,000 Near Rockdale, Texas."
            American Business 23, no. 3: 26-27, 37-40.   (47)

64. Graham, David Ralph
    1973   "The Role of Business in the Economic Redevelopment
            of the Rural Community." Research Monograph no.
            36. Austin, Tex.: University of Texas, Bureau of
            Business Research, Graduate School of Business.   (64)

65. Gray, Irwin
    1969   "Employment Effect of a New Industry in a Rural Area."
            Monthly Labor Review 92, no. 6: 26-30.   (53)

66. Gray, Ralph
    1962   "Community Impact of New Industry." Arkansas
            Economist 4, no. 3: 17-24.   (6)

67. Haga, William J., and Clinton L. Folse
    1971   "Trade Patterns and Community Identity." Rural
            Sociology 36, no. 1: 42-51.   (11)

68. Hagerman, L. Dale, and Curtis H. Braschler
    1966   "Part One: An Analysis of the Impact of Industrializa-
            tion on a Small Town Economy. A Case Study of Ava,
            Missouri. Part Two: The Impact of Industrialization
            of a Small Town on Local Government. A Case Study
            of Ava, Missouri." Research Bulletin no. 910. Re-
            search Project 507. Columbia, Mo.: University of
            Missouri, Department of Agricultural Economics.   (29)

69. Helgeson, Delmer L., and Maurice J. Zink
    1973   "A Case Study of Rural Industrialization in Jamestown,
            North Dakota." Agricultural Economics Report no. 95.
            Fargo, N. Dak.: North Dakota State University, De-
            partment of Agricultural Economics, Agricultural
            Experiment Station.   (36)

70. Holley, Cynthia N.
    1973   "Religious Commitment and Psychosomatic Impair-
            ment." Master's thesis, University of South Florida,
            Department of Sociology.   (11)

71. Hoover, Herbert
    n.d.a. "Rural Industrialization in West Virginia: Case Study
            of a New Particle Board Plant in Braxton County,
            West Virginia." Washington, D.C.: U.S. Department
            of Agriculture, Economic Research Service, Economic
            Development Division.   (52)

72. Hoover, Herbert
    n.d.a. "Rural Industrialization in Kentucky: Case Study of a
            New Bedding Plant at Munfordville, Kentucky."
            Washington, D.C.: U.S. Department of Agriculture,
            Economic Research Service, Economic Development
            Division.   (20)

73. Hough, Richard L.
    1968   "Religion and Social Integration in a Rural American
            Setting." Master's thesis, University of Illinois.   (11)

74. Hough, Richard L.
    1969   "Structural Stress, Anomia and Psychological Disorder."
            Ph.D. dissertation, University of Illinois.   (11)

75. Hough, Richard L., E. M. Beck, and Gene F. Summers
    1972   "Status Inconsistency: A Two-Step Regression Ap-
            proach." Working paper no. 72.10. Madison, Wis.:
            University of Wisconsin, Department of Rural Sociol-
            ogy, Center of Applied Sociology. (11)

76. Hough, Richard L., and John P. Clark
    1969   "Some Determinants of Attitudes Toward Industriali-
            zation in a Rural Community." Working paper no.
            69.3. Madison, Wis.: University of Wisconsin, De-
            partment of Rural Sociology, Center of Applied
            Sociology. (11)

77. Hough, Richard L., and Gene F. Summers
    1970   "Structural Stress and Psychological Impairment."
            Working paper no. 70.1. Madison, Wis.: University
            of Wisconsin, Department of Rural Sociology, Center
            of Applied Sociology. (11)

78. Hough, Richard L., Gene F. Summers, and James O'Meara
    1969   "Parental Influence, Youth Contraculture and Rural
            Adolescent Attitudes Toward Minority Groups."
            Rural Sociology 34: 383-86. (11)

79. Howard, William C.
    1973   "The Staffing Experience of a New Industrial Plant:
            A New Technique for Determining Manpower Avail-
            ability and Characteristics." Norman, Okla.: Uni-
            versity of Oklahoma, Industrial Development Institute
            (American Industrial Development Council thesis). (69)

80. Irwin, Thomas K., II
    1965   "Benefits Derived by Banks from Industrial Growth."
            Norman, Okla.: University of Oklahoma, Industrial
            Development Institute (American Industrial Develop-
            ment Council thesis). (18)

81. Johnson, Doyle Paul
    1968   "Social Control in the Hennepin Area." Working paper
            no. 68.4. Madison, Wis.: University of Wisconsin,
            Department of Rural Sociology, Center of Applied
            Sociology. (11)

82. Johnson, Doyle Paul
    1969   "The Response of Clergymen to Industrial Development."
            Ph.D. dissertation, University of Illinois. (11)

83. Johnson, Doyle Paul
     1972   "Social Class and Attitudinal Vs. Behavioral Religios-
             ity." Working paper no. 72.2. Madison, Wis.: Uni-
             versity of Wisconsin, Department of Rural Sociology,
             Center of Applied Sociology. (11)

84. Johnson, Doyle Paul, and Gene F. Summers
     1971   "Industrial Development and Goal Modification in
             Church Congregations." Working paper no. 71.2.
             Madison, Wis.: University of Wisconsin, Department
             of Rural Sociology, Center of Applied Sociology. (11)

85. Johnson, Maxine C.
     1960   "The Effects of the Anaconda Aluminum Company Plant
             on Flathead County, Montana." Regional Study no. 12.
             Missoula, Mont.: Montana State University, School of
             Business Administration, Bureau of Business and Eco-
             nomic Research. (31)

86. Jordan, Max F.
     1967   "Rural Industrialization in the Ozarks: Case Study of
             a New Shirt Plant at Gassville, Arkansas." Agricul-
             tural Economic Report no. 123. Washington, D.C.:
             U.S. Department of Agriculture, Economic Research
             Service. (7)

87. Kaldor, Donald R., and Ward W. Bauder
     1963   "What Happens When . . . New Industry Comes to a
             Rural Community?" Iowa Farm Science 18, no. 5:
             3-559. (14)

88. Kaldor, Donald R., Ward W. Bauder, and Marvin W. Trautwein
     1964   "Impact of New Industry on an Iowa Rural Community.
             Part 1. Farming and Farm Living." Special Report
             no. 37. Department of Economics and Sociology,
             Center for Agricultural and Economic Development.
             Ames, Iowa: Iowa State University, Agricultural and
             Home Economics Experiment Station. (14)

89. Kaldor, Donald, and Mike Dahlke
     1973   "Industrial Efforts and Experiences in Iowa's Rural
             Communities." Rural Development Special Series.
             Ames, Iowa: Iowa State University, Center for Agri-
             cultural and Rural Development. (15)

90. Kayser, Brian D.
     1971   "Educational Aspirations: Markov and Poisson Models."
            Master's thesis, University of Minnesota.   (11)

91. Kayser, Brian D.
     1972a "Educational Aspirations on Rural High School Students:
            A Markovian Approach Using Independent Variables and
            Panel Data." Ph.D. dissertation, University of
            Minnesota. (11)

92. Kayser, Brian D.
     1972b "Religious Identification and Changes in Achievement
            Motivation: A Panel Study." Working paper no. 72.1.
            Madison, Wis.: University of Wisconsin, Department
            of Rural Sociology, Center of Applied Sociology. (11)

93. Kayser, Brian D.
     1972c "The Change in Educational Aspirations Over Time."
            Working paper no. 72.4. Madison, Wis.: University
            of Wisconsin, Department of Rural Sociology, Center
            of Applied Sociology. (11)

94. Kayser, Brian D.
     1973a "Educational Aspirations as a Stochastic Process."
            Working paper no. 73.16. Madison, Wis.: University
            of Wisconsin, Department of Rural Sociology, Center
            of Applied Sociology. (11)

95. Kayser, Brian D.
     1973b "The Maintenance of Educational Aspirations Over
            Time: A Longitudinal Study." Working paper no.
            73.12. Madison, Wis.: University of Wisconsin, De-
            partment of Rural Sociology, Center of Applied Sociol-
            ogy. (11)

96. Kayser, Brian D., and Gene F. Summers
     1974   "The Stability of Adolescent Personality Characteris-
            tics." Working paper no. 74.2. Madison, Wis.:
            University of Wisconsin, Department of Rural Sociol-
            ogy, Center of Applied Sociology. (11)

97. Klein, William E., Jr.
     1959   "The Effect of Local Industrialization in a Rural Low-
            Income County." Master's thesis, Oklahoma State
            University. (39)

98. Klimasewski, Theodore
    1974   "The Significance of Manufacturing Activity in a Rural
           Area in East Tennessee." Ph.D. dissertation, Uni-
           versity of Tennessee.   (45)

99. Kuehn, John A., Lloyd D. Bender, Bernal L. Green, and
    Herbert Hoover
    1972   "Impact of Job Development on Poverty in Four De-
           veloping Areas, 1970." Agricultural Economic Report
           no. 225. Washington, D.C.: U.S. Department of
           Agriculture, Economic Research Service.   (4, 63)

100. Lonsdale, Richard E.
     1966   "Two North Carolina Commuting Patterns." Economic
            Geography 42, no. 2: 114-38.   (34)

101. McArthur, J'Wayne, and Robert O. Coppedge
     1969   "Employment Impacts of Industrial Development: A
            Case Study of Box Elder County, Utah, from 1950 to
            1966." Utah Economic and Business Review 29, no.
            2: 1-6, 9-10. Salt Lake City: University of Utah,
            College of Business, Bureau of Economic and Busi-
            ness Research.   (50)

102. McElveen, Jackson V.
     1970   "Rural Industrialization in the Southeast Coastal Plain:
            Case Study of a New Brick Factory in Summerville,
            South Carolina." Agricultural Economic Report no.
            174. Washington, D.C.: U.S. Department of Agri-
            culture, Economic Research Service.   (43)

103. Maitland, Sheridan, and James Cowhig.
     1958   "Research on the Effects of Industrialization in Rural
            Areas." Monthly Labor Review 81, no. 10: 1121-24.
            (14, 21, 28, 37, 49, 50)

104. Maitland, Sheridan, and Reed E. Friend
     1961   "Rural Industrialization: A Summary of Five Studies."
            Agriculture Information Bulletin no. 252. Washington,
            D.C.: U.S. Department of Agriculture, Economic Re-
            search Service.   (13, 21, 28, 49, 50)

105. Maitland, Sheridan, and George L. Wilber
     1958   "Industrialization in Chickasaw County, Mississippi:
            A Study of Plant Workers." Bulletin 566. State

College, Miss.: Mississippi State University, Mississippi Agricultural Experiment Station. (28)

106. Martin, Joe A.
1960   "The Impact of Industrial Development upon Agriculture. Lawrence County: A Progress Report on Industrial Development in a Rural Area of Special Interest to Farmers and Community Leaders." Progress report no. 33, Tennessee Farm and Home Science. Knoxville: University of Tennessee, Agricultural Experiment Station. (46)

107. Matz, Earl Luke
1957   "The Impact of a Large Industrial Plant upon a Small Agrarian Community." Ph.D. dissertation, Ohio State University. (68)

108. Merrill, Kenneth E., and David L. Ryther
1961   "Plant Location and Community Changes." Kansas Business Review 14, no. 7: 10-13. (17)

109. Merrill, Kenneth E., and David L. Ryther
1961   "Plant Location and Community Changes." Lawrence, Kans.: University of Kansas, Center for Research in Business. (17)

110. Metz, Donald C.
1968   "A Study of Industrial Branch Plants in the Countryside of Minnesota." Marshall, Minn.: Southwest Minnesota State College, Division of Engineering Technology. (24)

111. Miernyk, William H.
1971   "Local Labor Market Effects of New Plant Locations." In Essays in Regional Economics. Edited by John F. Kain and John R. Meyer. Cambridge, Mass.: Harvard University Press. (14, 21, 28, 49, 50, 53, 62)

112. Miller, Daniel Frank
1967   "The Influence of Industrialization and the Buying Habits of Industrial Employees, Tarboro, North Carolina." Greenville, N.C.: Eastern North Carolina University, Eastern North Carolina Development Institute. (35)

113. Morris, Robert Bremner, Jr.
    1960   "The Economic Effect of a New Industry on a Small
            City." Master's thesis, Massachusetts Institute of
            Technology.   (23)

114. Niagara Mohawk Power Corporation
    1967   "A Report: Impact of a Manufacturing Plant on the
            Economy of an Upstate Community." Niagara Mohawk
            Power Corporation.   (33)

115. Olsen, Duane A., and John A. Kuehn
    1974   "Migrant Response to Industrialization in Four Rural
            Areas, 1965-70." Agricultural Economic Report no.
            270. Washington, D.C.: U.S. Department of Agricul-
            ture, Economic Research Service, in cooperation with
            the University of Missouri Agricultural Experiment
            Station.   (63)

116. Osborne, Harold W.
    1959   "The Impact of a Village Factory on a Selected Area
            of Rural Louisiana." Ph.D. dissertation, Louisiana
            State University.   (21)

117. Paden, David, Donald Krist, and Michael Seaton
    1972   "Impact of Industrial Development on Selected Iowa
            Communities." Final report. Ames, Iowa: Iowa
            Development Commission.   (15)

118. Peterson, John M., and Earl Wright
    1967   "Dynamics of Small Area Labor Supply: A Case Study."
            Little Rock, Ark.: University of Arkansas, Industrial
            Research and Extension Center, College of Business
            Administration, Publication H-18.   (1, 63)

119. Peterson, John M.
    1974   "Effects of Rural Industrialization on Labor Demand
            and Employment." In Rural Industrialization: Prob-
            lems and Potentials. Edited by Larry R. Whiting.
            Ames, Iowa: Iowa State University Press.   (1, 63)

120. Pittman, B. W.
    1965   "Industrial Development in an Agricultural Economy--
            A Study of Industrial Growth in Leflore County,
            Mississippi." Norman, Okla.: University of Okla-
            homa, Industrial Development Institute (American In-
            dustrial Development Council thesis).   (26)

121. Plaxico, James Samuel
    1947   "Some Economic Aspects of Rural Industrialization."
            Master's thesis, Clemson Agricultural College.   (42)

122. Pray, Hubert Q.
    1965   "Impact of Industrial Growth on the Labor Force of
            Washington County, Mississippi, 1950-1963." Norman,
            Okla.: University of Oklahoma, Industrial Develop-
            ment Institute (American Industrial Development Coun-
            cil thesis).   (25)

123. Ramana, K. V.
    1968   "Industrialization and Social Change in the Hennepin
            Area." Working paper no. 68.3. Madison, Wis.:
            University of Wisconsin, Department of Rural Sociol-
            ogy, Center of Applied Sociology.   (11)

124. Rathburn, Arthur C.
    1972   "Industrial Development Process in Willamette Valley,
            Oregon: Three Cases." Portland, Ore.: Oregon
            State University. (Mimeographed paper).   (41)

125. Rinehart, James R.
    1963   "Rates of Return on Municipal Subsidies to Industry."
            The Southern Economic Journal 24, no. 4: 297-306.
            (59)

126. Ritzenthaler, Robert E.
    1953   "The Impact of Small Industry on an Indian Community."
            American Anthropologist 55, no. 1: 143-48.   (54)

127. Rojek, Dean G.
    1973   "The Social and Psychological Consequences of Intra-
            generational Mobility." Working paper no. 73.4.
            Madison, Wis.: University of Wisconsin, Department
            of Rural Sociology, Center of Applied Sociology.   (11)

128. Rojek, Dean G., Frank Clemente, and Gene F. Summers
    1974   "Community Satisfaction in a Rural Setting: Dimension-
            ality and Correlates." Working paper RID 74.1.
            Madison, Wis.: University of Wisconsin, Department
            of Rural Sociology, Center of Applied Sociology.   (11)

129. Ryan, Robert H., Charles T. Clark, and L. L. Schkade
    1963   "Paris, Texas, from Farm to Factory." Area Eco-

nomic Survey no. 14. Austin, Tex.: University of
Texas, Bureau of Business Research. (48)

130. Saltzman, Lloyd R.
       1964   "Economic Case Studies of Community Sponsored Ef-
              forts to Develop Industry." Tulsa, Okla.: University
              of Tulsa. (38)

131. Schneiderman, James A.
       1971   "The Impact of Rural Industrial Development on Agri-
              cultural Land Use and Labor Mobility." Master's
              thesis, Illinois State University.

132. Scott, John T., Jr.
       1968   "Economic Impact of Industrialization on Traditional
              Rural Areas." Journal of the American Society of
              Farm Managers and Rural Appraisers 32, no. 2: 8-13.
              (11)

133. Scott, John T., Jr.
       1973   "Profile Change When Industry Moves into a Rural
              Area." Working paper RID 73.7. Madison, Wis.:
              University of Wisconsin, Department of Rural Sociol-
              ogy, Center of Applied Sociology. (11)

134. Scott, John T., Jr., and C. T. Chen
       1973   "Expected Changes in Farm Organization When Indus-
              try Moves into a Rural Area." Illinois Agricultural
              Economics (January): 41-47. (11)

135. Scott, John T., Jr., and Gene F. Summers
       1974   "Problems in Rural Communities after Industry
              Arrives." In Rural Industrialization: Problems and
              Potentials. Edited by Larry R. Whiting. Ames, Iowa:
              Iowa State University Press, for the North Central
              Regional Center for Rural Development. Reprinted in
              U.S. Senate, Committee on Agriculture and Forestry,
              Subcommittee on Rural Development. Rural Indus-
              trialization: Prospects, Problems, Impacts, and
              Methods. Committee print (April 19, 1974). (11)

136. Scott, John T., and P. L. Wahi
       1972   "Factors Affecting Labor Supply in an Industrializing
              Rural Area." Working paper RID 72.6. Madison, Wis.:
              University of Wisconsin, Department of Sociology, Cen-
              ter of Applied Sociology. (11)

137. Seiler, Lauren H.
    1970   "Social Structure and Anomie: Social Isolation as 'Retreatism'." Ph.D. dissertation, University of Illinois. (11)

138. Seiler, Lauren H.
    1974   "Community Verticalization: On the Interface between Corporate Influence and Horizontal Leadership." Working paper no. 74.3. Madison, Wis.: University of Wisconsin, Department of Rural Sociology, Center of Applied Sociology. (11)

139. Seiler, Lauren H., and Gene F. Summers
    1974a   "Locating Community Boundaries: An Integration of Theory and Empirical Research." Sociological Methods and Research 2, no. 3: 259-80. (11)

140. Seiler, Lauren H., and Gene F. Summers
    1974b   "Toward an Interpretation of Items Used in Field Studies of Mental Illness." Social Science and Medicine 8, no. 8: 459-67. (11)

141. Shaffer, Ronald Earl
    1972   "The Net Economic Impact of New Industry on Rural Communities in Eastern Oklahoma." Ph.D. dissertation, Oklahoma State University. (40)

142. Shaffer, Ronald, and Luther Tweeten
    1972   "Net Economic Impact of New Industry on Rural Communities with Emphasis on the Cost of Industrialization." In 1972 Proceedings of the Western Agricultural Economics Association. Edited by Samuel H. Logan. Logan, Utah: Utah State University. (40)

143. Shaffer, Ronald E.
    1973   "Estimating the Economic Spillovers of Industrial Expansion in Rural Areas." Madison, Wis.: University of Wisconsin-Extension, Department of Agricultural Economics. (40)

144. Shaffer, Ronald E.
    1974   "Rural Industrialization: A Local Income Analysis." Southern Journal of Agricultural Economics 6, no. 1: 97-102. (40)

145. Shaffer, Ronald E.
    n.d.   "Net Income and Employment Effects of New Industry on Rural Counties and Communities in Eastern Oklahoma." Mimeographed. Madison, Wis.: University of Wisconsin, Department of Agricultural Economics. (40)

146. Shaffer, Ronald E., and Luther G. Tweeten
    1974   "Economic Changes from Industrial Development in Eastern Oklahoma." Bulletin B-715. Stillwater, Okla.: Oklahoma State University, Agricultural Experiment Station.   (40)

147. Shaffer, Ronald, and Luther Tweeten
    1974   "Measuring the Net Economic Changes from Rural Industrial Development in Oklahoma." Journal of Land Economics 50: 261-71.   (40)

148. Shasta County Economic Development Corporation
    1973   "Overall Economic Development Program Progress Report." Redding, Calif.: Economic Development Corporation of Shasta County.   (10)

149. Sizer, Leonard M., and William B. Clifford
    1966   "Rural Industrialization: A Case Study in Educational Values and Attitudes." Bulletin No. 521. Morgantown, W. Va.: West Virginia University, Agricultural Experiment Station.   (53)

150. Sizer, Leonard M., and Edward A. Smith
    n.d.   "Toward an Integration of Migration and Location Theory." Mimeographed. Morgantown, W. Va.: Department of Sociology, Agricultural Experiment Station.   (53)

151. Somers, Gerald
    1958   "Labor Recruitment in a Depressed Rural Area." Monthly Labor Review 81, no. 10: 1113-20.   (53)

152. Sorkin, Alan L.
    1969   "American Indians Industrialize to Combat Poverty." Monthly Labor Review 92, no. 3: 19-25.   (71)

153. Stengel, Kathryn Brooke
    1970   "Rural Trade Patterns: An Examination of Reilly's Law." Master's thesis, University of Illinois.   (11)

154. Stepp, J. M., and J. S. Plaxico
  1948   "The Labor Supply of a Rural Industry: A Case Study
          of the McCormick (S. C.) Spinning Mill." Bulletin 376.
          Clemson, S.C.: Clemson Agricultural College, Agri-
          cultural Experiment Station.   (42)

155. Stevens, J. B., and L. T. Wallace
  1964   "Impact of Industrial Development on Howard County,
          Indiana, 1947-1960." Research Bulletin no. 784.
          Lafayette, Ind.: Purdue University, Agricultural Ex-
          periment Station.   (13)

156. Stuart, Alfred W.
  1971   "Rural Industrialization and Population Growth: The
          Case of Arkansas." Civil Defense Research Project
          ORNL-AUD-4. Oak Ridge, Tenn.: Oak Ridge National
          Laboratory.   (5)

157. Summers, Gene F.
  1973   "Large Industry in a Rural Area: Demographic, Eco-
          nomic and Social Impacts." Working paper no. 73.19.
          Final report to the Office of Economic Research, Eco-
          nomic Development Administration, U.S. Department
          of Commerce. Madison, Wis.: University of Wis-
          consin, Department of Rural Sociology, Center of Ap-
          plied Sociology. (Available from the National Techni-
          cal Information Service, no. COM-74-10214.) Re-
          printed in U.S. Senate, Committee on Agriculture and
          Forestry, Subcommittee on Rural Development. Rural
          Industrialization: Prospects, Problems, Impacts, and
          Methods. Committee print (April 19, 1974).   (11)

158. Summers, Gene F.
  1974   "A Social System Perspective of Rural Industrial De-
          velopment." Working paper no. 74.4. Madison, Wis.:
          University of Wisconsin, Department of Rural Sociol-
          ogy, Center of Applied Sociology.   (11)

159. Summers, Gene F., and Elwood M. Beck, Jr.
  1972   "Industrial Development and Urbanization: A U.S.
          Case." Working paper RID 72.8. Madison, Wis.:
          University of Wisconsin, Department of Rural
          Sociology, Center of Applied Sociology.   (11)

160. Summers, Gene F., Marianne Burke, Suzanne Saltiel, and
     John P. Clark
     1971   "Stability of the Structure of Work Orientations Among
            High School Students." Multivariate Behavioral Re-
            search 6: 35-50.   (11)

161. Summers, Gene F., and Frank Clemente
     1973   "Rapid Industrial Development, Competition, and
            Relative Economic Status: A Study in Human Ecology."
            Working paper RID 73.10. Madison, Wis.: University
            of Wisconsin, Department of Rural Sociology, Center
            of Applied Sociology.   (11)

162. Summers, Gene F., Richard L. Hough, Doyle P. Johnson,
     and Kathryn A. Veatch
     1970   "Ascetic Protestantism and Political Preference: A
            Re-Examination." Review of Religious Research 12:
            17-25.   (11)

163. Summers, Gene F., Richard L. Hough, John T. Scott, Jr.,
     and Clinton L. Folse
     1969   "Before Industrialization: A Rural Social System Base
            Study." Bulletin 736. Urbana-Champaign, Ill.: Uni-
            versity of Illinois, Agricultural Experiment Station.
            (11)

164. Summers, Gene F., Lauren H. Seiler, and Richard L. Hough
     1969   "Psychiatric Symptoms and the Use of Mental Health
            Services." Working paper no. 69.6. Madison, Wis.:
            University of Wisconsin, Department of Rural Sociol-
            ogy, Center of Applied Sociology.   (11)

165. Summers, Gene F., Lauren H. Seiler, and Richard L. Hough
     1971   "Psychiatric Symptoms: Cross-Validation with a Rural
            Sample." Rural Sociology 36: 367-78.   (1)

166. Summers, Gene F., Lauren H. Seiler, and Glenn Wiley
     1970   "Validation of Reputational Leadership by the Multitrait-
            Multimethod Matrix." In Sociological Methodology.
            Edited by E. F. Borgatta and G. W. Bohrnstedt. San
            Francisco: Jossey-Bass.   (11)

167. Summers, Gene F., Ronald Shaffer, Frank Clemente, and
     James L. Moore
     1973   "Social and Economic Effects of Industrial Develop-
            ment." In Information Methods and Procedures for

the Evaluation of the Environmental Effects of Industrial Development. Edited by James L. Moore. Madison, Wis.: University of Wisconsin, School of Natural Resources. (11)

168. Tennessee Town and City
    1957   "Rx for Prosperity: Cash Register Hums. Lawrence County's Out-Migration Grinds to a Halt as New Plants Put Men to Work." Vol. 8. (46)

169. Till, Thomas E., Jr.
    1972   "Rural Industrialization and Southern Rural Poverty: Patterns of Labor Demand in Southern Non-Metropolitan Labor Markets and Their Impact on the Poor, 1959-1969." Ph.D. dissertation, University of Texas. (58)

170. Trautwein, Marvin W.
    1961   "Effects of Industrialization on the Agriculture of an Eastern Iowa Community." Ph.D. dissertation, Iowa State University. (14)

171. Uhrich, Dwight G.
    1974   "Economic Impact of New Industry on the Brookings Community: 3M, a Case Study." Master's thesis, South Dakota State University. (44)

172. Wadsworth, H. A.
    1966   "The Effects of New Industry in a Rural Area." Indiana Business Review 41: 7-11. (12)

173. Wadsworth, H. A., and J. M. Conrad
    1965   "Leakages Reducing Employment and Income Multipliers in Labor-Surplus Rural Areas." Journal of Farm Economics 47, no. 5: 1197-1202. (12)

174. Wadsworth, H. A., and J. M. Conrad
    1966   "Impact of New Industry on a Rural Community." Research Bulletin no. 811. Lafayette, Inc.: Purdue University Agricultural Experiment Station. (12)

175. Wahi, Purushotam Lal
    1969   "An Analysis of Factors Affecting Supply Price of Labor in an Industrializing Area." Master's thesis, University of Illinois. (11)

176. Walker, James L.
     1973   Economic Development, Black Employment, and
             Black Migration in the Nonmetropolitan Deep South.
             Austin, Tex.: University of Texas, Center for the
             Study of Human Resources.   (57)

177. Walker, Mabel
     1956   "The Plant, the Office, and the City. Part II. Indus-
             trial Location Impacts." Tax Policy 23, nos. 2-3:
             3-35.   (70)

178. Walraven, Kornelis J.
     1962   "Impact of New Plants on Local Labor Supply: North-
             west Arkansas." Fayetteville, Ark.: University of
             Arkansas, College of Business Administration, In-
             dustrial Research and Extension Center. (1, 2)

179. Walraven, Kornelis J., and John H. Opitz
     1960   "Labor Supply in Northwest Arkansas, 1960."
             Fayetteville, Ark.: University of Arkansas, College
             of Business Administration, Industrial Research and
             Extension Center.   (1)

180. Wanner, Richard A., and E. M. Beck, Jr.
     1972   "Least-Squares Estimation of Effects on Inter- and
             Intra-Generational Occupational Transition Probabili-
             ties." In Proceedings of the American Statistical
             Association. 1972 Social Statistics section. Washing-
             ton, D.C.: American Statistical Association.   (11)

181. Wheaton, Blair, Duane F. Alwin, and Gene F. Summers
     1974   "Specification and Estimation of Panel Models In-
             corporating the Reliability and Stability of Multi-Wave
             Variables." Working paper no. 74.5. Madison, Wis.:
             University of Wisconsin, Department of Rural Sociol-
             ogy, Center of Applied Sociology.   (11)

182. Wilber, George L., and Sheridan Maitland
     1958   "Effects of a New Industry on a Mississippi Com-
             munity." Information Sheet 597. State College,
             Miss.: Mississippi State University, Department of
             Sociology, Agricultural Experiment Station.   (28)

183. Wilber, George L., and Sheridan Maitland
     1963   "Industrialization in Chickasaw County Mississippi:

A Study of Rural Residents." State College, Miss.:
Mississippi State University, Agricultural Experiment
Station.   (28)

184. Wilcock, Richard C.
     1954   "New Firms and the Labor Supply in Small Communi-
             ties." Current Economic Comment 16, no. 4: 3-15.
             (66)

185. Wilson, Charles MacArthur
     1965   "The Impact of Industrial Development on Lawrence
             County, Tennessee." Master's thesis, University of
             Tennessee.   (46)

186. Yantis, Betty L.
     1972   "The Economic Impact of Industry on Community
             Services in Seven Municipalities in the Ozarks Region
             of Arkansas." Ph.D. dissertation, University of
             Arkansas.   (1, 2, 3)

Abt Associates, Inc.
1968   "The Industrialization of Southern Rural Areas: A Study
          of Industry and Federal Assistance in Small Towns with
          Recommendations for Future Policy." Washington, D.C.:
          U.S. Department of Commerce, Economic Development
          Administration, Office of Economic Research.

Alexander, John W.
1954   "The Basic-Nonbasic Concept of Urban Economic Func-
          tions." Economic Geography 30: 246-61.

Andrews, Richard B.
1953-56   "Mechanics of the Urban Economic Base." Land Eco-
          nomics 29-31.

Andrews, R. B., I. V. Fine, A. C. Johnson, and E. E. Werner
1959   "The Effects of Industrialization on Six Small Wisconsin
          Cities," Wisconsin Commerce Papers, vol. 2, no. 3.
          Madison, Wis.: Wisconsin Business Research Council
          Committee for Economic Development; University of Wis-
          consin, School of Commerce, Bureau of Business Re-
          search and Service.

Andrews, Wade H., and Ward W. Bauder
1968   "The Effects of Industrialization on a Rural County: Com-
          parisons of Social Change in Monroe and Noble Counties
          of Ohio." Department Series A.E. 407. Wooster, Ohio:
          Ohio Agricultural Research and Development Center.

Arkansas Department of Labor, Employment Security Division.
1958   "The Effect of an Industry on a Small Rural Community:
          Byrd Manufacturing Corporation and Star City, Arkansas."
          Little Rock: Reports and Analysis Section, Employment
          Security Division, Arkansas Department of Labor.

Beale, Calvin
1969   "Demographic and Social Considerations for U.S. Rural
          Economic Policy." American Journal of Agricultural
          Economics 51: 410-27.

REFERENCES

Beck, Elwood M., Jr.
1972a   "A Study of Rural Industrial Development and Occupational
         Mobility." Ph.D. dissertation, University of Tennessee.

Beck, Elwood M.
1972b   "Industrial Development and Occupational Movers and
         Stayers." Working paper RID 72.17. Madison, Wis.:
         University of Wisconsin, Department of Rural Sociology,
         Center of Applied Sociology.

Beck, Elwood M.
1975   Personal Communication from Elwood M. Beck to Gene F.
         Summers.

Beck, Elwood M., Louis E. Dotson, and Gene F. Summers.
1973   "Effects of Industrial Development on Heads of House-
         holds." Growth and Change 4: 16-19.

Beck, Elwood M., and Jennifer H. Madans
1975a   "On the Relationship Between First Occupation and Cur-
         rent Occupational Status." Sociology of Work and Occupa-
         tions 1, no. 4: 372-95.

Beck, Elwood M., and Jennifer H. Madans
1975b   "Affluence, Equality, and Equity: A Case Study of Rural
         Development and Economic Status." Working paper RID
         75.9. Madison, Wis.: University of Wisconsin, Depart-
         ment of Rural Sociology, Center of Applied Sociology.

Bender, Lloyd, Bernal L. Green, and Rex R. Campbell
1971   "Trickle-Down and Leakage in the War on Poverty."
         Growth and Change 2, no. 4: 34-41.

Bender, Lloyd, Bernal L. Green, and Rex R. Campbell
1973   "Ghettos of Poverty in the Ozarks." Planning 39, no. 7:
         13-15.

Bertrand, Alvin L., and Harold W. Osborne
1959   "Rural Industrialization in a Louisiana Community." Bul-
         letin No. 524. Baton Rouge, La.: Louisiana State Uni-
         versity, Agricultural Experiment Station.

Bertrand, Alvin, and Harold W. Osborne
1959   "The Impact of Industrialization on a Rural Community."
         Journal of Farm Economics 41, no. 5: 1127-34.

Bertrand, Alvin L., and Harold W. Osborne
1960   "Rural Industrialization: A Situational Analysis." Rural
        Sociology 25, no. 4: 387-93.

Bertrand, Alvin L., Paul H. Price, and Harold W. Osborne
1958   "The Impact of Industrial Development on Rural Levels of
        Living (A Study of Plant Employees in a Sample Area in Ru-
        ral Louisiana)." Mimeographed. Baton Rouge, La.: Lou-
        isiana State University, Department of Rural Sociology.

Bird, Alan R.
1973   "Deployment of Economic Activity." Paper presented at
        meeting of Southern Regional Science Association, New
        Orleans.

Black, Therel R., Carmen Fredrickson, and Sheridan Maitland
1960   "Industrialization of Box Elder County." Agricultural Ex-
        periment Station Bulletin 420. Logan, Utah: Utah State
        University.

Brady, Guy, Jr.
1974   "The Economic Impact of Industrialization on a Rural Town
        Economy, Wynne, Arkansas." Masters thesis, University
        of Arkansas.

Brann, W. Paul
1964   "Helena, West Helena, Arkansas: A Case Study in Eco-
        nomic Readjustment." In Community Economic Develop-
        ment Efforts: Five Case Studies. Supplementary paper
        no. 18. New York: Committee for Economic Development.

Brinkman, George
1973   "Effects of Industrializing Small Communities." Journal of
        Community Development Society 4, no. 1: 69-80.

Bryant, W. Keith
1969   "Industrialization As a Poverty Policy: Toward a Micro
        Analysis," Papers on Rural Poverty, API Series 37, Agri-
        cultural Policy Institute, School of Agriculture and Life
        Sciences, North Carolina State University: 71-82.

Bucher, Norman J.
1971   "Impact of New Industrial Plants: Eight Case Studies."
        Office of Industrial Development Studies, University of
        Missouri. Jefferson City, Mo.: Missouri Division of
        Commerce and Industrial Development.

REFERENCES

Bureau of Population and Economic Research
1956   "The Impact of Industry in a Southern Rural County:
          Changes in Road Use, Travel Habits and Socioeconomic
          Characteristics in Charlotte County, Virginia, Five Years
          after the Establishment of a New Manufacturing Plant."
          Bureau of Population and Economic Research, University
          of Virginia. Richmond: Virginia Department of Highways.

Carroll, John J., and Seymour Sacks
1962   "The Property Tax Base and the Pattern of Local Govern-
          ment Expenditures: The Influence of Industry." In Papers
          and Proceedings of the Regional Science Association, vol. 9.

Chamber of Commerce of the United States, Economic Research De-
          partment
1960   "What New Industrial Jobs Mean to a Community." Wash-
          ington, D.C.: U.S. Chamber of Commerce.

Chamber of Commerce of the United States, Economic Analysis and
          Study
1968   "What New Industrial Jobs Mean to a Community." Wash-
          ington, D.C.: U.S. Chamber of Commerce.

Chamber of Commerce of the United States, Economic Analysis and
          Study
1973   "What New Jobs Mean to a Community." Washington,
          D.C.: U.S. Chamber of Commerce.

Chinitz, Benjamin, and Raymond Vernon
1960   "Changing Forces in Industrial Location." Harvard Busi-
          ness Review 38: 126-36.

Christiansen, John R., Sheridan Maitland, and John W. Payne
1959   "Industrialization and Rural Life in Two Central Utah
          Counties." Bulletin 416, Utah Agricultural Experiment
          Station. Logan, Utah: Utah State University.

Clark, John P., Gene F. Summers, and Richard L. Hough
1968   "Perceptions of Social Control in a Rural Area." Working
          paper no. 68.1. Madison, Wis.: University of Wisconsin,
          Department of Rural Sociology, Center of Applied Sociology.

Clemente, Frank, and Gene F. Summers
1973a   "A Comment on Palmore and Whittington's Relative Status
          of the Aged." Social Forces 51: 494-95.

Clemente, Frank, and Gene F. Summers
1973b   "An Exploratory Note on Family Status and Work-Residence
         Separation." Working paper RID 73.14. Madison, Wis.:
         University of Wisconsin, Department of Rural Sociology,
         Center of Applied Sociology.

Clemente, Frank, and Gene F. Summers
1973c   "Industrial Development and the Elderly: A Longitudinal
         Analysis." Journal of Gerontology 28, no. 4: 479-83.

Clemente, Frank, and Gene F. Summers
1973d   "Large Industries in Small Towns: Who Benefits?" Work-
         ing paper RID 73.9. Madison, Wis.: University of Wis-
         consin, Department of Rural Sociology, Center of Applied
         Sociology.

Clemente, Frank, and Gene F. Summers
1973e   "Rural Industrial Development and Commuting Patterns."
         Working paper RID 73.15 (August). Madison, Wis.: Uni-
         versity of Wisconsin, Department of Rural Sociology,
         Center of Applied Sociology.

Clemente, Frank, and Gene F. Summers
1974   "Age and the Journey to Work." The Gerontologist 14.

Clemente, Frank, and Gene F. Summers
1975   "The Journey to Work of Rural Industrial Employees: A
         Test of the Metropolitan Model of Commuting." Social
         Forces 54, no. 1: 212-19.

Commission on Population Growth and the American Future
1972   Population and the American Future. Washington, D.C.:
         U.S. Government Printing Office.

Creamer, Daniel
1963   "Changing Location of Manufacturing Employment." Studies
         in Business Economics, no. 83. New York: National In-
         dustrial Conference Board.

Crecink, John C.
1970   "Rural Industrialization: Case Study of a Tissue Paper Mill
         in Pickens, Miss." Agricultural Economic Report no. 189.
         Washington, D.C.: United States Department of Agriculture,
         Economic Research Service.

Daoust, Charles F.
1954   "Transition in Central Michigan: Agriculture to Industry."
            Master's thesis, University of Chicago.

Davis, James Nathaniel, Jr.
1963   "Effects of Industrialization upon the Economy of Searcy,
            Arkansas: A Case Study." Ph.D. dissertation, University
            of Arkansas.

Dean, Robert D.
1973   Suburbanization of Industry in the U.S. Oak Ridge, Tenn.:
            Oak Ridge National Laboratory.

Debes, Leroy J.
1973   "The Impact of Industrialization upon Real Estate in Par-
            sons, Kansas." Master's thesis, Kansas State University.

Dietz, John Leslie
1971   "Tractors to Capacitors: An Analysis of the Impact of New
            Manufacturing Plants on Small Agricultural Communities
            in the Northern Great Plains." Ph.D. dissertation, Syra-
            cuse University.

Dietz, John Leslie
1972   "Rural Area Development: Analysis of the Impact of New
            Factories on Agricultural Towns in the Northern Great
            Plains." Great Plains-Rocky Mountain Geographical
            Journal 1: 19-25.

Erickson, William L.
1969   "Alienation, Participation and Environmental Satisfaction:
            A Path Analysis." Master's thesis, University of Illinois.

Fuchs, Victor R.
1962   Changes in Location of Manufacturing in the U.S. New
            Haven, Conn.: Yale University Press.

Funk, Herbert Joseph
1964   "Effects of New Manufacturing Plant on Business Firms in
            an Eastern Iowa Community." Ph.D. dissertation, Iowa
            State University.

Garrison, Charles B.
1967   "Economic Impact of New Industry on Small Towns." Ph.D.
            dissertation, University of Kentucky.

Garrison, Charles B.
1970   "The Impact of New Industry on Local Government Finances
            in Five Small Towns in Kentucky." Agricultural Economic
            Report no. 191. Washington, D.C.: U.S. Department of
            Agriculture, Economic Research Service.

Garrison, Charles B.
1971   "New Industry in Small Towns: The Impact on Local Gov-
            ernment." National Tax Journal 24, no. 4: 493-500.

Garrison, Charles B.
1972   "The Impact of New Industry: An Application of the Eco-
            nomic Base Multiplier to Small Rural Areas." Land Eco-
            nomics 47, no. 4: 329-37.

Garth, John
1953   "When Big Business Comes to a Country Town: Why Alcoa
            Spent $80,000,000 near Rockdale, Texas." American
            Business 23, no. 3: 26-27, 37-40.

Graham, David Ralph
1973   "The Role of Business in the Economic Redevelopment of
            the Rural Community." Research monograph, no. 36.
            Austin, Tex.: University of Texas, Bureau of Business
            Research, Graduate School of Business.

Gray, Irwin
1969   "Employment Effect of a New Industry in a Rural Area."
            Monthly Labor Review 92, no. 6: 26-30.

Hagerman, L. Dale, and Curtis H. Braschler
1966   "Part One: An Analysis of the Impact of Industrialization
            on a Small Town Economy. A Case Study of Ava, Missouri.
            Part Two: The Impact of Industrialization of a Small Town
            on Local Government. A Case Study of Ava, Missouri."
            Research Bulletin no. 910 (July), Research Project 507.
            Columbia, Mo.: University of Missouri, Department of
            Agricultural Economics.

Hansen, Niles
1970   Rural Poverty and the Urban Crisis. Bloomington: Indiana
            University Press.

Hansen, Niles
1972   Intermediate Size Cities as Growth Centers. New York:
            Praeger Publishers.

REFERENCES

Hansen, Richard, and Gary M. Munsinger
1972   "A Prescriptive Model for Industrial Development," Land
          Economics 48: 76-81.

Haren, Claude C.
1970   "Rural Industrial Growth in the 1960's." American Journal
          of Agricultural Economics 52: 431-37.

Haren, Claude C.
1973   "Rural Industrial Growth in the Southeast since 1962."
          Paper read at Rural Development Center, Tifton, Georgia.

Helgeson, Delmer L., and Maurice J. Zink
1973   "A Case Study of Rural Industrialization in Jamestown,
          North Dakota." Agricultural Economics Report no. 95.
          Fargo, N.D.: North Dakota State University, Department
          of Agricultural Economics, Agricultural Experiment Station.

Hirsch, Werner Z.
1961   "Regional Fiscal Impact of Local Industrial Development."
          In Papers and Proceedings of the Regional Science Asso-
          ciation, vol. 7.

Hirsch, Werner Z.
1967   "The Supply of Urban Services." In Issues in Urban Eco-
          nomics. Edited by Harvey S. Perloff and Lowden Wingo.
          Baltimore: Resources for the Future.

Hirsch, Werner Z.
1969   "Fiscal Impact of Industrialization on Local Schools."
          Review of Economics and Statistics (May): 191-99.

Hoover, Edgar M. and Raymond Vernon
1959   Anatomy of a Metropolis. Cambridge, Mass.: Harvard
          University Press.

Hoover, Herbert
n.d.a   "Rural Industrialization in West Virginia: Case Study of
          a New Particle Board Plant in Braxton County, West
          Virginia." Washington, D.C.: U.S. Department of Agri-
          culture, Economic Research Service, Economic Develop-
          ment Division.

Hoover, Herbert
n.d.b   "Rural Industrialization in Kentucky: Case Study of a New
          Bedding Plant at Munfordville, Kentucky." Washington,

D.C.: U.S. Department of Agriculture, Economic Research Service, Economic Development Division.

Hough, Richard L., and John P. Clark
1969   "Some Determinants of Attitudes Toward Industrialization in
           a Rural Community." Working paper no. 69.3. Madison,
           Wis.: University of Wisconsin, Department of Rural So-
           ciology, Center of Applied Sociology.

Howard, William C.
1973   "The Staffing Experience of a New Industrial Plant: A New
           Technique for Determining Manpower Availability and Char-
           acteristics." Norman, Okla.: University of Oklahoma,
           Industrial Development Institute (American Industrial De-
           velopment Council thesis).

Isard, Walter
1960   Methods of Regional Analysis: An Introduction to Regional
           Science. New York: The Technology Press of M.I.T. and
           John Wiley & Sons.

Johnson, Doyle Paul
1968   "Social Control in the Hennepin Area." Working paper no.
           68.4. Madison, Wis.: University of Wisconsin, Depart-
           ment of Rural Sociology, Center of Applied Sociology.

Johnson, Doyle Paul
1969   "The Response of Clergymen to Industrial Development."
           Ph.D. dissertation, University of Illinois.

Johnson, Doyle Paul, and Gene F. Summers
1971   "Industrial Development and Goal Modification in Church
           Congregations." Working paper no. 71.2. Madison, Wis.:
           University of Wisconsin, Department of Rural Sociology,
           Center of Applied Sociology.

Johnson, Maxine C.
1960   "The Effects of the Anaconda Aluminum Company Plant on
           Flathead County, Montana." Regional Study no. 12. Mis-
           soula, Mont.: Montana State University, School of Business
           Administration, Bureau of Business and Economic Research.

Jordan, Max. F.
1967   "Rural Industrialization in the Ozarks." Agricultural Eco-
           nomic Report 123. Washington, D. C.: U.S. Government
           Printing Office.

Jordan, Max F.
1967   "Rural Industrialization in the Ozarks: Case Study of a
            New Shirt Plant at Gassville, Arkansas." Agricultural
            Economic Report no. 123. Washington, D.C.: U.S. De-
            partment of Agriculture, Economic Research Service.

Kain, John F.
1969   "Distribution and Movement of Jobs and Industry." In
            The Metropolitan Enigma. Edited by J. Q. Wilson. Cam-
            bridge, Mass.: Harvard University Press.

Kaldor, Donald R., Ward W. Bauder, and Marvin W. Trautwein
1964   "Impact of New Industry on an Iowa Rural Community.
            Part 1. Farming and Farm Living." Special Report no.
            37. Department of Economics and Sociology, Center for
            Agricultural and Economic Development. Ames, Iowa:
            Iowa State University, Agricultural and Home Economics
            Experiment Station.

Keynes, John Maynard
1965   The General Theory of Employment, Interest and Money.
            New York: Harcourt, Brace and World, Inc.

Klein, William E., Jr.
1959   "The Effect of Local Industrialization in a Rural Low-
            Income County." Master's thesis, Oklahoma State Univer-
            sity.

Klimasewski, Theodore
1974   "The Significance of Manufacturing Activity in a Rural Area
            in East Tennessee." Ph.D. dissertation, University of
            Tennessee.

Kuehn, John A., Lloyd D. Bender, Bernal L. Green, and Herbert
            Hoover
1972   "Impact of Job Development on Poverty in Four Developing
            Areas, 1970." Agricultural Economic Report no. 225.
            Washington, D.C.: United States Department of Agricul-
            ture, Economic Research Services.

Kuznets, Simon
1955   "Economic Growth and Income Inequality." American
            Economic Review 45: 1-28.

Kuznets, Simon
1966   "Consumption, Industrialization, and Urbanization." In
          Industrialization and Society. Edited by Bert Hoselitz and
          Wilbert E. Moore. Paris: UNESCO-Mouton.

Lonsdale, Richard E.
1966   "Two North Carolina Commuting Patterns." Economic
          Geography 42, no. 2: 114-38.

Lonsdale, Richard E., and C. E. Browning
1971   "Rural-Urban Locational Preferences of Southern Manufac-
          turers." Annals of American Association of Geographers:
          255-68.

McArthur, J'Wayne, and Robert O. Coppedge
1969   "Employment Impacts of Industrial Development: A Case
          Study of Box Elder County, Utah, from 1950 to 1966."
          Utah Economic and Business Review 29, no. 2: 1-6, 9-10.
          Salt Lake City, Utah: University of Utah, College of
          Business, Bureau of Economic and Business Research.

McElveen, Jackson V.
1970   "Rural Industrialization in the Southeast Coastal Plain:
          Case Study of a New Brick Factory in Summerville, South
          Carolina." Agricultural Economic Report no. 174. Wash-
          ington, D.C.: U.S. Department of Agriculture, Economic
          Research Service.

McLaughlin, Glenn E.
1938   Growth of Manufacturing Areas. Pittsburgh: University of
          Pittsburgh Press.

McLaughlin, Glenn E., and Stefan Robock
1949   Why Industry Moves South. Washington, D.C.: National
          Planning Association.

Maitland, Sheridan, and Reed E. Friend
1961   "Rural Industrialization: A Summary of Five Studies."
          Agriculture Information Bulletin no. 252. Washington,
          D.C.: U.S. Department of Agriculture, Economic Re-
          search Service.

Maitland, Sheridan, and George L. Wilber
1958   "Industrialization in Chickasaw County, Mississippi: A
          Study of Plant Workers." Bulletin 566. State College,

Miss.: Mississippi State University, Mississippi Agricultural Experiment Station.

Martin, Joe A.
1960   "The Impact of Industrial Development upon Agriculture.
            Lawrence County: A Progress Report on Industrial Devel-
            opment in a Rural Area of Special Interest to Farmers and
            Community Leaders." Progress report no. 33, Tennessee
            Farm and Home Science (January, February, March).
            Knoxville, Tenn.: University of Tennessee, Agricultural
            Experiment Station.

Marshall, Douglas
1965   "Migration and Older People in a Rural Community." In
            Older People and their Social World. Edited by A. Rose
            and W. Peterson. Philadelphia: F. A. Davis.

Matz, Earl Luke
1957   "The Impact of a Large Industrial Plant upon a Small
            Agrarian Community." Ph.D. dissertation, Ohio State
            University.

Maxwell, James A.
1965   Financing State and Local Governments. Washington,
            D.C.: The Brookings Institute.

Merriam, Ida C.
1968   "Welfare and Its Measurement." In Indicators of Social
            Change. Edited by Eleanor B. Sheldon and Wilbert E.
            Moore. New York: Russell Sage Foundation.

Merrill, Kenneth E., and David L. Ryther
1961   "Plant Location and Community Changes." Kansas Busi-
            ness Review 14, no. 7: 10-13.

Merrill, Kenneth E., and David L. Ryther
1961   "Plant Location and Community Changes." Lawrence,
            Kans.: University of Kansas, Center for Research in
            Business.

Metz, Donald C.
1968   "A Study of Industrial Branch Plants in the Countryside of
            Minnesota." Marshall, Minn.: Southwest Minnesota State
            College, Division of Engineering Technology.

Miernyk, William H.
1971   "Local Labor Market Effects of New Plant Locations." In
        Essays in Regional Economics. Edited by John F. Klein
        and John R. Meyer. Cambridge, Mass.: Harvard Univer-
        sity Press.

Milkman, Raymond H., Christopher Bladen, Beverly Lyford, and
        Howard L. Walton
1972   Alleviating Economic Distress: Evaluating a Federal Effort.
        Lexington, Mass.: D. C. Heath and Co.

Miller, Daniel Frank
1967   "The Influence of Industrialization and the Buying Habits of
        Industrial Employees, Tarboro, North Carolina." Green-
        ville, N.C.: Eastern North Carolina University, Eastern
        North Carolina Development Institute.

Miller, Herman P.
1970   "Recent Trends in Family Income." In The Logic of Social
        Hierarchies. Edited by Edward O. Lauman, Paul M.
        Siegel, and Robert W. Hodge. Chicago, Ill.: Markham
        Publishing Co.

Moes, John E.
1962   Local Subsidies for Industry. Chapel Hill, N.C.: Uni-
        versity of North Carolina Press.

Moore, James L., ed.
1973   Information, Methods and Procedures for the Evaluation of
        the Environmental Effects of Industrial Development.
        Madison, Wis.: Environmental Awareness Center, School
        of Natural Resources, University of Wisconsin.

Morris, Robert Bremner, Jr.
1960   "The Economic Effect of a New Industry on a Small City."
        Master's thesis, Massachusetts Institute of Technology.

Moses, L. N., and H. Williamson
1967   "The Location of Economic Activity in Cities." American
        Economic Review 57: 211-22.

Olsen, Duane A., and John A. Kuehn
1974   "Migrant Response to Industrialization in Four Rural Areas,
        1965-70." Agricultural Economic Report no. 270. Wash-
        ington, D.C.: United States Department of Agriculture,

Economic Research Service, in cooperation with the University of Missouri Agricultural Experiment Station.

Osborne, Harold W.
1959   "The Impact of a Village Factory on a Selected Area of Rural Louisiana." Ph.D. dissertation, Louisiana State University.

Paden, David, Donald Krist, and Michael Seaton
1972   "Impact of Industrial Development on Selected Iowa Communities." Final report. Ames, Iowa: Iowa Development Commission.

Palmer, Edgar Z., Gerald E. Thompson, Moon H. Kang, and William H. Strawn
1958   "The Economic Base and Multiplier." Business Research Bulletin no. 63. Lincoln, Neb.: College of Business Administration, University of Nebraska.

Patrick, Charles H.
1973   Decentralization of Manufacturing Employment. Oak Ridge, Tenn.: Oak Ridge National Laboratory.

Perloff, Harvey S., Edgar S. Dunn, Jr., Eric E. Lampard, and Richard F. Muth.
1960   Regions, Resources and Economic Growth. Baltimore: Johns Hopkins Press.

Peterson, John M.
1974   "Effects of Rural Industrialization on Labor Demand and Employment." In Rural Industrialization: Problems and Potentials. Edited by Larry R. Whiting. Ames, Iowa: Iowa State University Press.

Pfouts, Ralph W., ed.
1960   The Techniques of Urban Economic Analysis. West Trenton, N.J.: Chandler-Davis Publishing Co.

Pickard, J.
1972   "Population in Appalachia." Washington, D.C.: Appalachian Regional Commission.

Pittman, B. W.
1965   "Industrial Development in an Agricultural Economy--A Study of Industrial Growth in Leflore County, Mississippi."

Norman, Okla.: University of Oklahoma, Industrial Development Institute (American Industrial Development Council thesis).

Plaxico, James Samuel
1947   "Some Economic Aspects of Rural Industrialization." Master's thesis, Clemson Agricultural College.

Pray, Hubert Q.
1965   "Impact of Industrial Growth on the Labor Force of Washington County, Mississippi 1950-1963." Norman, Okla.: University of Oklahoma, Industrial Development Institute (American Industrial Development Council thesis).

Ramana, K. V.
1968   "Industrialization and Social Change in the Hennepin Area." Working paper no. 68.3. Madison, Wis.: University of Wisconsin, Department of Rural Sociology, Center of Applied Sociology.

Rathburn, Arthur C.
1972   "Industrial Development Process in Willamette Valley, Oregon: Three Cases." Mimeographed. Portland, Ore.: Oregon State University.

Ritzenthaler, Robert E.
1953   "The Impact of Small Industry on an Indian Community." American Anthropologist 55, no. 1: 143-48.

Rojek, Dean G., Frank Clemente, and Gene F. Summers
1974   "Community Satisfaction: A Study of Contentment with Local Services." Rural Sociology 40, no. 2: 177-92.

Ryan, Robert H., Charles T. Clark, and L. L. Schkade
1963   "Paris, Texas, from Farm to Factory." Area Economic Survey no. 14. Austin, Tex.: University of Texas, Bureau of Business Research.

Saltzman, Lloyd R.
1964   "Economic Case Studies of Community Sponsored Efforts to Develop Industry." Tulsa, Okla.: University of Tulsa.

Schneiderman, James A.
1971   "The Impact of Rural Industrial Development on Agricultural Land Use and Labor Mobility." Master's thesis, Illinois State University.

Scott, John T., Jr., and Gene F. Summers
1974   "Problems in Rural Communities after Industry Arrives."
            In Rural Industrialization: Problems and Potentials.
            Edited by Larry R. Whiting. Ames, Iowa: Iowa State Uni-
            versity Press, for the North Central Regional Center for
            Rural Development. Reprinted in U.S. Senate, Committee
            on Agriculture and Forestry, Subcommittee on Rural De-
            velopment. Rural Industrialization Prospects, Problems,
            Impacts, and Methods. Committee print (April 19, 1974).

Seiler, Lauren H.
1974   "Community Verticalization: On the Interface Between
            Corporate Influence and Horizontal Leadership." Working
            paper no. RID 74.3. Madison, Wis.: University of Wis-
            consin, Department of Rural Sociology, Center of Applied
            Sociology.

Shaffer, Ronald Earl
1972   "The Net Economic Impact of New Industry on Rural Com-
            munities in Eastern Oklahoma." Ph.D. dissertation,
            Oklahoma State University.

Shaffer, Ronald Earl
1974   "Rural Industrialization: A Local Income Analysis."
            Southern Journal of Agricultural Economics 6, no. 1:
            97-102.

Sizer, Leonard M., and William B. Clifford
1966   "Rural Industrialization: A Case Study in Educational
            Values and Attitudes." Bulletin no. 521. Morgantown,
            W. Va.: West Virginia University, Agricultural Exper-
            ment Station.

Sizer, Leonard M., and Edward A. Smith
n.d.   "Toward an Integration of Migration and Location Theory."
            Mimeographed. Morgantown, W. Va.: Department of
            Sociology, Agricultural Experiment Station.

Smith, Cortland L., Thomas C. Hogg, and Michael J. Reagan
1971   "Economic Development: Panacea or Perplexity for Rural
            Areas?" Rural Sociology 36: 173-86.

Smith, David M.
1972   Industrial Location: An Economic Geographical Analysis.
            New York: John Wiley and Sons.

Somers, Gerald
1958   "Labor Recruitment in a Depressed Rural Area." Monthly
          Labor Review 81, no. 10: 1113-20.

Stepp, J. M., and J. S. Plaxico
1948   "The Labor Supply of a Rural Industry: A Case Study of the
          McCormick (S. C.) Spinning Mill." Bulletin 376. Clemson,
          S. C.: Clemson Agricultural College, Agricultural Experi-
          ment Station.

Stevens, J. B., and L. T. Wallace
1964   "Impact of Industrial Development on Howard County,
          Indiana, 1947-1960." Research Bulletin no. 784. Lafayette,
          Ind.: Purdue University, Agricultural Experiment Station.

Stuart, Alfred W.
1971   "Rural Industrialization and Population Growth: The Case
          of Arkansas." Civil Defense Research Project ORNL-
          AUD-4. Oak Ridge, Tenn.: Oak Ridge National Laboratory.

Summers, Gene F.
1973a   "Large Industry in a Rural Area: Demographic, Economic
          and Social Impacts." Working paper no. RID 73.19. Final
          report to the Office of Economic Research, Economic De-
          velopment Administration, U.S. Department of Commerce.
          Madison, Wis.: University of Wisconsin, Department of
          Rural Sociology, Center of Applied Sociology. (Available
          from the National Technical Information Service, no.
          COM-74-10214.) Reprinted in U.S. Senate, Committee on
          Agriculture and Forestry, Subcommittee on Rural Develop-
          ment. Rural Industrialization: Prospects, Problems,
          Impacts, and Methods. Committee print (April 19, 1974).

Summers, Gene F.
1973b   Large Industry in a Rural Area. Madison, Wis.: Univer-
          versity of Wisconsin, Department of Rural Sociology,
          Center of Applied Sociology.

Summers, Gene F., and Elwood M. Beck, Jr.
1972   "Industrial Development and Urbanization: A U.S. Case."
          Working paper no. RID 72.8. Madison, Wis.: University
          of Wisconsin, Department of Rural Sociology, Center of
          Applied Sociology.

Summers, Gene F., and Frank Clemente
1973   "Rapid Industrial Development, Competition, and Relative
            Economic Status: A Study in Human Ecology." Working
            paper no. RID 73.10. Madison, Wis.: University of Wis-
            consin, Department of Rural Sociology, Center of Applied
            Sociology.

Summers, Gene F., John P. Clark, and Lauren H. Seiler
1970   "The Renewal of Community Sociology." Rural Sociology
            35: 218-31.

Summers, Gene F., Lauren H. Seiler, and Glenn Wiley
1970   "Validation of Reputational Leadership by the Multitrait-
            Multimethod Matrix." In Sociological Methodology. Edited
            by E. F. Borgatta and G. W. Bohrnstedt. San Francisco:
            Jossey-Bass.

Tennessee Town and City
1957   "Rx for Prosperity: Cash Register Hums. Lawrence
            County's Out-Migration Grinds to a Halt as New Plants Put
            Men to Work." Vol. 8.

Thompson, Tracy
1933   Location of Manufacturing, 1899-1929. Washington, D.C.:
            U.S. Government Printing Office.

Thompson, Wilbur R.
1968   "Internal and External Factors in the Development of Urban
            Economics." In Issues in Urban Economics. Edited by
            Harvey S. Perloff and Lowden Wingo. Baltimore: Johns
            Hopkins Press, for Resources for the Future, Inc.

Thompson, Wilbur R., and John M. Mattila
1959   Econometric Model of Postwar State Industrial Develop-
            ment. Detroit: Wayne State University Press.

Tiebout, Charles M.
1956a   "Exports and Regional Economic Growth," Journal of Po-
            litical Economy 54: 160-65.

Tiebout, Charles M.
1956b   "The Urban Economic Base Reconsidered," Land Econom-
            ics 31: 95-99.

Tiebout, Charles M.
1962   The Community Economic Base Study. New York: Com-
          mittee for Economic Development.

Till, Thomas E., Jr.
1972   "Rural Industrialization and Southern Rural Poverty: Pat-
          terns of Labor Demand in Southern Non-Metropolitan Labor
          Markets and Their Impact on the Poor, 1959-1969." Ph.D.
          dissertation, University of Texas.

Till, Thomas E., Jr.
1973   "Extent of Industrialization in Southern Labor Markets in
          the 1960's." Journal of Regional Science 13: 453-61.

Uhrich, Dwight G.
1974   "Economic Impact of New Industry on the Brookings Com-
          munity: 3M, A Case Study." Master's thesis, South
          Dakota State University.

U.S. Congress
1970   Appalachian Regional Development Act of 1965. U.S.
          Code, vol. 8.

U.S. Congress
1970   Public Works and Economic Development Act of 1966.
          U.S. Code, vol. 9.

U.S. Congress, House
1972   "Rural Development Act of 1972." Pub. L. 92-419, 92d.
          Cong., 2d. sess., 1972, H.R. 12931.

U.S. Department of Agriculture
1971   Yearbook of Agriculture, 1971. Washington, D.C.: U.S.
          Government Printing Office.

Vernon, Raymond
1959   Metropolis. New York: Doubleday.

Wadsworth, H. A., and J. M. Conrad
1965   "Leakages Reducing Employment and Income Multipliers in
          Labor-Surplus Rural Areas." Journal of Farm Economics
          47, no. 5: 1197-1202.

Wadsworth, H. A. and J. M. Conrad
1966   "Impact of New Industry in a Rural Community." Research

Bulletin no. 811.   Lafayette, Ind.: Purdue University,
Agricultural Experiment Station.

Walker, James L.
1973   Economic Development, Black Employment, and Black
          Migration in the Nonmetropolitan Deep South. Austin,
          Tex.: University of Texas, Center for the Study of Human
          Resources.

Walker, Mabel
1956   "The Plant, the Office, and the City. Part II. Industrial
          Location Impacts." Tax Policy 23, nos. 2-3: 3-35.

Walraven, Kornelis J.
1962   "Impact of New Plants on Local Labor Supply: Northwest
          Arkansas." Fayetteville, Ark.: University of Arkansas,
          College of Business Administration, Industrial Research
          and Extension Center.

Wheat, Leonard F.
1973   Regional Growth and Industrial Location. Lexington,
          Mass.: D. C. Heath and Co.

Wilber, George L., and Sheridan T. Maitland
1963   "Industrialization in Chickasaw County Mississippi: A
          Study of Rural Residents." State College, Miss.: Missis-
          sippi State University, Agricultural Experiment Station.

Wilcock, Richard C.
1954   "New Firms and the Labor Supply in Small Communities."
          Current Economic Comment 16, no. 4: 3-15.

Wilson, Charles MacArthur
1965   "The Impact of Industrial Development on Lawrence County,
          Tennessee." Master's thesis, University of Tennessee.

Yantis, Betty L.
1972   "The Economic Impact of Industry on Community Services
          in Seven Municipalities in the Ozarks Region of Arkansas."
          Ph.D. dissertation, University of Arkansas.

household size and industrial development, 43
household size, nonmetropolitan industrial
workers, 3

Idaho, 176
Illinois, 15, 16, 34, 68, 112, 113, 128, 176;
Bureau County, 61; Hennepin, Putnam
County, 137; Hennepin, 16, 109, 115, 121,
189, 195; Iroquois County, 186; Kankakee,
175; LaSalle County, 61; Putnam County,
61, 63, 65, 66, 100; Tuscola, 175
income and migration, 28
income changes, 62, 63
income equality, 5
income, 62-71; median family, 66; per
capita, 64
increase in public school enrollment,
100-01
Indiana, 15, 16, 99, 128; Howard County, 56,
64, 66, 78, 86, 91, 101, 199; Kokomo,
Howard County, 138-39; Linton, Greene
County, 138; Linton, 48, 56, 78, 81, 86,
91, 96
induced demand for governmental services,
97-98
Industrial Development Bonds, 94, 95, 96
industrial employment and poverty, 48
industrial location and climate, 9
industrial location trends, 6
industrial location, regional shifts, 7, 8-9
industrialization and urbanization, 29
inmigrants, 2, 25
immigration, 25, 26, 69-70
intergovernmental transfer payments, 89-91;
highway funds, 90; sales tax, 90
Iowa, 15, 16, 33, 48, 128, 187, 190, 194,
201; Centerville, Appanoose County, 140;
Creston, Union County, 140; Creston, 49;
Decorah, Winneshiek County, 140; Decorah,
49; Grinnell, Poweshiek County, 140;
Grinnell, 48; Jackson County, 61; Jefferson, Greene County, 140; Jefferson, 48, 49;
Lake Mills, Winnebago County, 140;
Maquoketa, Jackson County, 139; Orange
City, Sioux County, 140; Orange City, 49

journey to work, 34-35; distance, 34-35;
time, 35

Kansas, 15, 16, 79, 84, 86, 101, 128, 142,
170, 175; Parsons, 83, 141, 186
Kentucky, 15, 16, 75, 77, 94, 101, 103, 128,
143, 169, 176, 187; Fleming County, 56,
64; Flemingsburg, Fleming County, 143;
Flemingsburg, 94; Hart County, 56; Laurel
County, 56, 61, 63, 64; Lebanon, Marion
County, 143; Lebanon, 94; Lincoln County,
56, 65; London, Laurel County, 143;
London, 94; Marion County, 56, 64;

Munfordville, Hart County, 144; Munford-
ville, 188; Russell County, 56, 64; Russell
Springs, Russel County, 143; Stanford,
Lincoln County, 143; Stanford, 77, 94

labor sheds, nonmetropolitan, 2-3
labor survey, 6
leadership, 111-12; changes in, 111-12
local community support, 13
locational costs, 72
Louisiana, 15, 16, 32, 51, 52, 108, 110, 120,
128, 168, 169, 176, 182, 194; Roseland,
Tangipahoa Parish, 145

manufacturing employment growth, 8
market location shifts, 9
Massachusetts, 16
median age, 39; female plant workers, 39;
male plant workers, 39
median family income, 66
Michigan, 15, 128, 172, 176, 185; Edmore,
Montcalm County, 145; Edmore, 79, 80,
82, 86, 87, 88, 102
migration, 28, 29; and income, 27; and poverty,
29; intentions, 27
migration of plant workers, 27
Minnesota, 15, 16, 118, 124, 128, 147, 176,
193; Rochester, Olmstead County, 146;
Rochester, 49, 57
minority training assistance programs, 6
Mississippi Delta, 50-51
Mississippi, 15, 16, 51, 52, 107, 128, 168,
169, 176, 202; Adams County, 52; Alcorn
County, 50, 52, 173; Chickasaw County, 51,
52, 108, 120, 192; Fayette, 174; Houston,
Chickasaw County, 149; Jefferson City, 52;
LeFlore County, 55, 56, 57, 148, 194, 217;
Pickens, Holmes County, 149; Pickens, 56,
57, 185; Tippah County, 50, 52, 173; Washington County, 61, 147, 195
Missouri, 15, 16, 183; Ava, Douglas County,
128, 175, 176; Ava, 84, 91, 99, 100, 101,
188; Douglas County, 67, 96; Lebanon,
Laclede County, 150
modal age, 39; female plant workers, 39;
male plant workers, 39
Montana, 15, 16, 128; Columbia Falls, Flathead County, 151; Flathead County, 63, 64,
190, 212
multipliers, employment, 54-59

National Land Use Policy, 7
Nebraska, 15, 170, 176; Custer County, 65;
Dawson County, 64; Keith County, 64
net migration, 25, 27
New Mexico, 15; San Juan County, 173; Ship-
rock, 174
New York, 15, 16, 128, 152; Honeoye, 152
nonmetropolitan industrial development, 11-13

willingness of industry, 13
Wisconsin, 15, 16, 22, 34, 38, 51, 57, 81, 84, 86, 90, 180; Fort Atkinson, Jefferson County, 166; Hartford, Washington County, 166; Lac du Flambeau Indian Reservation, Vilas County, 166; Monroe, Green County, 166; Prairie du Chien, Crawford County, 166; Richland Center, Richland County, 166; West Bend, Washington County, 166

GENE F. SUMMERS is Professor of Rural Sociology and Director of the Center of Applied Sociology in the University of Wisconsin, Madison. He is editor of <u>Attitude Measurement</u> and co-author of <u>Before Industrialization</u>. He also has contributed numerous articles to professional journals in sociology and other social sciences. For the past ten years his work has been focused on examining the social and psychological impacts of industrial expansion in small cities and towns and rural areas.

Professor Summers received his Ph.D. from the University of Tennessee.

SHARON D. EVANS is a graduate student and research assistant in sociology and rural sociology at the University of Wisconsin, Madison. Her master's thesis is an investigation of the demographic impacts of nonmetropolitan industrial development in the United States between 1950 and 1970. Ms. Evans received her B.A. from the University of Otago, New Zealand.

FRANK CLEMENTE is Associate Professor of Sociology, Pennsylvania State University. Previously he was Visiting Associate Professor of Rural Sociology, University of Wisconsin, Madison. He edited <u>Rural America</u>, published by the American Academy of Political and Social Science, and has contributed to a number of sociological journals. He is currently studying the socioeconomic effects of nuclear power plants in rural America.

Dr. Clemente holds a Ph.D. from the University of Tennessee.

E. M. BECK is Assistant Professor, Department of Sociology, at the University of Michigan, and director of the Detroit Area Study. He has held positions as a research specialist at the Center of Applied Sociology, University of Wisconsin, Madison, and as a research associate at the Institute of Behavioral Science, University of Colorado. He has published works in quantitative analysis, complex organizations, stratification, and economic development in numerous academic and professional journals. Currently he is working on a longitudinal investigation of changes in the distribution of income in nonmetropolitan America from 1950 to 1970.

Professor Beck received his Ph. D. from the University of Tennessee.

JON MINKOFF is a graduate student and Social Organization Trainee in Sociology at the University of Wisconsin, Madison. His contribution to the present volume reflects an active pursuit of issues in political economics and social change. Mr. Minkoff received his B.A. from the University of California, Berkeley.

RELATED TITLES
Published by
Praeger Special Studies

POLICY EVALUATION FOR COMMUNITY
DEVELOPMENT: Decision Tools for Local
Government
Shimon Awerbach and William A. Wallace

REGIONAL ECONOMIC DIVERSIFICATION
Michael E. Conroy

INDUSTRIAL LOCATION DECISIONS: Detroit
Compared with Atlanta and Chicago
Lewis Mandell

THE EXODUS OF CORPORATE HEADQUARTERS
FROM NEW YORK CITY
Wolfgang Quante